PHOTOS
MAGI

By Sherry London and Rhoda Grossman

Contributions by Robert Barnes, Michel Bohbot, Helen Golden, Dot Krause, Kelly Loomis, Cher Threinen-Pendarvis, Al Ward, Phil Williams, David Xenakis, and Sandy Young

201 West 103rd Street, Indianapolis, Indiana 46290
An Imprint of Pearson Education
Boston ▪ Indianapolis ▪ London ▪ Munich ▪ New York ▪ San Francisco

PHOTOSHOP 7 MAGIC

FIRST EDITION: May, 2002

International Standard Book Number: 0-7357-1264-6

Library of Congress Catalog Card Number: 2001099568

06 05 04 03 02 7 6 5 4 3 2 1

Interpretation of the printing code: The rightmost double-digit number is the year of the book's printing; the rightmost single-digit number is the number of the book's printing. For example, the printing code 02-1 shows that the first printing of the book occurred in 2002.

Printed in the United States of America

Trademarks

All terms mentioned in this book that are known to be trademarks or service marks have been appropriately capitalized. New Riders Publishing cannot attest to the accuracy of this information. Use of a term in this book should not be regarded as affecting the validity of any trademark or service mark. Photoshop is a registered trademark of Adobe.

Warning and Disclaimer

This book is designed to provide information about Photoshop 7. Every effort has been made to make this book as complete and as accurate as possible, but no warranty of fitness is implied.

The information is provided on an as-is basis. The authors and New Riders Publishing shall have neither liability nor responsibility to any person or entity with respect to any loss or damages arising from the information contained in this book or from the use of the discs or programs that may accompany it.

Publisher
David Dwyer

Associate Publisher
Stephanie Wall

Production Manager
Gina Kanouse

Managing Editor
Sarah Kearns

Senior Acquisitions Editor
Linda Anne Bump

Development Editor
John Rahm

Project Editor
Michael Thurston

Copy Editor
Jill Batistick

Indexer
Larry Sweazy

Product Marketing Manager
Kathy Malmloff

Publicity Manager
Susan Nixon

Manufacturing Coordinator
Jim Conway

Book Designer
Steve Gifford

Cover Designer
Aren Howell

Proofreader
Marcia Deboy

Composition
Gloria Schurick

Media Developer
Jay Payne

CONTENTS AT A GLANCE

About the Authors

Sherry London

Sherry London is an artist, writer, and teacher—which is exactly what a going-into-college aptitude test predicted. (It also correctly predicted that she would make a rotten housekeeper!) She was a contributing editor for *Computer Artist* magazine (before that publication's untimely death) and has written for *Electronic Publishing*, *Pre*, *MacWeek*, *MacUser*, *Digital Vision*, and the combined *MacWorld/MacUser* magazine. She currently writes for *Photoshop User* and *Mac Design* magazines. She has taught Photoshop, prepress, and QuarkXPress at Moore College of Art and Design and at Gloucester County College. She has spoken at a number of conferences, including the Thunder Lizard Photoshop Conference and the Professional Photographers of America convention. She has written a number of books on Photoshop, Illustrator, and Painter. She teaches online Photoshop courses for Education to Go (**www.ed2go.com**). You can reach her at **slondon@earthlink.net** or visit her web site at **www.sherrylondon.com** (if she ever has the time to get it up and working!).

Rhoda Grossman

With a background in traditional fine art, illustration, and cartooning, Rhoda began to transfer those skills to the Macintosh in 1989. She demonstrated digital caricature at numerous computer graphics trade shows in the early '90s and contributed step-by-step artwork to books on Photoshop and Painter. She wrote *Photoshop Effects Magic* (1997, Hayden Books) and more recently co-authored (with Sherry London) *Photoshop 6 Effects Magic* and *Painter f/x and Design*. This is the fourth collaboration for Rhoda and Sherry.

Rhoda teaches digital art and graphic design at the Center for Electronic Art in San Francisco and at the Foothill College in Los Altos Hills, California. She still does on-the-spot caricature at events. Rhoda is a member of the Graphic Artists Guild, the San Francisco Society of Illustrators, and the National Caricaturists Network. In recent years, she played a role in creating fair tax regulations for artists in California. Her portfolios and a cartoon autobiography can be seen at **www.digitalpainting.com**.

Robert Barnes

Robert Barnes is an award-winning visual artist who has made the transition from professional photography to digital fine art. A graduate of Eckerd College with a B.A. in art and photography, Mr. Barnes became chief photographer/cinematographer for Turner Broadcasting in 1972. He earned the Emmy Award for Outstanding Documentary in 1976.

In 1979, he joined the founding team at Cable News Network (CNN), where he championed the effort to build the world's first computerized television newsroom.

In 1986, he moved to Apple Computer and spent the next 10 years working in advanced technology. In 1995, he became product manager for QuickTime VR Authoring Studio, a revolutionary software product that takes normal 35 mm photographs and stitches them together to create a 360 degree panoramic image.

Mr. Barnes moved to Boulder, Colorado, in 1997, and after nearly three decades of detours, Barnes has returned to his first true calling... working as a full-time artist.

Mr. Barnes has been a guest lecturer on digital art and video production at the University of Georgia, the University of Colorado at Denver, Eckerd College, and the University of Colorado at Boulder.

His art can be seen on his web site at **www.barnesgallery.com**.

Michel Bohbot

Michel is an award-winning illustrator who combines digital with traditional rendering skills. Michel is a recent president of the San Francisco Society of Illustrators. He has taught courses in illustration and business practices at the Academy of Art College in San Francisco. He also contributed to the *Photoshop 6 Effects Magic* book. Real-world examples were also the inspiration for this year's tutorial. He and his brother have completed an illustrated fantasy novel and are looking for a publisher (hint, hint). See more of Michel's work at **www.mbohbot.com**.

Helen Golden

Artist Helen Golden, a pioneer in the digital art realm, exhibits in solo, curated, and invited exhibitions and is often cited in newspapers, magazines, books, television, and on the Internet. Her artwork is in private and corporate collections and has been accessed by the National Museum of American Art at the Smithsonian Institution in Washington, DC. It has been shown and sold in exhibitions nationally and internationally, including those at the Triton Museum of Art, the San Jose Museum of Art, the Fuller Museum of Art, Stanford University, the Ansel Adams Museum, the Silicon Valley Art Museum, and venues in New York City, Europe, Japan, and Canada.

In July 1997, she was a co-organizer of "Digital Atelier: A Printmaking Studio for the 21st Century" at the National Museum of American Art, where she was an artist-in-residence for 21 days along with the artists of "Unique Editions," the digital collective of which she is a co-founder. The event was enabled and supported by 31 technology corporations.

She is a Laureate of the 1998 Computerworld Smithsonian Information Technology Innovation Distinction and, in 1998, she was the recipient of the André Schellenberg Award in Fine Art. She was the first curator/director of "Art At the Pond," a San Francisco gallery that pioneered in featuring digital art. She serves to educate the public, collectors, and galleries about the new digital tools. As a research consultant for many corporations, she has had opportunities to try emerging technologies and to provide feedback from an artist's perspective.

Dot Krause

Dot Krause is a painter, collage artist, and printmaker who incorporates digital mixed media into her art. Her work is exhibited regularly in galleries and museums and is featured in more than three dozen current periodicals and books. She is professor emeritus at Massachusetts College of Art, where she founded the Computer Arts Center, and a member of Unique Editions and Digital Atelier, which are digital artists collaboratives, with Bonny Lhotka and Karin Schminke. She is a frequent speaker at conferences and symposia and a consultant for manufacturers and distributors of products that may be used by fine artists.

In July 1997, Krause organized "Digital Atelier: A Printmaking Studio for the 21st Century" at the National Museum of American Art at the Smithsonian Institution and was an artist-in-residence there for 21 days. For that work, she received a Smithsonian Technology in the Arts Award. That same year, she worked with a group of curators to help them envision the potential of digital printmaking in "Media for a New Millennium," a work-tank/think-shop organized by the Vinalhaven Graphic Arts Foundation.

In June 2001, with Digital Atelier, Krause demonstrated digital printmaking techniques at the opening of the "Brooklyn Museum of Art 27th Print National, Digital: Printmaking Now."

Kelly Loomis

Kelly is an award-winning graphic designer and artist based in the San Francisco Bay area. Her traditional work includes stained glass, for which she used to do business as Paine in the Glass. Her work has been published in numerous books and exhibited in art shows in and around Northern California. You can see more of her work on her website at **http://www.7rings.com**.

Cher Threinen-Pendarvis

Cher is a designer, fine artist, author, and educator based in San Diego, California. She has worked with both traditional and electronic tools for nearly 30 years. Her digital fine art and design has been exhibited as large format hand-worked prints worldwide and published in many publications, including *The Photoshop WOW! Book*, *The Official Photoshop Handbook*, *Photoshop 6 Magic*, *EFX Art and Design*, *Design Graphics*, *Digital Fine Art* magazine, *Contact* magazine, *MacWeek*, *MacUser Macworld*, *Publish*, *Step-by-Step Publications*, and *Computer Artist* magazine. Cher holds a BA with Highest Honors and Distinction in Art specializing in painting and printmaking. She is Principal of the consulting firm Cher Threinen Design, is an enthusiastic teacher, and is author of *The Painter 7 WOW! Book*, the fifth edition of this highly praised volume of techniques, and inspiration. You can see her work at **http://www. pendarvis-studios.com**. Photo by Michael Antorietto.

Al Ward

Al Ward, a certified Photoshop addict and webmaster of Action FX Photoshop Resources (**www.actionfx.com**), hails from Missoula, Montana. A former submariner in the U.S. Navy, Al now spends his time creating add-on software for Photoshop and writing about graphics-related topics. Al is the co-author (with Colin Smith) of *Photoshop Most Wanted*, a manual of popular Photoshop special effects, and *Foundation Photoshop 6.0*, both from Friends of Ed Publishing. He has been a contributor to *Photoshop User* magazine, a contributing writer for *Inside Photoshop 6* from New Riders Publishing, and a writer for several Photoshop-related web sites, including Planet Photoshop (**www.planetphotoshop.com**). Al was also a panelist at the Photoshop World 2001 Los Angeles Conference, and he contributes to the official NAPP web site as the actions area coordinator (**www.photoshopuser.com**).

Al lists Scott Kelby as his hero, coffee as his favorite food group, and sleep as the one pastime he'd like to take up some day.

In his off time, he enjoys his church, his family, fishing the great northwestern United States, and scouring the web for Photoshop-related topics.

Phil Williams

After graduating from a coordinated program between the Pennsylvania Academy of Fine Arts and the Graduate School of Fine Arts at the University of Pennsylvania in Philadelphia, Mr. Williams began his professional career as a commissioned portrait painter.

After several years of portrait painting, he became very involved with sound as a medium of art and found that freelancing as a sound engineer in the film industry provided the free time, the materials, and the sound palette to pursue his interest in sound as an art form. Part of working in the film industry involves traveling to ordinary and extraordinary places throughout the country and the world. It was during those travels that he collected the sound effects that became his sound palette. Several times a year during this period, he produced sound shows in various avante garde locations and galleries in and around Philadelphia, Pennsylvania.

In the mid 1980s, while attempting to computerize his sound effects library built up over 12 years in the business, he got totally involved with computer programming. Soon thereafter, he sold his sound business and equipment, bought some computers, and became a freelance computer programmer. In the early '90s, when desktop computers began to show promise as tools for graphic design and artwork, he went full circle back to the visual arts, becoming a digital illustrator and web site designer. Today he spends most of his time digitally painting artwork and portraits.

David Xenakis

David Xenakis is Vice President for Production for XRX, Inc. David's company produces *Knitter's Magazine*, XRX Books, and puts on Stitches Fair and Consumer shows. The publications of XRX are known in their industry as unusually high-quality print presentations. This is partly due to the fact that XRX has been involved in digital printing for a long time: *Knitter's Magazine*, for example, was the first nationally distributed publication to be done entirely in QuarkXPress. David is the author of *Photoshop 6 In Depth* and has co-authored previous editions of that book with Sherry London. David has also served as a technical editor for several books on Adobe Photoshop and Adobe Illustrator, and has contributed material for several books on these topics.

Sandy Young

Sandy Young is an award-winning digital and mixed-media artist working out of Studio Y, the digital studio she founded in 1991. Sandy creates digital images for clients such as The 2002 Cotton Bowl, Sony Music, Pepsi Co., Minolta, and Simon & Schuster.

Accomplished in both the fine art and commercial arenas, Sandy's accolades include awards by PRINT, ASCI, Fractal Design, California Works, and the Luther Burbank Center for the Arts. You can see Sandy's work at **www.studio-y.com**.

About the Technical Reviewers

These reviewers contributed their considerable hands-on expertise to the entire development process of *Photoshop 7 Magic*. As the book was being written, these dedicated professionals reviewed all the material for technical content, organization, and flow. Their feedback was critical to ensuring that *Photoshop 7 Magic* fit our readers' need for the highest-quality technical information.

Jon McFarland

Jon McFarland manages the design department for a national developer/owner/manager of retail, office, and residential properties. His experience in the CAD industry has branched into a career in computer graphics and animation. Jon also teaches at the Virginia Marti College of Art and Design and authors books on computer animation. He lives in Cleveland, Ohio, with his sons Zachary and Jacob.

Brian Sierkowski

Brian lives in Bloomington, Indiana, where he works as a web designer and programmer for Indiana University's School of Education. He does freelance work as a web site developer, is an avid photographer, and teaches a class on Photoshop for amateur photographers. He recently returned to college to complete a degree in psychology. Any free time he has left after everything just mentioned is spent with his dog Benny.

Dedication

Sherry London

To my husband Norm for love, loyalty, and growing old together.

—Sherry London

Rhoda Grossman

To the students, faculty, and staff of the Center for Electronic Art in San Francisco, California.

Acknowledgments

Sherry London

I would like to thanks the folks at New Riders for letting us do this again! It is always a pleasure to work with you.

I want to express my appreciation of and admiration for all of the contributing authors. Their work adds so much to this book.

I want to thank my co-author, Rhoda, for teaming up again. As always, I can't imagine doing this without you!

Margot Maley Hutchinson, our agent at Waterside, deserves a warm note of appreciation. Your help is valued!

I also want to thank Chris Setlock for permission to use his wonderful displacement maps, Judy Donovan for her willingness to be my model, and Linda Kamholz for her expertise and advice on traditional marbling.

Finally, to my husband, Norm. You make everything else possible. Thank you for putting up with me.

Rhoda Grossman

Thanks to my mother and my cousin Jerry Portnoy and his wife, Eli, for allowing me to mess with their likenesses.

I also want to thank the companies who provided demo copies of plug-in software to enhance Photoshop's capabilities.

Once again, thanks to Sherry for collaborating with me. You are not just a partner, but a valued friend.

Special thanks to the contributing authors. You have all taught me so much about this wonderful program.

Finally, thanks to everyone at Adobe Systems who helped create this version of Photoshop.

A Message from New Riders

As the reader of this book, you are our most important critic and commentator. We value your opinion and want to know what we're doing right, what we could do better, in what areas you'd like to see us publish, and any other words of wisdom you're willing to pass our way.

As Associate Publisher at New Riders, I welcome your comments. You can fax, email, or write me directly to let me know what you did or didn't like about this book—as well as what we can do to make our books better. When you write, please be sure to include this book's title, ISBN, and author, as well as your name and phone or fax number. I will carefully review your comments and share them with the authors and editors who worked on the book.

Please note that I cannot help you with technical problems related to the topic of this book, and that due to the high volume of email I receive, I might not be able to reply to every message. Thanks.

Fax: 317-581-4663

Email: stephanie.wall@newriders.com

Mail: Stephanie Wall
Associate Publisher
New Riders Publishing
201 West 103rd Street
Indianapolis, IN 46290 USA

Visit Our Web Site: www.newriders.com

On our web site, you'll find information about our other books, the authors we partner with, book updates and file downloads, promotions, discussion boards for online interaction with other users and with technology experts, and a calendar of trade shows and other professional events with which we'll be involved. We hope to see you around.

Email Us from Our Web Site

Go to **www.newriders.com** and click on the Contact Us link if you

- Have comments or questions about this book.
- Want to report errors that you have found in this book.
- Have a book proposal or are interested in writing for New Riders.
- Would like us to send you one of our author kits.
- Are an expert in a computer topic or technology and are interested in being a reviewer or technical editor.
- Want to find a distributor for our titles in your area.
- Are an educator/instructor who wants to preview New Riders books for classroom use. In the body/comments area, include your name, school, department, address, phone number, office days/hours, text currently in use, and enrollment in your department, along with your request for either desk/examination copies or additional information.

INTRODUCTION

Photoshop 7 Magic highlights projects from some of the top innovative professionals in computer art, and these professionals teach you to enhance both your Photoshop and artistic skills. Its purpose is to facilitate your exploration of new features and deepen your understanding of more familiar tools.

Who We Are

The two lead authors of this book are Sherry London and Rhoda Grossman, who have co-authored *Painter 5 f/x* and *Painter 6 f/x & Design* (Coriolis) and *Photoshop 6 Effects Magic*. This book is not merely an update of *Photoshop 6 Effects Magic*. It has ALL NEW techniques!

Rhoda is also the author of *Photoshop Effects Magic* (covering version 4). She brings her experience in traditional fine art and illustration to the computer. Sherry has written numerous books on a wide variety of CG applications. Sherry's background in fiber art makes her a "whiz-kid" with patterns and textures.

Sherry and Rhoda are joined by many very talented contributors, including Robert Barnes, Michel Bohbot, Helen Golden, Dot Krause, Kelly Loomis, Cher Threinen-Pendarvis, Al Ward, Phil Williams, David Xenakis, and Sandy Young.

Everyone on the writing team of *Photoshop 7 Magic* does more than just write. We are all working artists. We share not only the technical savvy we have developed using Photoshop in real-world assignments, but our creative process as well.

Who You Are

This book is intended for intermediate to advanced users of Photoshop and assumes you have a familiarity with the program's fundamentals. You're reading this because you want to get a deeper understanding of those fundamentals, as well as a solid grasp of new features.

We are aware that there is no such thing as a "generic" user of Photoshop. You might be advanced in the tools and features you use everyday, but intermediate on others. You might even be a beginner in a few areas. For that reason, we have included some basics where needed. As a result, advanced users and beginners with a sense of adventure can all benefit from this book.

What's in This Book

Every project in *Photoshop 7 Magic* is a step-by-step project that shows you how to create realistic and fantastic effects, ranging from altering photographs to liquid painting. While flipping through these pages, you'll see images developing for each project. You can work a project from start to finish, even if all you do is read the captions on the figures! We do, of course, give you more complete instructions in the text, including notes and tips, that will make you an insider in short order.

We've divided the book into sections based on the methods described: "Artistic Techniques," "Web Techniques," and "Image Manipulation Techniques."

The Companion CD

Included on the CD that comes with this book are all the files, presets, and images necessary to complete the projects, including several demos and plug-ins. Please note that the project files are for learning purposes only. Copyrights for the images are held by the artists who created them and you may not republish them in any form without written permission from the authors. For more information, please see the "What's on the CD-ROM" appendix at the back of this book.

Our Assumptions as We Wrote the Book

We had four assumptions when we wrote this book, based on our collective experience learning and working with graphics software.

You Like to Learn Visually

A picture used to be worth a thousand words. Even at today's exchange rate, it's still a lot more valuable to see an image than it is to have it described to you. You won't have to guess whether you've done a step correctly. We've included a figure adjacent to as many steps as necessary to make sure you stay on track.

Your Time Is Valuable

You don't want to spend forever learning one effect, and you don't want to wade through a lot of incidental material before you get to the good stuff. The projects in this book are focused and self-contained. Each project begins with a short paragraph explaining what you will be doing, as well as a brief summary of what tools and techniques will be used to achieve the effect. Find a project that fascinates you and plunge right in.

You Want a Deeper Understanding of Photoshop

It's not enough to learn a recipe for an effect. You need to know how a command or feature works. One of the goals of this book is not only to take you through the steps toward an end result, but also to make sure you understand how you got there. Most steps include a short explanation about why you are using a given tool or setting.

You Want to Learn Techniques You Can Really Use

We want to help you apply these techniques in your own work. To that end, each project includes a variation or two. Try them and then come up with a few of your own. This will enable you to master the techniques and not just the specific images presented here.

Conventions Used in This Book

Every computer book has its own style of presenting information. We begin each project by showing you the end result in all its glory. Next, you'll find the step-by-step instructions for completing the project, including succinct and extremely valuable explanations. That text is in the left column. In the corresponding column to the right are the screen captures and stages of the image as they develop.

We include the complete path for a command the first time it is used in a project and then just refer to the command itself. For example, "Image/Adjust/Levels" becomes "Levels" the next time it's mentioned. Keyboard shortcuts are given as PC/Macintosh equivalents. For example, Ctrl+L/Cmd+L will bring up the Levels dialog.

Join the Revolution

How can we refer to the industry's most widely used and established 2D graphics program as revolutionary? This upgrade, Photoshop 7, provides a powerful and versatile Brush engine for the first time. New features include Tool Presets and a Presets Manager. There are enhancements for the Liquify feature and improvements to Image Ready's capability to work with web graphics. There are even more Blending modes (can't have too many of those)! Photoshop 7 represents a quantum leap in overall features and possibilities. When you try a few projects and you learn what Text Warp, Liquify, and Art History can do, you'll understand why we're so excited.

TRANSLUCENCY IN TYPOGRAPHY

"Give me a museum, and I'll fill it."

—PABLO PICASSO

A Romantic Look for Text

This project teaches you how to create a blend of romantic script with a collage of old letters, stamps, and postmarks.

You will make a script title selectively translucent so that it can interact with its background in interesting ways. The technique relies on variations of the background image to mask parts of the foreground display text. By altering values within the mask, you can choose which parts of the image are visible through the text. This technique is especially effective when the background image contains linear forms such as the handwriting shown in this image.

Project 1

Translucency in Typography

by Sandy Young

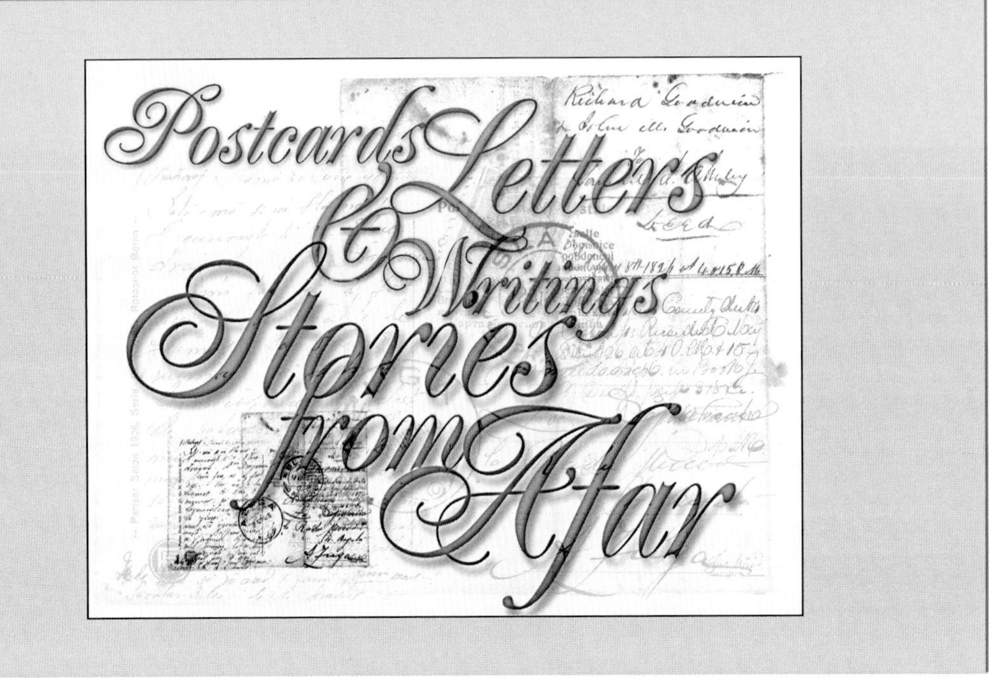

Getting Started

The image you'll start with is already an interesting collage of scanned handwriting, type, shapes, and symbols. There are a variety of hues and saturation levels, including mottled browns and yellows that show the age of the materials.

Much of the contrast and detail of this collage is reduced as you develop the script title. Although the finished project depends less on the clarity of these items, their richness remains perceptible as—dare I say it?—subtext.

1. Quit Photoshop and load the Porte Light font into your computer. Launch Photoshop again.

2 Open the file Writings.tif.

Begin with the collage of old letters, postcards, and stamps.

Creating Type

You will make several text layers using the Porte Light typeface and then merge them into a single rasterized layer.

1 Choose the Horizontal Type tool and select the Porte Light font, with the size set to 120 points. Make sure the font color is black. Type **Postcards**.

2 Type **Letters & Writings**, putting each word and the ampersand on a separate layer so that you can rearrange them easily on the page. I used Porte Light at 120 points for the word "Writings." The word "Letters" and the ampersand were set at 180 points.

Tip: You can make a new layer for each word by switching to another tool (any tool) for a moment after typing a word. Then, you can switch back to the Type tool and continue typing.

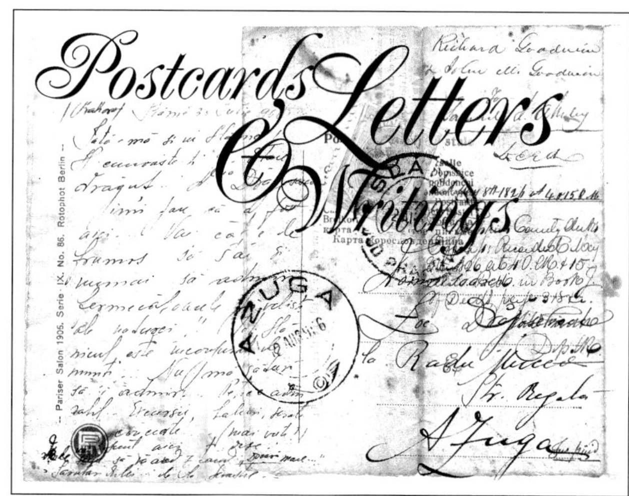

3 Position all the type the way you want, and then merge all four type layers into one. The easiest way to do this is to make the background layer invisible and then use the Merge Visible command in the Layers pop-up menu. Name the merged layer **Text**.

The resulting layer is rasterized, no longer capable of further editing with type options such as font.

4 Use the Eyedropper tool to sample the purple color in the postmark stamp on the background image. You can also enter these values for CMYK: C 100, M 99, Y 2, and K 2. If you are working in RGB, use these values: R 45, G 48, and B 141.

5 Lock Transparency in the Layers palette and fill the type layer with purple. A handy shortcut for filling with foreground color is Alt+Backspace/ Option+Delete. Locking Transparency prevents the color from filling the entire layer.

In the next steps, you'll add some volume to the title.

6 Make a copy of the Text layer (Ctrl+J/Cmd+J). Change the text fill in the copy to white.

7 Prepare to blur the white text layer by unlocking Transparency. Apply Filter > Blur > Gaussian Blur using a radius of 4.5 pixels.

Unlocking Transparency is necessary for pixels to extend beyond the confines of the type.

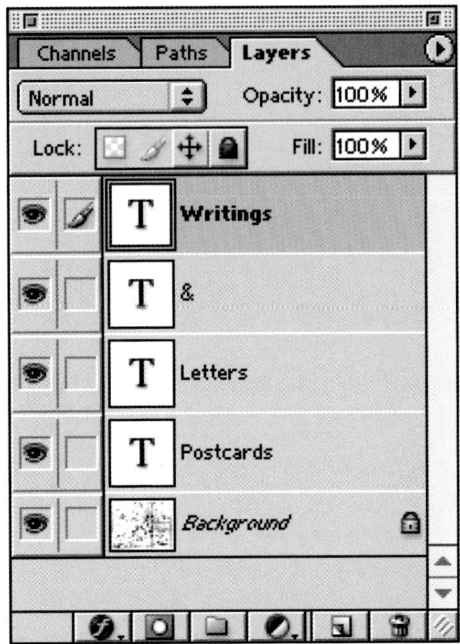

Type each word on its own layer.

8. Change Opacity of the white text to 75%. Offset the layer by shifting it 1 pixel up and 1 pixel to the left, using the arrow keys with the Move tool selected.

   The result is soft highlights in the center of the type.

9. For more dimensionality, add a drop shadow to the main (purple) text layer. Use the "f" menu at the bottom of the Layers palette to choose the Drop Shadow effect. Accept Multiply for the Blend mode, keep the angle at 120 degrees, and change Opacity to 50%. Use a default distance of 5 pixels and a spread of 0%. Change Size to 13 pixels. Use Global Light and Layer Knocks Out Drop Shadow.

Add highlights to the purple text.

> **Tip:** You can use arrow keys to nudge a layer without switching to the Move tool. Just hold down the Ctrl/Cmd key.

Making Translucency Effects

You'll use the background to create a mask to apply to the type. The original collage will be pasted into the Layer Mask for the text. This is the key to creating variations in translucency based on the luminosity (brightness or value) of the background image.

1. With purple text still the target layer, add a Layer Mask by clicking the Mask icon at the bottom of the Layers palette.

2. Make the background collage the active layer. Select > All and copy it to the Clipboard (Ctrl+C/Cmd+C).

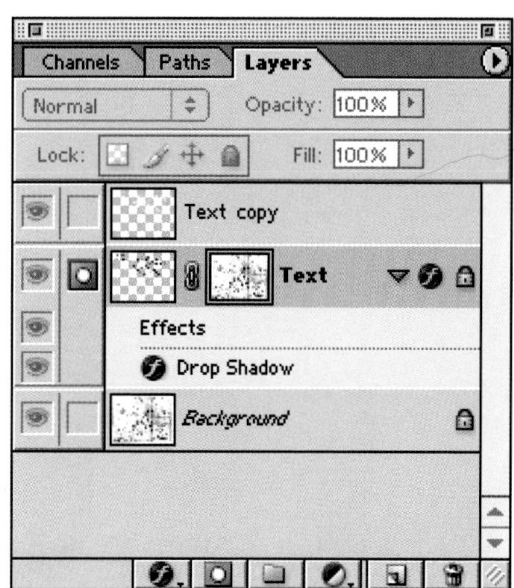

3 Alt-click/Option-click the Layer Mask thumbnail to make the mask visible. It is completely white at this point. Paste the background image into the mask. A grayscale version of the collage appears.

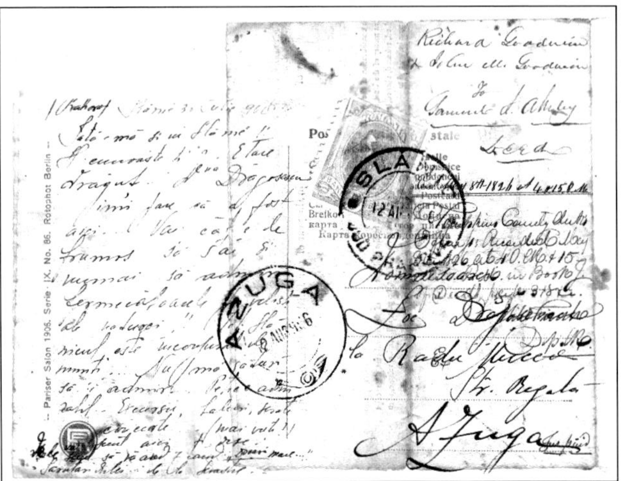

Paste the background collage into the Text layer's Layer Mask.

4 Alter the gray values in the mask with the Levels adjustment (Ctrl+L/Cmd+L). Move the black point slider of the Output Levels bar to 170.

The mask is now composed of much lighter gray tones. Because black masks 100 percent, this has provided a way to assure that all parts of the title are visible to some extent.

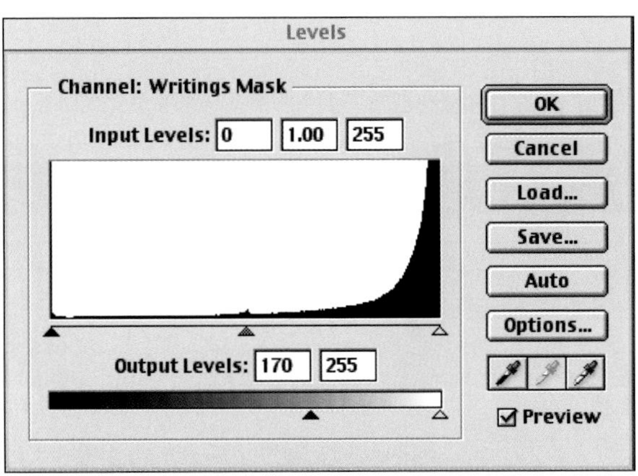

Adjust Levels to lighten the Layer Mask.

5 Make a Layer Mask for the white blurred text layer. Copy the original background image into this new mask.

The background image is still on the Clipboard, unless you used the Purge command or copied something else since Step 3.

6 Alter the gray values in this new mask with Levels Adjustments. This time move the black point slider of the Output Levels bar to 100.

The translucency of "Postcards, Letters & Writings" is complete. You will add more type and apply the same effects with slightly different settings.

Note: If you're not familiar with Layer Masks, here's how they work. Black pixels on the mask hide the corresponding pixels of the image layer completely. White pixels on the mask enable pixels of the image to show completely. As expected, intermediate shades of gray have a partial effect on hiding the image pixels.

Because you made the mask from the background image, there is more translucency in the type where there is darker detail in the background. The type is at full strength over blank areas. This effect cannot be achieved by simply reducing the Opacity of the type layers uniformly. You also can't do it with a change in Blending mode. Compare your Layer Mask effect to the result of merging the type layers and switching to Multiply mode or the new Linear Burn.

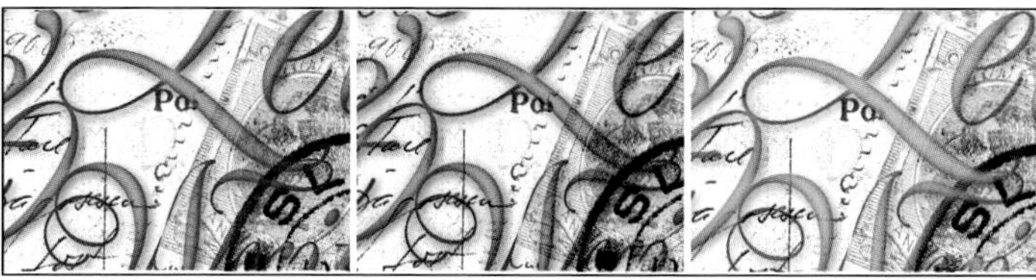

Compare the Masking effect (left) with Multiply (center) and Linear Burn modes.

7 Create additional title script using the words "Stories from Afar." Make this title larger than the first, and put each word on a new layer so that you can arrange the words creatively on the page. I used the Porte Light font at 240 points for the words "Stories" and "Afar." The word "from" is set at 180 points. Set the text color to black.

8 When you are satisfied with their positions, merge all three new type layers into one. The resulting layer will be rasterized.

9 Repeat the steps for adding depth and volume, with the following changes from earlier settings: blur the white-filled copy of the type by 6.0 pixels, give the drop shadow a distance of 23 pixels, set the size to 16 pixels, and set Opacity to 30%.

A larger blur is needed because of this type's increased point size. Putting the drop shadow farther away from the type and at lower opacity gives the illusion that the type is raised from the surface more so than the original type.

Add more words to the title.

10 Prepare Layer Masks exactly as you did before.

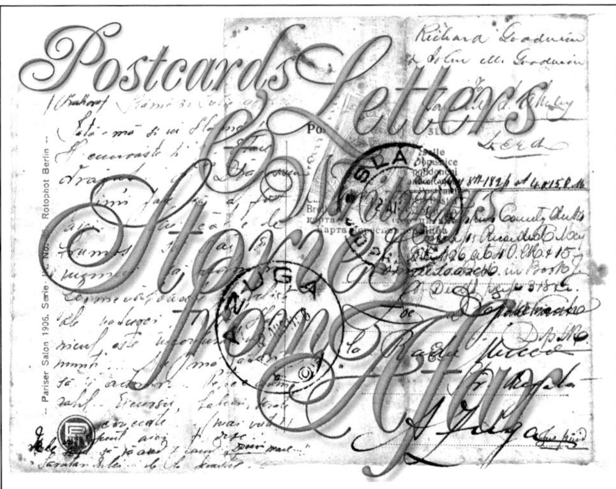

Apply Blur, Drop Shadow, and Layer Mask effects.

Softening the Background

OK, this is a bit of a visual mess. Even so, you should be able to see how the title text interacts with the background. Next you'll make the background more subtle.

1 Create a new layer and drag it down to just above the background image. Fill it with a cream color sampled from the aging paper in the background. You also can enter the values I used: C 0, M 1, Y 24, and K 0. The RGB equivalents are R 25, G 248, and B 204. Set the layer opacity to 75%.

Make the background more interesting by having it show more clearly at the upper-right corner and fade out toward the center of the image. Again you'll use Layer Mask techniques.

2 Increase Opacity of the cream layer to 90%. Give it a Layer Mask.

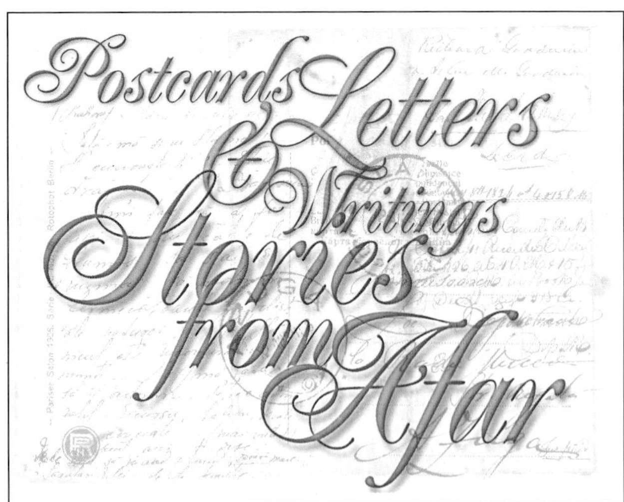

Add a cream-filled layer at 75% opacity.

3. Use the Gradient tool with Radial style and the Black, White color preset. Drag diagonally from the upper-right corner, stopping at the top of the "t" in the word "Stories." It is not necessary to make the Layer Mask visible for this step.

   Now the upper-right corner of the cream layer is transparent, which enables the background to show at full strength, gradually fading out to cream near the center.

4. Make a copy of the background image layer.

5. Select All and use the Free Transform command (Ctrl+T/Cmd+T). Enter 30% in both the Width and Height fields on the Options Bar.

6. Sharpen the layer using Filter > Sharpen > Unsharp Mask. Enter these values: Amount 80%, Radius 1.0 pixels, and Threshold 3 Levels.

7. Move the small copy of the background into position as shown in the finished image at the beginning of this project. Change the Blending mode to Multiply. Flatten the image and you're done!

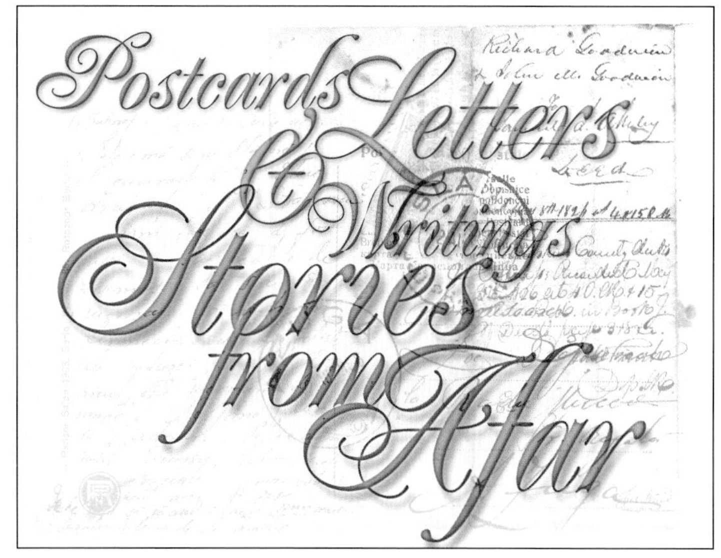

Blend the background into the cream layer with a gradient in the Layer Mask.

Warp Type Tricks

Here's a project with a bold contemporary look. It combines the translucency techniques you just learned with Photoshop's Warp Text feature. You'll create a public service piece called "fine print."

1. Make a new RGB file with a white background approximately 7.5 inches wide by 5 inches high at 150 pixels per inch.

   You'll start by typing three separate layers of text using a bold san serif font such as Arial Black. This font is available, if you need it, on the book's CD-ROM.

2 Type **examine** on the first layer, using these choices on the Options Bar: Regular, 90 pt., Strong, and black color.

3 On the second layer, type **the** with the same options for the Type tool. Type **fine print** on the third layer. Position the type on the page as shown in the figure.

examine
the
fine print

Create "examine the fine print" on three type layers.

4 Create a fourth text layer, using Arial (a slimmer version of Arial Black). Set the size to 10 points, leaving the other options unchanged. Click the Palettes button on the Options Bar to access Character settings. Set the leading (line spacing) to 12 points. Type **fine print fine print** many times across most of the page. Repeat on the next line. Copy and paste the text repeatedly until you have a block of text about half the height of the page. Center and position this text block under the word "examine." Set the layer opacity to 31%.

Create the tiny fine print on a fourth layer.

5 Name this layer **fine print fine print**, and then drag it to the bottom of the stack in the Layers palette so that the other text layers remain solid black.

6 To avoid confusion as we continue working, rename the original 90-point "fine print" text as **fine print BOLD**.

In the next steps, you use the Warp Text feature. This option cannot be used on bitmapped or rasterized text.

7 Target the "fine print BOLD" layer. Choose the Type tool and click the Warp Text button on the Options Bar. Find Fisheye in the style pop-up menu, and then move the bend slider to +60. Horizontal and vertical distortion should remain at 0.

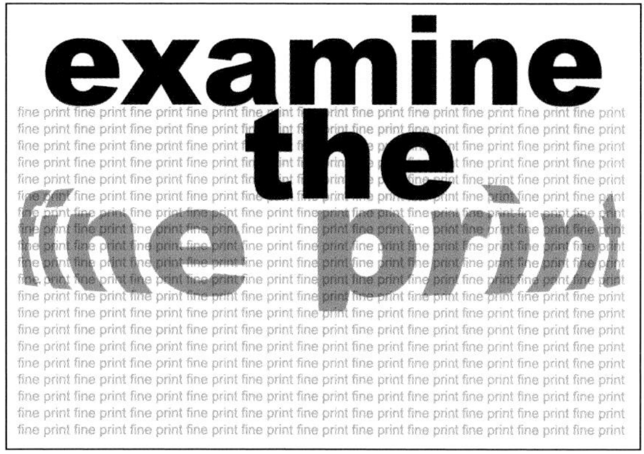

Use a Fisheye warp.

8 Set the opacity of the warped text to 38%.

9 Create a new layer, fill it with white, and place it just over the "fine print fine print" layer.

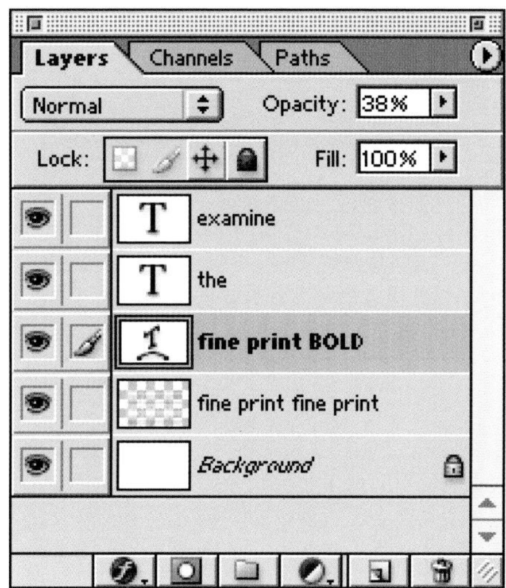

Reduce opacity of the warped text layer.

10 Use the Elliptical Marquee tool to make a selection as wide as the warped "fine print BOLD" type and about half as high. Use the arrow keys to center the selection over the warped text and then delete it.

This layer is serving as a mask, so rename it **mask layer**. All the "fine print fine print" is still there, but only the portion that shows through the elliptical hole is visible.

Tip: You can move a selection Marquee without moving any image pixels as long as a Selection tool (not the Move tool) is active. If your ellipse is in position but not quite the perfect size, use Expand or Contract from the Select > Modify menu.

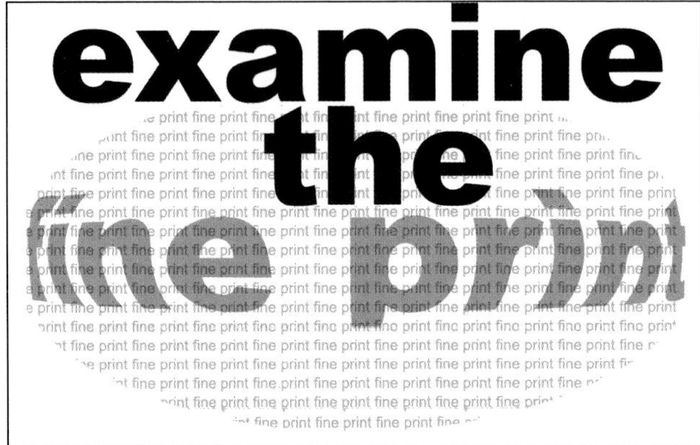

Make a new white layer with an elliptical hole to serve as a mask.

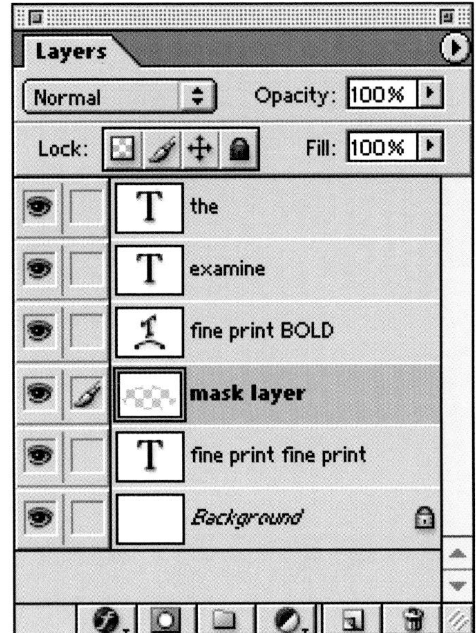

11 Make a copy of the "fine print fine print" layer (Ctrl+J/Cmd+J). Apply Text Warp to the copy, using the Bulge style. Make sure the Bend slider is at +50. Horizontal and vertical distortion should remain at 0. Set the layer opacity to 100%.

Use the bold Fisheye warped text as a mask for the two "fine print fine print" layers.

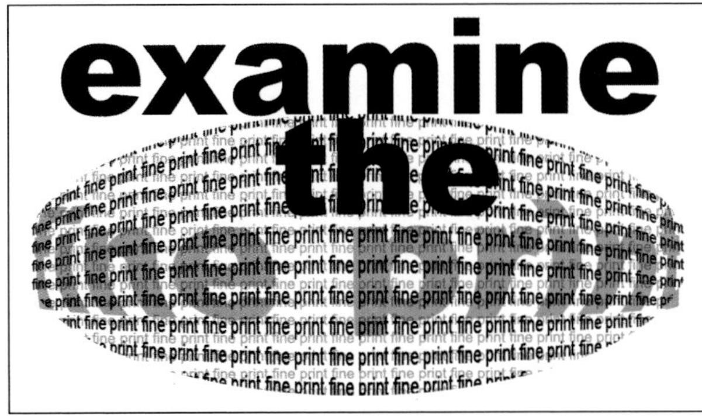

Apply Bulge warp to a copy of the "fine print fine print" layer.

12 Make a copy of the bold Fisheye warped layer. Set the layer opacity to 100%. Create a new layer and fill it with white. Position the new white layer just below the bold, warped copy. Link the two together and choose Merge Linked from the Layers drop-down menu. Name this merged layer **Mask 2**.

You're ready to apply Mask 2 to both "fine print fine print" layers—once direct and once inverted.

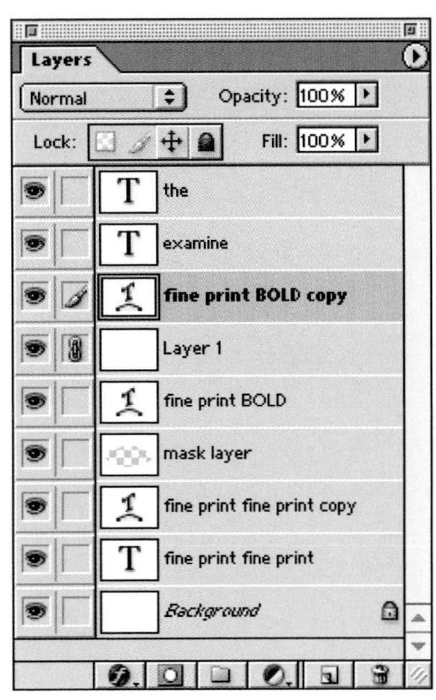

Copy the Fisheye warp text and link it with a new white layer.

Tip: To make sure you are still on track, hide all layers except the new Mask 2. The easiest way to do this is to press the Alt/Option key while clicking the visibility eyeball for Mask 2. You should see the Fisheye warped text in 100% black on a white background. Alt-click/Option-click again to toggle the visibility of all layers.

Hide visibility of all layers except the new Mask 2.

13 Copy the contents of Mask 2 to the paste buffer (Ctrl+C/Cmd+C), and then turn off its visibility.

14 Create a Layer Mask for the warped "fine print fine print" layer. Alt-click/Option-click the Layer Mask thumbnail to view it, and then click Paste. Invert the Layer Mask (Ctrl+I/Cmd+I).

Now the Layer Mask has white text on a black background. Only the portion of the image layer corresponding to the white areas is visible.

15 Paste Mask 2 into the Layer Mask for the Bulge warped layer, and then invert it.

16 Create a Layer Mask for the original "fine print fine print" layer. Alt-click/Option-click the Layer Mask thumbnail to view the mask. Paste the content again, but do not invert.

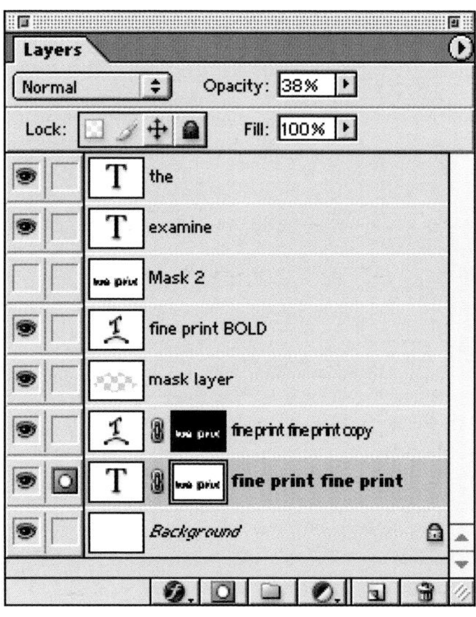

Paste Mask 2 into a Layer Mask for the original "fine print fine print" layer.

17 Flatten the image.

This image will serve as the background for the following set of steps.

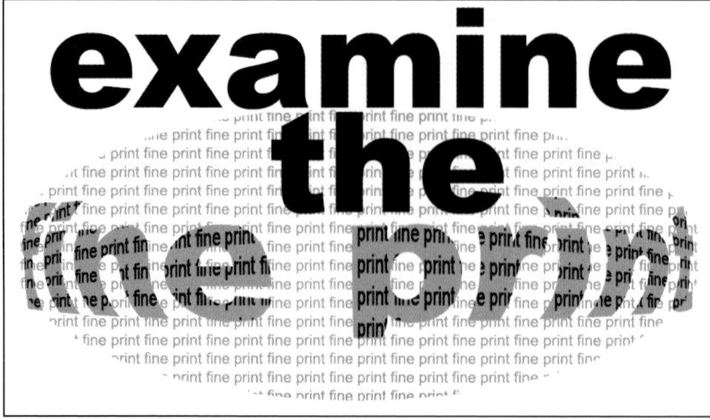

Finish the black-and-white stage of the image by flattening all layers.

Seeing Through the Fine Print

Complete the service announcement by adding some additional text in color and using the translucency technique.

1. Type **before you sign** in bright red. Make the font Arial Black, Regular, 48 point, and Strong.
2. Change the font size to 10 points and type **protect your interests. examine the fine print before you sign.** on another layer. Select the "examine the fine print" portion and change its color to black. Position the type layers on the page as shown.
3. Copy the contents of the Background layer to the paste buffer.
4. Make a Layer Mask for the "before you sign" layer. Alt-click/Option-click the Layer Mask thumbnail in the Layers palette and paste the background into it.
5. Change Levels in the Layer Mask. Enter these values for Input Levels: 150/1.00/255. Make all layers visible again.

   The Levels adjustment made the "fine print" on the Layer Mask bold and dark, resulting in greater transparency. Thus, the gray fine print on the Background layer shows more strongly against the red text.
6. Finally, flatten and save the image.

If you like working with type, don't miss Project 15, "Satin Beveled Type," which is Cher Pendarvis' project on custom Layer Styles.

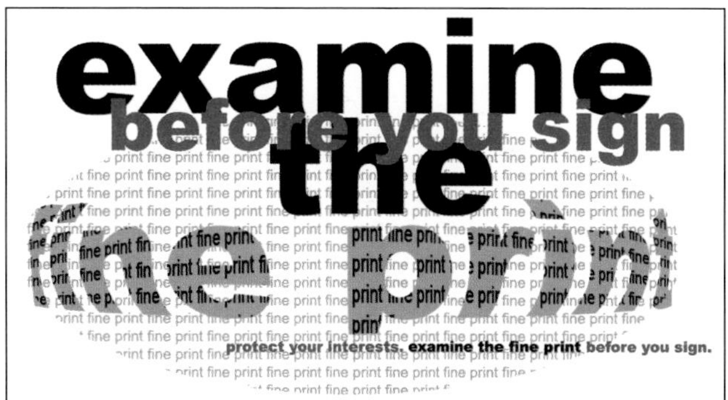

Add new text in red.

Create transparency in the red text.

"There are no facts, only interpretations."

—FRIEDRICH NIETZSCHE

BRUSH TECHNIQUES

Customizing Your Painting Tools with the New Brush Engine

Take full advantage of Photoshop's new Brush engine. Create new Brush tips and customize Brush Presets for a wide variety of drawing and painting effects.

Photoshop's new Brush architecture provides greatly enhanced control of brush behavior. Effects that were once difficult to achieve, such as painting with texture, can now become built-in Brush qualities with a single mouse click. Incidentally, if you are using a mouse, you can have almost as much fun with brushes as you can with a pressure-sensitive tablet.

Project 2

Brush Techniques

by Rhoda Grossman

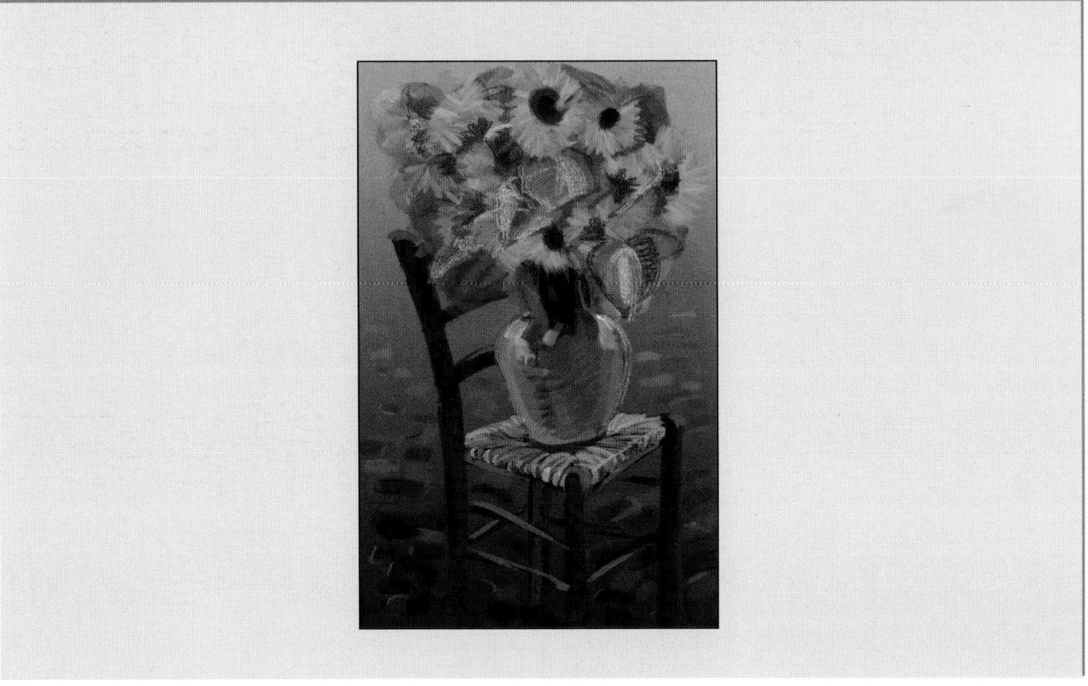

Getting Started

Photoshop 7 offers numerous brush presets divided into several categories or libraries. New libraries include Dry Media, Wet Media, and Thick Heavy brushes. There are about 240 brush presets, which ought to be enough to satisfy most users, but to paraphrase a T-shirt I once saw, "Whoever dies with the most brushes wins."

Your first step is to familiarize yourself with the new brush variables by altering the qualities of a default brush.

1 Use File > New (Ctrl+N/Cmd+N) to make a new RGB image with a white background. 8×8 inches at 72 ppi should be big enough to give lots of room for testing brush strokes.

2 Choose the Brush tool from the main tool palette. Open the Brushes palette by clicking the Brushes tab in the palette at the extreme right of the Options Bar.

The Stroke Thumbnail at the bottom of the Brushes palette updates to reflect any changes you make in the shape or dynamics of the brush.

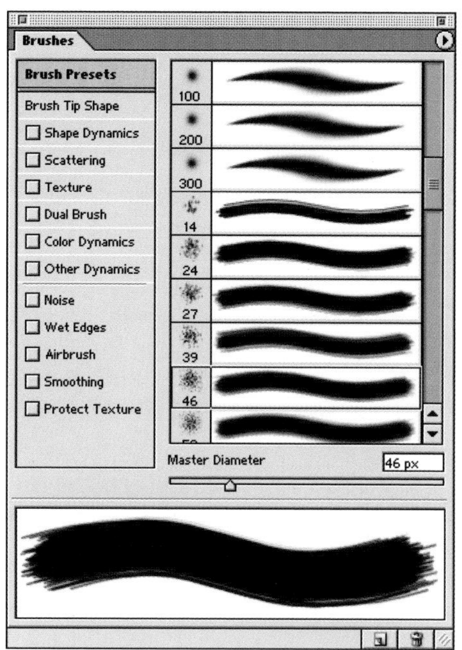

Open the Brushes palette.

Tip: Drag the Brushes tab down and away from the Option strip so that it will remain open while you work.

3 Choose the Spatter 39 pixels preset and make a black stroke.

Notice that your stroke and the Stroke Thumbnail show no variation in thickness. The stroke looks like it's made of bristles, not spatters. A footprint of the brush tip, however, is a roughly circular spatter of tiny dots—hence the name.

Make a stroke with the Spatter 39 pixels brush.

4 Highlight Shape Dynamics in the Brushes palette. Set Size Jitter to 0% and choose Pen Pressure for Control. Now the Stroke Thumbnail is thinner at both ends, indicating that you can vary thickness with stylus pressure.

Notice that there are controls for Tilt and Thumbwheel to accommodate advanced tablets that have these options.

5 Highlight Scattering, and the Stroke Thumbnail shows a slightly roughened edge. The default value for scatter is 33%. This can be decreased or increased to taste. Make a few test strokes with a variety of scatter amounts.

6 Highlight Texture. The preview square shows the current pattern being used as texture. You can switch to any item in this Pattern library or load an alternative library from the pop-up list. Make test strokes with a number of different patterns as texture.

Shown in the left column are strokes made with Satin, Nebula, Herringbone, and Optical Checkerboard. All are from the default Pattern library. On the right are strokes made with patterns in the Artist Surfaces library: Gauze, Parchment, and Wax Crayon on Charcoal Paper. Finally, you see the Web texture from the Texture Fill 2 library.

7 Your brush has changed considerably from the original preset. If you like the changes, save them. Use the New Brush command in the Brushes palette pop-up menu and give your new custom brush a descriptive name.

Practice adding Texture to brush strokes.

Tip: A new pattern is easily created from a rectangular selection in a photo, drawing, or scan. Edit > Define Pattern adds your selection as a pattern tile in the current library. It is immediately available as a brush texture.

Keep the image you have been using for practice open. You will continue testing brush dynamics here. Whenever this "scratch paper" gets too full, just clear it with Select > All (Ctrl+A/Cmd+A) and Delete.

Creating a Leafy Brush

Many of the most exciting brush presets are not based on simple circular dabs. Instead, they are sampled. The Spatter brush you just worked with is a good example. Any mark you make, or a collection of marks, or a tiny image element can become a brush tip.

You'll continue to customize brush dynamics, and you'll make a new brush from the scanned image of a leaf.

1 Highlight Brush Presets. This makes alternative Brush libraries available when you open the pop-up list. Load the Special Effect Brushes.

Notice the sampled brushes, such as Hypno Lines, Ducks Not in a Row, and Butterfly.

2 Choose the Butterfly brush and make a stroke, using a bright, saturated color.

Color variation within the stroke is the result of 87% Hue Jitter in Color Dynamics. Color changes don't show in the Stroke Thumbnail.

3 Alter the color variation by reducing Hue Jitter to 0% and raising Saturation Jitter to about 90%. Make another test stroke.

4 Change the Brightness Jitter to 90% and reduce Saturation Jitter.

5 Load the F X Magic Brushes.abr library found in the Projects/02_Brush_Techniques folder on the accompanying CD-ROM.

6 Open LEAF.tif, which is found in the Projects/02_Brush Techniques folder on the accompanying CD.

7 Click the white background with the Magic Wand tool and use Select > Inverse to select only the Leaf.

Adjust Color Dynamics for the Butterfly brush.

Tip: The Load Brushes command enables you to navigate anywhere to access Brush preset libraries. A more efficient way to switch Brush libraries is to use the list of available preset groups at the bottom of the Brushes pop-up menu. Make the F X Magic Brushes part of this list by quitting Photoshop, dragging the F X Magic Brushes.abr file into the Brushes folder in the Presets folder of the Adobe Photoshop 7 application. Launch Photoshop and you'll find the new Brush library in the list.

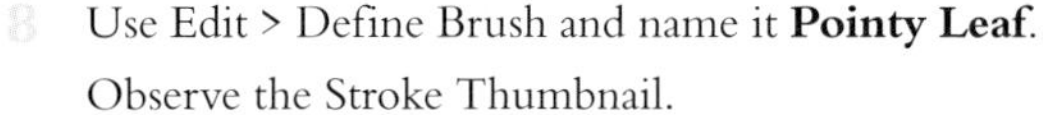

8 Use Edit > Define Brush and name it **Pointy Leaf**. Observe the Stroke Thumbnail.

Your new brush appears at the bottom of the current Brush library. The stroke it makes isn't very interesting...yet. It will become much more exciting after adjustments to size, angle, scatter, and color dynamics.

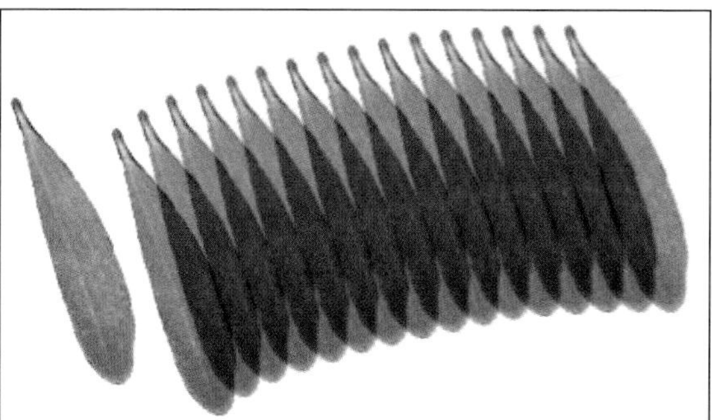

Make a new Brush tip from the Leaf image.

9 Highlight Brush Tip Shape. Adjust the pixel diameter and spacing of the leaf dabs.

I used 90 pixels and 25% spacing.

10 Highlight Shape Dynamics. Use the settings shown to alter the Stroke Thumbnail. Make a few test strokes.

A circular stroke clearly shows that the angle of the leaves varies as a function of direction. This relationship works whether you use a stylus or a mouse. An interesting feature of the Direction variable is that a clockwise stroke differs from a counterclockwise stroke. Notice that the pointy ends of the leaf are on the outer edge of a clockwise stroke, but they are at the center of a counterclockwise stroke.

11 Highlight Scattering and move the Scatter slider to about 33%.

This gives the stroke a small amount of variability in the placement of dabs.

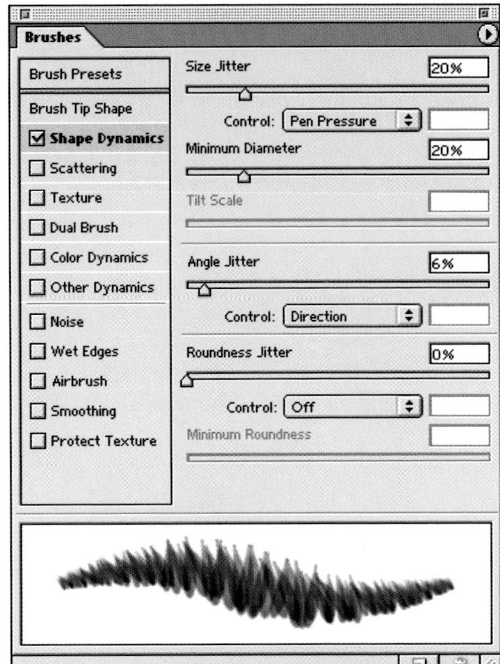

Adjusting Shape Dynamics.

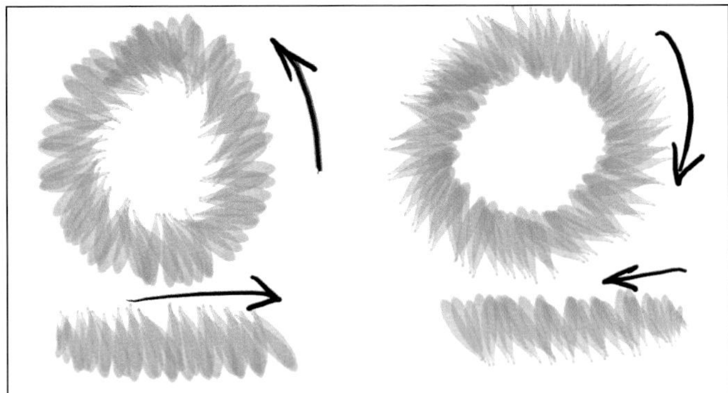

Make circular strokes to see the angle as a function of direction.

12 Add some color variation to the stroke in the Color Dynamics section. Set Hue Jitter to 7% and set both Saturation and Brightness Jitter to 16%. Make test strokes with several foreground colors.

13 Save your settings with the New Brush command in the Brushes palette pop-up menu.

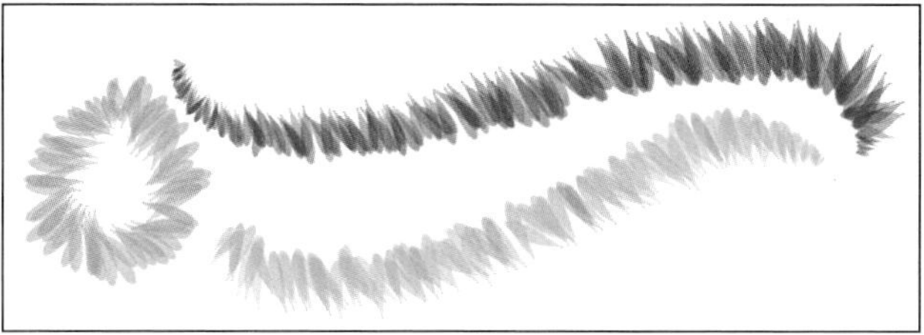

Test the effect of color variation.

Note: The New Brush command is a little clunky. Every time you want to save changes to a brush quality or behavior, you are prompted to give the brush a name. Even if you give it the same name as before, the older version isn't replaced. You can have several brushes with the same name, each with different characteristics. This can be confusing. You will need to eliminate each earlier version of the brush with the Delete Brush command.

Creating Textured Brushes

A basic brush can get a personality makeover quickly when you apply Texture dynamics. Here is the same brush with an assortment of patterns assigned as texture.

1 Restore the default Brushes library with the Reset Brushes command. Photoshop presents a warning box where you can choose either to replace the current library or append to it. Çlick OK to replace.

Change a brush dramatically by giving it a specific texture.

2 Make a test scribble with the Chalk 60 pixels brush.

Even without any added dynamics, the stroke has a somewhat bristly look at the beginning and end and where it changes direction. This is due to the sampled brush tip.

Scribble with the Chalk 60 pixels brush, with no dynamics enabled.

3 Use the Shape Dynamics section to set Angle Jitter to 3%. This roughens the edges of the stroke just a bit.

4 Activate the Texture section. Load the Rock Patterns library to replace the current set of textures. Choose Textured Tile and set the Mode to Hard Mix. Make some practice strokes.

Increase Angle Jitter to add rough edges.

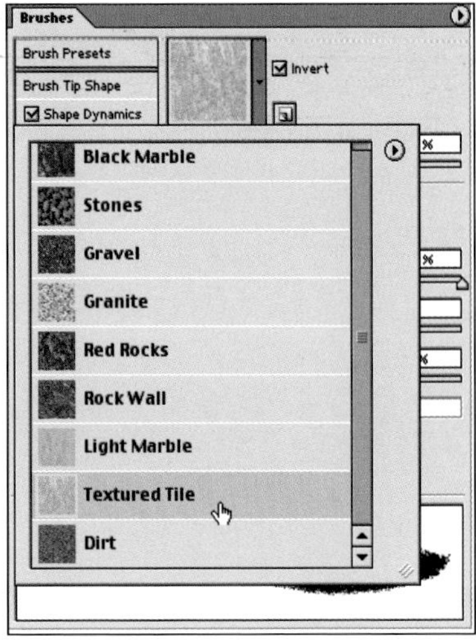

Choose Textured Tile from the Rock Patterns library.

5 Save your changes with the New Brush command.

Practice using the new Brush preset.

Customizing Brush Libraries

Suppose you want to create a new family of brushes that contains only your own custom brushes. Maybe you'd like to reorganize Photoshop brushes into different categories that are more convenient for the way you like to work.

You can't simply drag brush presets from one library to another. That would be too easy! The process can be considerably more tedious. I reduced the 54 presets in the default Brush library to my favorite 15 items. I had to choose the unwanted brushes one by one and use the Delete Brush command on each one. The remaining brushes were saved as a new library, using the Save Brushes command.

1 Choose Thick Heavy Brushes in the presets list to replace your current library.

   There are only five items in this group, so it will be quick to rename the set and replace some or all of them with your own presets.

2 Delete as many as four of the Thick Heavy Brushes. (You cannot completely empty out a library.) Use Save Brushes and call the new set **My Brushes** or anything you like.

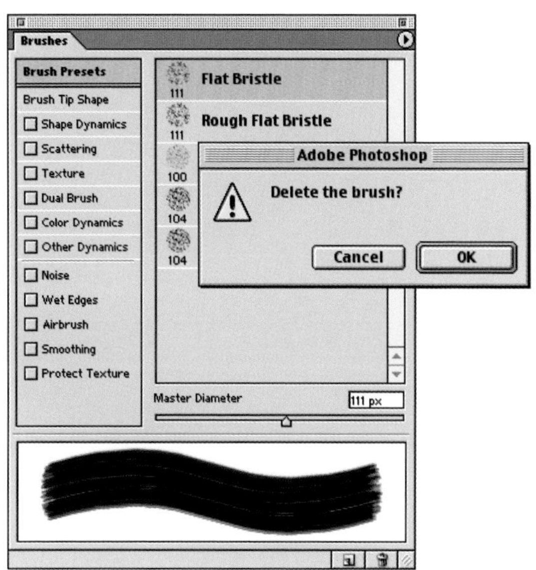

Load Thick Heavy Brushes and delete all but one of them.

Tip: Save "My Brushes" to the Brushes folder in Photoshop's Presets folder; that way, "My Brushes" will appear in the Brushes pop-up list the next time you launch Photoshop.

Using Brushes to Create a Still Life Painting

The painting shown at the beginning of this section was inspired by a photograph, but was created "from scratch" entirely with brushwork.

1 Load the F X Magic Brushes.abr library of presets from the Projects/02_Brush Techniques folder on the accompanying CD.

2 Open the source image Sunflowr.tif.

3 Set foreground color to gray-blue (R 157, G 171, B 186) and background color to dark green (R 20, G 54, B 32).

4 Make a new layer and fill it with the foreground to background linear gradient, dragging vertically from the top of the image to the bottom.

5 Reduce Opacity of the layer to about 95%, just enough to be able to see the underlying source image.

Your painting will be created on this new layer. The photo is used only as reference.

6 Make a rough sketch of the basic forms of the vase and flowers using the Soft Wet 31 pixel brush and a dark gray color.

Notice that this brush has Wet Edges enabled, giving the strokes more density at the edges, emulating a watercolor stroke.

7 Switch the foreground color to dark blue and use the Textured Chalk brush you made earlier to lay out the chair in bolder strokes. Change Brush diameter as needed to make each line of the chair's frame in a single stroke.

Note: My intention is to interpret the photo rather freely and to get a mixed media look by using a variety of brushes. At this stage, it's easier to open the original reference photo as a separate file so that you can glance at it without having to turn off your working layer. You can also sample colors with the Eyedropper more quickly.

8 Continue with Textured Chalk to block out color in the vase, using the Eyedropper tool to pick up colors from the photo. You can soften the effect by scribbling over some areas with the Soft Wet brush.

Use the Sunflowers photo for reference.

Quickly lay out the major shapes.

9 Use the Soft Wet brush to paint the cane seat of the chair.

10 Block in the foliage and stems with the Textured Chalk brush, using three shades of green for highlights, midtones, and shadows.

11 Use the Eyedropper tool to pick up a golden yellow from the flower petals in the photo. You can also key in R 209, G 161, B 42 in the Color Picker. Add textured Chalk strokes for the major flower shapes.

Develop the form of the vase and the texture of the chair seat.

12 Use Dodge and Burn, with the Soft Wet brush preset, to begin showing a hint of the cobblestone street background.

13 Return to the Brush tool, using the Scattered Leaves preset. Make the following adjustments to the default in Shape Dynamics: Increase Master Diameter in the Brush Presets section to about 400 pixels, in Shape Dynamics set Minimum Diameter to about 30%, make Angle a function of Direction, in the Scattering section decrease Scattering to about 185%, and in the Color Dynamics section make Jitter for Hue 30%, Saturation Jitter 45%, and Brightness Jitter at about 20%. Save your changes as a new brush.

14 Use the Magic Wand tool to select the yellow flowers you painted in Step 11. Be sure to disable the Contiguous option. Select > Inverse so that only the yellow strokes are unselected.

Paint rough shapes for flowers and leaves and thin edges for cobblestones.

15 Now that the flowers are protected, make several strokes with the new Scattered Leaves brush. Paint with a few different greens as the foreground color. Deselect when you are satisfied with this stage.

Even with all the adjustments you made, there is still a great deal of randomness resulting from the Scattered Leaves brush. You might need to undo strokes and reapply them a few times or use History to return to earlier stages.

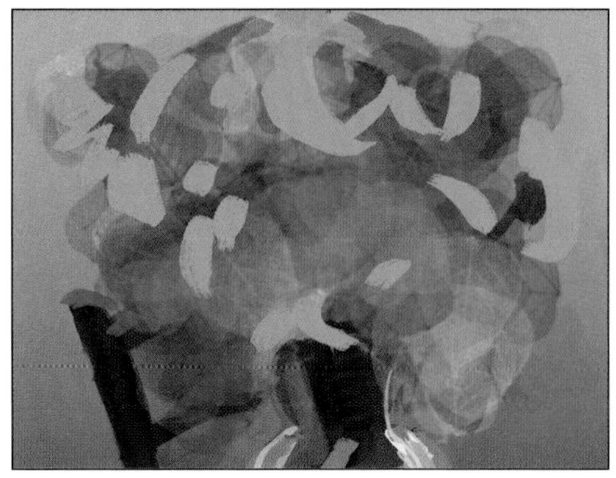

Add foliage with the customized Scattered Leaves brush.

16 Choose the Pointy Leaf brush you made earlier, and work with a golden yellow color. Paint over the sunflower petals, using curving strokes. For more variation, highlight the Brush Tip Shape section of the Brushes palette and increase pixel diameter and the spacing between leaf dabs.

Tip: Another useful setting in the Color Dynamics section is Foreground/Background Jitter. With this value increased, and with green as your background color, you can make strokes that blend petals and leaves nicely.

Paint petals with the Pointy Leaf brush.

Finishing Touches

You still need to add the dark centers to the flowers and develop more shadows and highlights.

1 Use Spatter 59 and Spatter 39 to apply dark brown for the flower centers. Use two shades of brown for the large flower at the top of the painting.

2 To add definition to the shapes of leaves and stems, choose the Hard Pastel on Canvas brush.

This brush has a strong texture, and its dry look will enhance the mixed media effect.

Now work on the vase. With some experimentation, it's possible to blend some of the scribbled strokes without losing too much of the rustic character of the pottery. Judicious use of Color Dodge and Color Burn modes will enhance the glaze.

Define edges with the Hard Pastel on Canvas brush.

3 Use Reset Brushes to load the default Brushes library. Choose the Watercolor Loaded Wet Flat Tip brush. Reduce Opacity in the Options Bar to about 60%. Make some strokes on the vase, using the Eyedropper frequently to vary color. Your strokes should follow the contours of the vase.

Tip: Try turning Wet Edges on. This automatically reduces opacity except for the edges of the stroke.

4 Continue using the Watercolor brush, switching to Color Dodge mode in the Options Bar to strengthen highlights and Color Burn mode to enrich dark areas. You'll need to turn the brush's Opacity way down, around 30%, to avoid a garish neon look! For thinner strokes, use the Watercolor Small Round Tip brush.

Your painting has variety in form, texture, and value. If you've been following along using your own image, you might be finished at this point, but my image could use a little more development in the chair seat and the cobblestone background.

Refine and add luster to the vase.

5 I added textured strokes to the seat of the chair with the Hard Pastel on Canvas brush, which was used earlier on the foliage. This time I chose the Woven Flat texture to emulate the cane fibers. It is found in the Patterns library.

Tip: You can fine tune Texture settings by adjusting size with the Scale slider. Like all other changes to a preset, the original texture will come back the next time you return to this brush, unless you use the New Brush command to save changes.

6. Create some depth in the cobblestone background. I used the Watercolor Loaded Wet Flat Tip brush with Size controlled by Pen Pressure and Angle controlled by Direction. Switch Blending Mode in the Options Bar to Color Dodge or Color Burn as needed. Multiply and Screen mode might work better in some areas.

Changing modes, foreground colors, opacity, pressure, and direction enables you to use one Brush preset for all the work needed on the cobblestones. Be sure to follow the contours of the stones and use less pressure as you paint stones that are farther away. Blues and purples are recommended for applying subtle tints to the stroke.

Develop the chair seat and paint some cobblestones.

MODIFICATIONS

Here's a quick way to paint an artistic variation of the Sunflowers photo, using the History Brush.

1. Open the original Sunflowr.tif photo.
2. Use Filter > Noise > Add Noise to the entire image to add a grainy texture. Settings are as follows: 36%, Gaussian, and Monochromatic.
3. Load the Special Effects Brushes library and highlight the Falling Ivy Leaves preset.

Apply a grainy texture with the Add Noise filter.

4. Choose the History Brush. Establish the Add Noise state as the source for History Brush strokes.

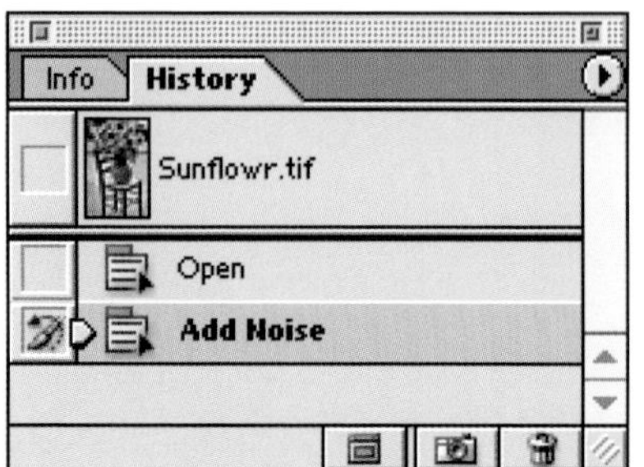

Make Add Noise the source state for the History Brush.

5 Paint using Difference mode, concentrating your strokes in the center of the image. This allows some of the leafy shapes of the brush to make a rough vignette at the edges of the image.

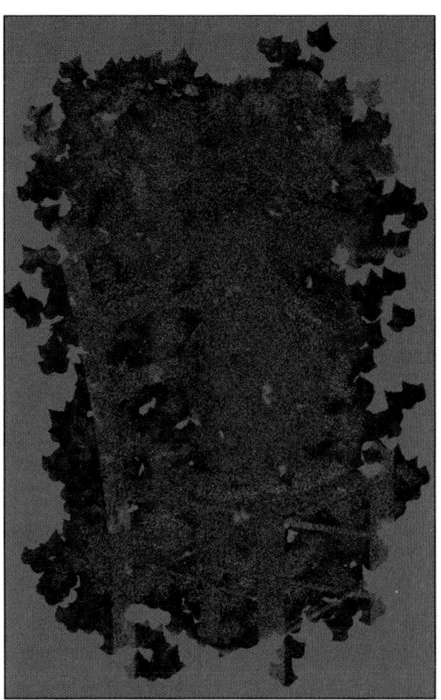

Paint with the Art History Brush in Difference mode.

6 Switch to Hard Light mode and paint some strokes over the flowers, vase, and chair seat. Let some of the Difference mode strokes remain in the chair frame and around the edges.

The Brush effects you learned here will be very useful when you work with the Art History Brush in the next project.

Paint a few Hard Light strokes to bring back some detail in the original colors.

"Our mind is capable of passing beyond the dividing line we have drawn for it. Beyond the pairs of opposites of which the world consists, other, new insights begin."

—HERMANN HESSE

ABSTRACT FIGURES AND PORTRAITS

Advanced Techniques with the Art History Brush

Tired of retouching and correcting images? Throw away the concept of "accuracy" for now and try painting more freely, with expressive effects. The exciting challenge of the Art History Brush is the unpredictability that seems built in. You are likely to have the "happy accidents" that make this a fine art exercise.

Project 3

Abstract Figures and Portraits

by Rhoda Grossman

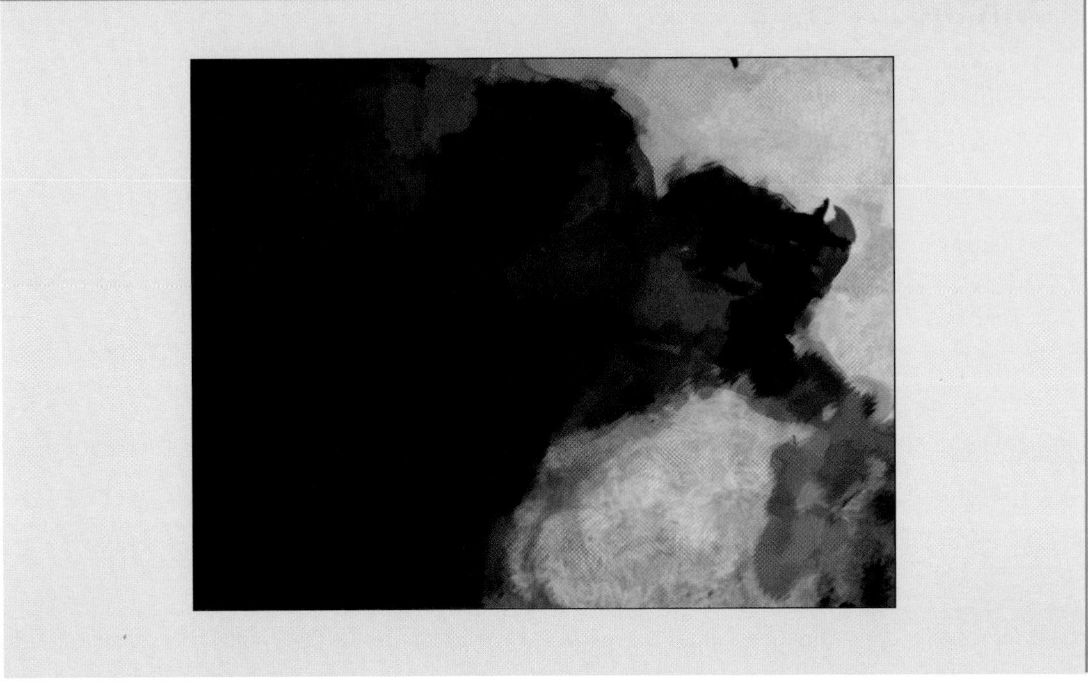

Getting Started

The Art History Brushes are affected by Photoshop's new Brush controls. Before you begin this project, brush up on these options with Project 2, "Brush Techniques." Though not absolutely necessary, a graphics tablet is recommended for this project.

Any kind of image can be altered and enhanced with Art History brushwork. My favorite subjects for painting and image manipulation are the human face and figure.

Making a Face

Take an ordinary vacation snapshot and turn it into a painting. You'll retain the original shapes and colors but recreate them with the Art History Brush. This section is a warm-up for more expressive effects later.

1. Open Ida_cafe.tif.

2. Sample a warm brown from the big umbrellas in the background. You can also type R 154, G 97, and B 80 in the Color Picker.

3. Fill the entire image with brown. The quickest way is with the keyboard shortcut of Alt+Backspace/ Option+Delete.

4. Edit > Fade Fill to about 90%, just enough to be able to see the original image as a guide for your brush strokes.

5. Use the Replace Brushes command in the Brush Preset Picker flyout menu. Choose F_X Magic Brushes.abr from the CD accompanying this book.

   This library provides a manageable number of interesting brush tips.

6. Choose the Art History Brush. Use the 63-pixel Watercolor Loaded Wet Flat Tip preset. On the Options Bar, accept the default Normal mode, 100% opacity, a 50-pixel area, and 100% tolerance. Set Style to Dab.

7. Scribble over the face and some of the surrounding areas.

   Notice that all the brush strokes are at the same angle, regardless of the direction of your brush strokes. That seems a bit too mechanical. In addition, some areas seem resistant to paint. You'll fix that in the next steps.

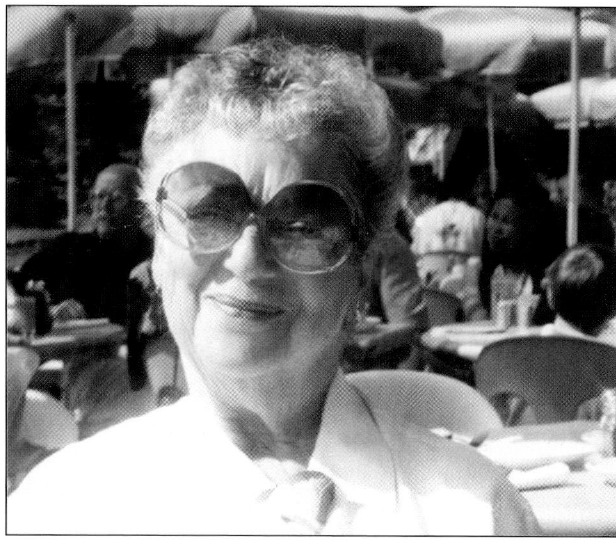

Begin with the close-up photo of Ida.

Tip: I prefer to have a relatively small number of brush presets at my fingertips to avoid spending time scrolling in search of just the right one. If you need to customize settings while you work, use the New Brush command to give each new preset a unique name. Eventually, you will develop a Brushes library that suits the way you like to paint.

8 Reduce Tolerance to 0% and paint again. This time no portion of the image resists paint. The strokes also seem richer and thicker.

9 To create variation in the angle of the brush tip, open the Brushes palette and highlight the Shape Dynamics field. Choose Direction in the Control menu for Angle Jitter. Repaint some of Ida's face with the new brush setting.

You will need frequent access to the Brushes palette. Drag it away from the palette well to keep it open while you work.

10 Switch to the Scattered Leaves brush. There's no need to change any settings in the Options strip. Paint over the background.

The translucent leaves that compose this brush tip are not intrusive or even apparent. The result is a soft focus background, ideal for this portrait.

Now eliminate the prickly strokes in the face that were caused by angle variation in the flat tip brush.

11 Switch to the Soft Wet 31 brush, and change Style from Dab to Tight Medium. Paint over Ida's face and neck.

12 Each time you brush over an area, the results are slightly different, even with the same settings. Continue working until you are satisfied with the effects.

13 The finished piece is still true to the original. Close this warm-up image. You can save it if you wish.

Reduce Tolerance in the Options Bar and set Angle Jitter to Direction control.

Use the Soft Wet brush with Tight Medium strokes to repaint the face.

Kissing Cousins

The photo of my cousin Jerry and his wife Eli provides the source image for a more abstract painting. Do not be concerned this time with keeping the likeness of the subjects. In fact, the farther away you get from Jerry and Eli, the better.

1. Open KISS.tif.

   This is a great image for developing with the Art History Brush. It's a good composition, with detail where it's needed—in the faces—and large, nearly flat areas of low saturation. The tonal range is broad, but the color range is restricted to a few warm browns and creams, with just a touch of pale green.

2. Start by painting the entire image with a large brush to eliminate detail (for now) and establish an interesting texture.

   I used the Texture 6 brush in the Assorted Brushes library, with size increased to about 70 pixels. The Options Bar settings are Normal mode, 100% Opacity, Dab style, 200-pixel area, and 0% Tolerance.

   Texture shows only at the edges where different colors meet. Jerry's black shirt and the smooth gradient on the wall are unchanged. You need to increase the color variability of the brush.

Reduce detail and apply strong texture with a large brush.

3 Highlight the Color Dynamics section of the Brushes palette. Move the Jitter sliders for Hue, Saturation, and Brightness to about 23%. Set the Purity slider to about 39%. Paint over everything except Jerry's and Eli's heads.

Now would be a good time to save your changes as a new preset. Use the New Brush command in the Brush Preset Picker flyout menu.

Tip: Color variability in the Art History Brush was managed differently in Photoshop 6. There was a field in the Options Bar for "Fidelity," meaning fidelity to the source color. With the new Color Dynamics controls in the Brush Presets section of the Brushes palette, there's no longer a need for the Fidelity slider.

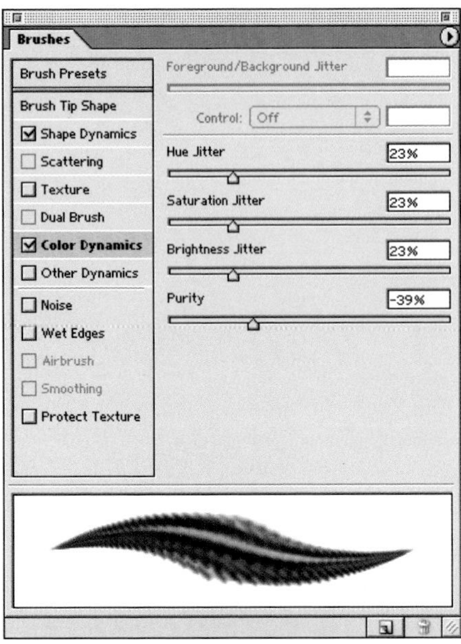

Adjust Color Dynamics and save all changes as a new preset.

At this stage, you have what could be considered an underpainting. You will develop it, as you would a traditional canvas, by emphasizing some areas while downplaying others. Variations in brushwork and the amount of detail will help.

4 Load the Natural Brushes library and choose the Charcoal 59 pixels brush. Set Style to Loose Long and paint on and around the two faces.

I like the bold strokes that loosely follow the basic forms of the faces. The fluffy texture from the underpainting looks good in Eli's shirt, so keep it, but return to a smoother look for Jerry's shirt.

Examine the underpainting and look for ways to develop it.

5 Switch to the Brush tool. You can continue using the Charcoal 59 pixels preset. Set Opacity in the Options Bar to about 50% and paint over Jerry's shirt with black. Vary the length and direction of your strokes slightly and use Edit > Fade as needed for just a bit of variation in tone and texture.

Yes, it's legal to use the "regular" brush on this project, especially if you know what you want and how to achieve it easily. Just be careful not to make your work look too slick.

Paint loose, long strokes over the faces and reduce variation in the black shirt.

6 Return to the Art History Brush configuration used in Step 4. Apply strokes to the upper-left background and to the area between Eli's shirt and the lower-right corner.

7 The painting is finished when you say so. If you feel you have created enough visually interesting shapes, tones, and textures, you might take a break and come back to give it a fresh look before deciding whether to work some more. It might be better to call the painting "finished" sooner rather than later to avoid overworking it.

Continue to develop the painting.

Modifications

Here are several quick variations you can make by combining two painted versions of the same source image.

1. Open the Kiss2.tif file. It is a version I painted earlier with different presets for the Art History Brush.

   There are strong similarities between the two paintings, of course, but there also are many differences. Those differences will reward us with some interesting combinations when you layer them and explore Blending mode changes.

2. Drag and drop (or copy and paste) your painting onto Kiss2.tif. Be sure the new layer is lined up accurately with the Background layer.

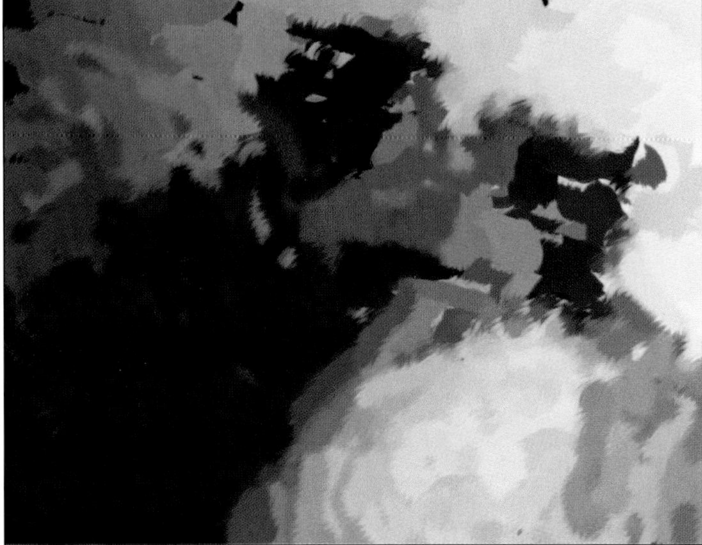

Use another painting or the Kiss file as a source for variations.

3. Explore Blending modes other than Normal, adjusting Opacity if needed to improve the effect. Especially promising choices include Darken, Lighten, Hard Light, and Difference.

4. Save a snapshot of each combination you like by using the Create new document icon at the bottom of the History palette.

   Darken mode at 100% mixes these two versions nicely, creating a more satisfying piece than either of the two layers alone.

Use Darken mode at 100%.

Hard Light mode at 100% creates vibrant skin tones and reduces detail in some areas.

Use Hard Light mode at 100%.

Difference mode at 50% produces moody effects, including cooler colors. You can expect that some cool, blue-green areas will result from Difference mode. Difference mode inverts color in many areas, and blue-green is the inverse of the warm, orangey flesh tones.

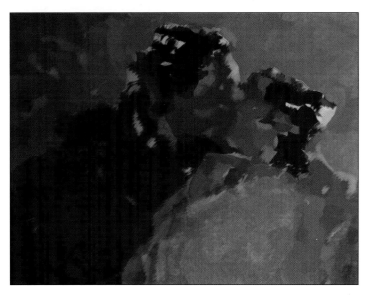

Use Difference mode at 50%.

Linear Burn, one of Photoshop's new modes, at 75% produces a dramatic passionate image, with rich creamy tones. It is shown as the opening image for this chapter.

There's almost no limit to the number of variations possible by combining two (or more) paintings with different Blending modes and opacities.

Another project that explores combining similar images is Project 6, "Abstract Imaging Using Liquify Tools." This project is about using the Liquify filter.

STILL-LIFE PAINTING FROM PHOTOS

"Time extracts various values from a painter's work. When these values are exhausted the pictures are forgotten, and the more a picture has to give, the greater it is."

—HENRI MATISSE

Photorealistic Paintings Using Photoshop's Expanded Brush Capabilities

A photograph of a traditional still-life setup is retouched and then painted in Layers. The result is a photorealistic painting with all the detail of the source image and the added richness that simply cannot be attained with photography alone.

Photoshop's expanded brush capabilities enable your skills in traditional drawing and painting to be expressed digitally.

Project 4

Still-Life Painting from Photos

by Phil Williams

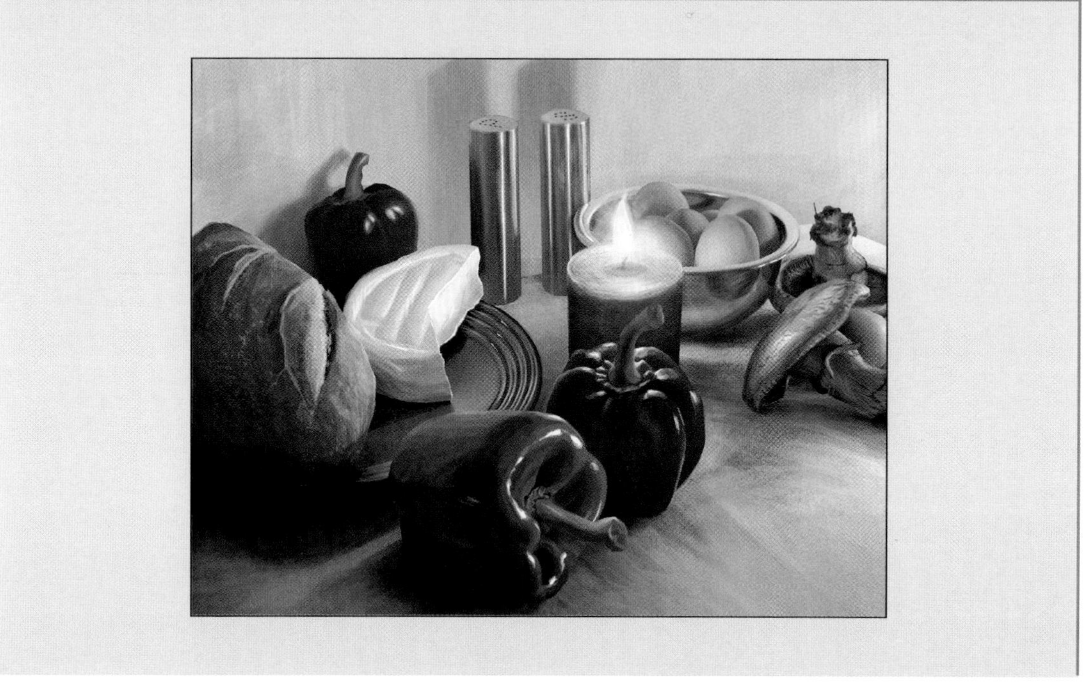

Getting Started

The photo you'll use as a reference needs a few small changes to improve it before you start painting.

1 Open StillLife.tif.

There are a few slight changes needed to improve the overall balance of the composition and create more interesting relationships between shapes.

2 Use any retouching tool, such as the Clone Stamp tool, to move the red pepper in the background to the left.

Note: Don't spend too much time making the photo manipulations look seamless. There is really no need for that because the photo will be used only as reference. Moving things around and even combining photographs can help you arrive at a better composition. Nonetheless, setting up a reference photo can be a creative part of the process.

3 Extend the candle up a bit, and move the pepper shaker slightly to the left.

4 When you have arrived at the composition, flatten the image, if needed, and use the Image Size command to enlarge it to 1400 pixels wide.

I like to work with images that are at least this size, so that I can get high-quality prints. The warning you might have heard against sampling up is not relevant here because the photo will be completely replaced by the painting.

5 Use Save As to name your altered photo **source photo** or something similar. Keep this file open while you work.

Improve the composition of the reference photo.

Making an Outline Drawing

We will use a copy of the source photo as the bottom layer of our working image. Two more layers are needed: a white layer with opacity turned down just enough to enable you to see the shapes of your composition and a transparent layer on top. You will trace simple outlines of the composition on the transparent layer.

1 Make a copy of the source photo. The easiest way is to use the Save As command and give the photo another name.

2 Make two new layers.

3 Fill the middle layer with white and set its Opacity to about 75%. Name this layer **onion skin**, a term used to describe translucent materials such as tracing paper.

This layer enables you to see the photo below and also to see your drawing as it develops.

4 Let the top layer remain transparent, and name it **outline**.

5 Choose the Brush tool and reset Brushes to the default library. Pick a Hard Round brush and set its Master Diameter setting to 8 pixels, or less, if you draw with a mouse. If you are using a graphics tablet, turn on Shape Dynamics and set Size Control to Pen Pressure.

6 Trace the major forms of the composition on the transparent outline layer. Concentrate on drawing the edges of shapes and a few additional contour lines.

7 When the tracing is finished, increase the onion skin layer to 100% opacity.

Now you will see just the line drawing.

Note: Notice that I fixed and lengthened the broken stem on the green pepper. Repairing the stem on the photo would have been tedious, but it's quick and easy in the line drawing. I'll simply add the stem when the painting begins.

Trace the shapes on the outline layer.

Creating the Base Painting

You will add light, dark, and medium tones on the onion skin layer. This is often how a traditional painter works at this stage. He or she just fills in some neutral tonality so that the white is not so overpowering.

1 Use the Lasso tool to select areas of various sizes and shapes and apply Levels changes to create tonal variation.

2 Switch to the Pencil tool and choose a Hard Round preset at various widths. Start large at about 60–100 pixels, and then reduce the size to 10–14 pixels as the shapes develop. Keep the opacity low, from 15% to 35%. Pick up color from the image by using the Modifier key (Alt/Option) as you paint.

Tip: If you are new to Photoshop 7's brush engine, this is a good chance to experiment with different settings. The only requirement is to keep the look roughly like the reference figure. Avoid being too precise; most of these strokes will be covered over before the painting is finished. It's just a nice loose way to get started.

Now layers become important.

3 Make a new layer for each major item in the still life. Give them corresponding names in the Layer Properties dialog box.

Note: Photoshop has layers; use them. They are certainly one of the main advantages that a digital painter has over a traditional painter. At this stage, use your layers liberally and label them accurately. In a still life like this one, I'll initially define each still life object on its own layer. As long as the layers remain transparent, that is until you paint on them, there is no increase in the file size, so make as many as you want without worrying about disk space.

Rather than painting with brushes at this stage, you'll use fills and adjustment commands to achieve colored midtones, highlights, and shadows for each layered item. This is an efficient way to apply basic color quickly and to simplify shapes.

Add overlapping brush strokes for basic tonality.

4. Target one of the transparent layers, such as the green pepper. Use the Lasso tool to follow the traced lines, creating a selection to fill with foreground color. Use the Eyedropper tool to sample the reference photo for the medium green (which is between the lightest and darkest greens).

5. Turn the Opacity of the onion skin layer down just enough to see the tonal variations of objects in the source photo. Use the Lasso tool to select all the areas of the object that are in shadow. Darken them with Levels.

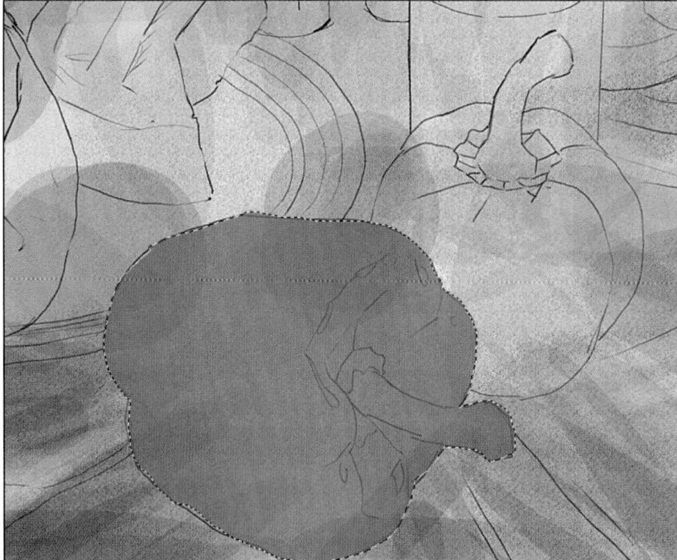

Fill a shape with its medium color.

6. Repeat Step 5, but select and adjust the lighter areas.

   Slight color shifts can occur as a result of Levels adjustments. Select a problem area with the Lasso tool and use Image > Adjustments > Color Balance. Move the appropriate sliders until you are satisfied.

Add lighter and darker shapes with Levels adjustments.

Note: You can expect to perform a great number of Levels and Color Balance adjustments throughout this project. Record an action to make it quick and easy to access these commands.

This action requires a selected area, so before you begin recording, make a selection on any image. In the Actions flyout menu, choose New Action. Give the action a name and assign it a function key.

Click the Record button. Choose Levels (Ctrl+L/Cmd+L). You will have to make some kind of adjustment for this to work, so change one of the options, and then click OK.

Press Ctrl+B/Cmd+B to bring up the Color Balance dialog box. Once again, make some kind of value change, and then click OK.

Now stop recording. You're not done yet. Notice two columns to the left of the Action names. At the far left is a check box. The column next to it is the Modal column. For your action to pause so that you can change settings, you must enable the Modal function.

Here are two peppers, each on its own layer and each modeled with lighter and darker colors and with suggestions of reflected lights. This has been accomplished using just the Lasso tool, the Levels Adjustments, and Color Balance Adjustments

Continue developing forms with Levels and Color Balance Adjustments.

When all the layers are developed to this point, you have the base painting. Many of the areas have overlapped other areas, so a rich combination of colors has begun to appear in the picture. With this much color, the picture itself becomes the palette for most subsequent color needs.

Complete the color fills and adjustments for the entire image.

ADDING REALISTIC LIGHT

At the lower right of the reference photo, notice the patch of reddish yellow candlelight that fades in and then spills off the corner. You'll use a Quick Mask technique to create the fade.

1 Select the area with the Lasso tool.

Select an area for enhancing candlelight.

Note: Photoshop's default settings for Quick Mask mode put the mask color over the unselected area rather than the selected area. There is an option to reverse that, which I prefer. I often paint in Quick Mask mode to create selections for Levels adjustments. With the default settings, it's more like erasing than painting, so I reverse the mask to achieve a more intuitive way of working.

2 Double-click the Quick Mask icon in the Tools palette to access Quick Mask Options. Click the Selected Areas button. Then change the color to cyan, and set the Opacity for the mask to 33%. Click OK and you'll see the selected area in 33% cyan.

These changes make it easier to see your work in progress when you use Quick Mask mode.

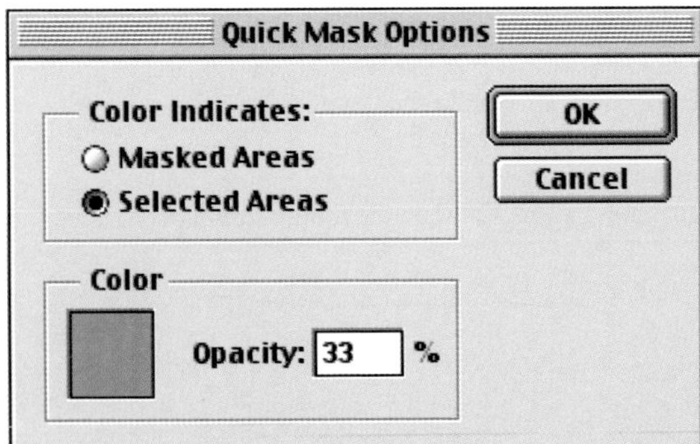

Make changes in the Quick Mask Options window.

Switch to Quick Mask mode.

3 In Quick Mask mode, lasso a large elliptical area with its center more or less at the point where the cyan mask touches the red pepper.

Make and feather a lasso selection in Quick Mask mode.

4 Give the selection a serious feather. At the resolution I am using, which is 4000 pixels wide, a serious feather is about 110 pixels. This gives the mask a gentle fade. Press the Delete key.

5 Toggle back to Standard mode by pressing Q.

The marching ants have changed as a result of the fade, but cannot accurately show the fade that we know is there.

Delete the selection to create a mask with a gradual fade.

6 Use Levels adjustments to lighten the selected area and Color Balance adjustments to boost the red and yellow.

The result is a convincing orange light that the candle throws on the surface.

Tip: Quick Mask mode can be used in a number of ways to create complex selections with fades and hard edges and to create various textures. You'll use Quick Mask mode again later, to add surface detail to the bread and mushrooms.

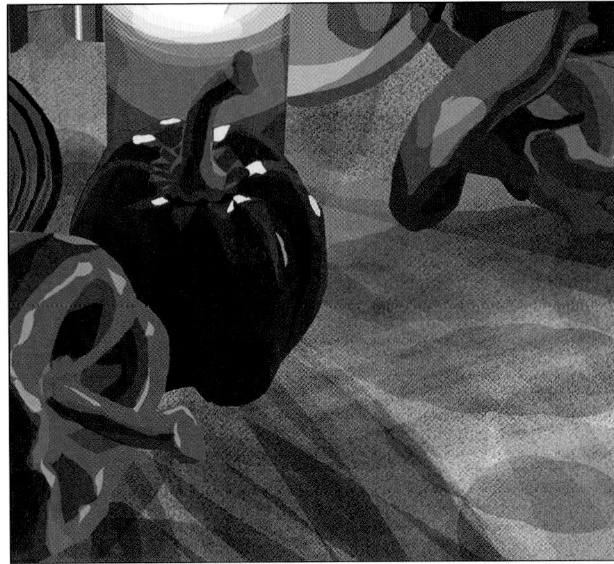

Brighten and warm up the color of the selection.

Painterly Techniques

At last, we start painting! When I paint high-resolution images digitally, I use a round, hard-edge brush (the Pencil tool, really) at low opacity almost exclusively.

1 Choose the Pencil tool and open Brush Presets. Enable Shape Dynamics and set Other Dynamics to Pen Pressure control. Change Master Diameter as needed.

With these settings, the Pencil tool acts very much like a real brush. The harder you press the pen to your tablet, the wider and darker the brush stroke.

Now work on the loaf of bread.

Note: A good trick to use when you're first starting to paint is to create a layer just above the one on which you intend to work. Paint on the new layer until you have what you want, and then merge it onto the intended layer. This technique enables you to take risks that you might not normally take because you can always simply delete the layer and start over. It's a great way to develop skill and even style. You'll find as you get comfortable with digital painting, you'll use the technique less and less as you become sure and confident with your painting tools.

2 Select the bread by clicking its layer in the Layers palette while holding down the Ctrl/Command key. This selects only the loaf of bread, not the transparent pixels. Thus, you don't have to worry about painting outside the bread loaf's boundary. Press Ctrl+H/ Cmd+H to hide the distracting marching ants.

3 Place your pencil over the area of color marked with the green "A" and switch to the Eyedropper tool by holding down the Alt/Option key. Sample the color.

4 Set the width of the Pencil tool to about 44 pixels and the opacity to about 33%. Paint strokes over the border that separates the "A" and "B" hues.

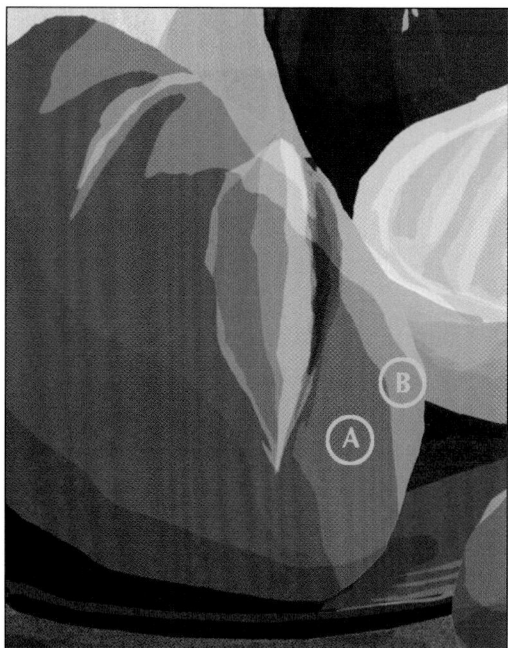

Sample color from the loaf of bread.

5 After a few strokes, sample the "B" color and paint across to the "A" area.

The brush strokes begin blending the two areas with a nice painterly look. Continue painting. Use the reference photo to guide your strokes.

Blend the hard lines between hues with overlapping strokes.

6 Work on the shadowed area where the bread meets the dark blue plate. Sample the dark blue, and paint strokes on the reddish brown bread. As you work, sample some of the new colors resulting from the strokes you just made.

This is a good demonstration of how your picture can become the palette from which you get your colors.

The bread needs a bit of texturing to suggest a crunchy crust.

7 Switch to Quick Mask mode.

Paint dark blue strokes from the plate onto the bread.

8 Load the Wet Media Brushes and choose the Large Texture Stroke. Use a Master Diameter of about 300 pixels, and set opacity to about 70%. Turn off Shape Dynamics and turn on Texture. Apply the brush to the surface of the bread by just touching it to various spots here and there.

This produces an irregular scatter effect and avoids any repeated patterns. The moldy look will disappear when you toggle back to Standard mode!

9 Return to Standard mode and hide the scattered marching ants.

10 Use Levels adjustments to gradually lighten the selected areas until you get the amount of texture you like.

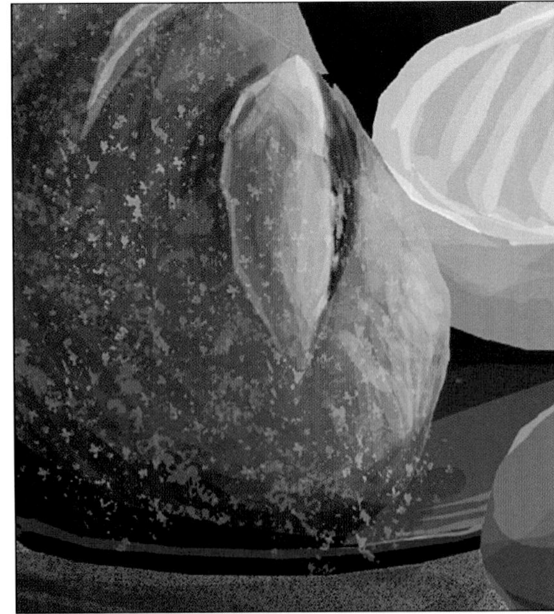

Paint irregular scattered textures in Quick Mask mode.

11 To add some darker areas in the crevices on top, toggle back to Quick Mask mode and paint a few squiggly areas in the crevices. Back in Standard mode, use Levels adjustments to darken the selection.

Continue painting and using the Quick Mask technique to add more interest and definition to the loaf of bread. When you are satisfied, move on to another object.

The mushroom in the back is upside down, so its fine inner structure shows a bit in the light. As usual in Photoshop, there is more than one way to add that fine detail. This method gives you more control over the effect than, for example, painting each line in Dodge mode.

12 In Quick Mask mode, use a small brush to draw lines that approximate the detailed structure. Use Levels adjustments to lighten the lines.

13 Add texture to the mushroom heads with the same basic techniques used on the loaf of bread.

14 When you are satisfied with each element in the still life, merge them into one layer, but leave the background separate.

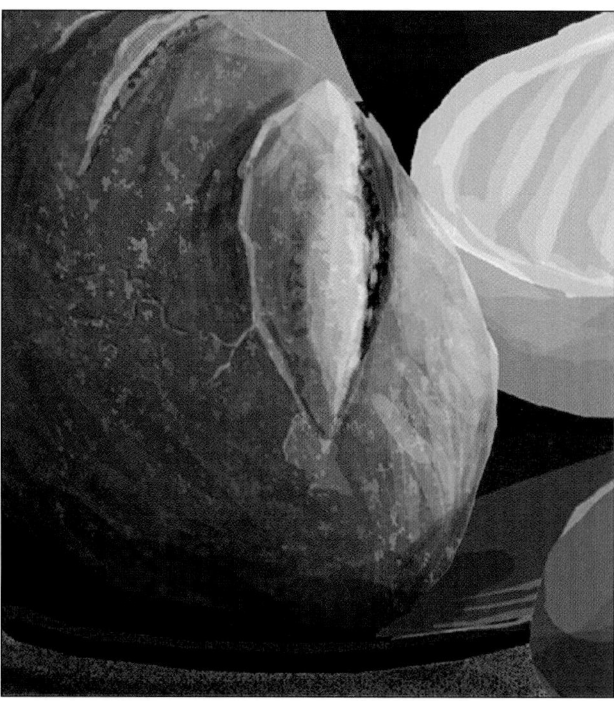

Finish adding texture to the bread.

Add detail to the mushroom in Quick Mask mode.

Finishing Touches

You've worked long and hard, and you're at the point where only a few areas of your painting could use some improvement. You might want to take a break, and then come back to look at the image with fresh eyes.

1. Examine the image, looking for boundaries between objects that need to be softened. Be especially careful in shadow areas, where the shift from object to shadow should be quite blurred.

2. Finally, look at the image as a whole and determine whether you need any overall changes in brightness, hue, or contrast.

   There's a good chance that after the layers are merged, you might want to change an item or two. I'd like to enrich the candle glow on the mushroom head slightly. Although that would have been easier with the item on its own layer, it's still doable. It just takes some finesse in creating selections.

3. Drag a Lasso selection that extends above the mushroom and that follows the edge of the candlelight along the mushroom head's edge.

4. Apply a large feather and switch to Quick Mask mode, where you can more easily see the selection fade.

5. Use the Lasso tool in Quick Mask mode to create a crisp selection edge at the top and bottom of the mushroom head. Do not use feathering this time. Press the Delete key to deselect the pixels that aren't needed.

   This creates a selection with a hard edge along the boundaries of the mushroom and a nice feathered fade on the head itself.

Make a selection with the perfect combination of hard edges and fades.

6 Return to Standard mode and make any appropriate Levels and Color Balance adjustments.

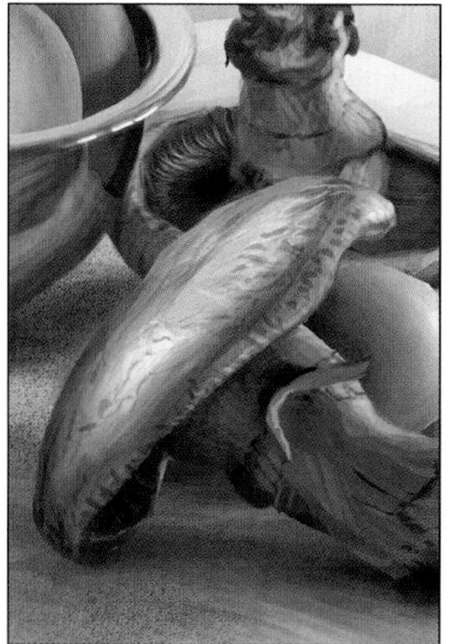

Increase candlelight on the mushroom.

Modifications

These techniques can be used successfully for a wide variety of fine art and commercial projects. These projects include portrait painting and product shot enhancements.

Photoshop artists are no longer dependent on filters to make painterly recreations of photographs. A combination of filters and brushwork can be effective, however, and quicker than painting everything from scratch. Apply a filter from the Artistic category, and then paint or adjust areas that still need work. Shown here, from left to right, are the Paint Daubs, Watercolor, and Fresco effects. The Paint Daubs effect requires adding detail, whereas the Watercolor effect needs some softening and smoothing.

Apply an Artistic filter to create the base painting.

If you wish to explore less realistic painting techniques, I recommend Project 3, "Abstract Figures and Portraits," which is about using the Art History Brush.

"I saw the angel in the marble and carved until I set him free."

—MICHELANGELO

MARBLED BACKGROUNDS

Using Photoshop to Reproduce Traditional Craft Techniques

Many cultures throughout time have been fascinated by the design possibilities that can be realized by dragging a stick through a bath of wet paint. Marbling has been practiced in Japan, China, Turkey, Persia, and throughout Europe. Today, marbled designs are used in items as varied as book endpapers and children's sneakers. It is a sought-after look. You can purchase stock photos of marbled papers for use on the computer, but you can also make some of your own. Here's a way to capture the beauty of marbling without the mess.

Project 5

Marbled Backgrounds

by Sherry London
with displacement maps by
Chris Setlock

Getting Started

The possibilities of marbling are endless. You can mix and match techniques and make an infinite number of combinations of colors and designs. One of the paradoxes of traditional marbling is that the inks used to create the marbled patterns do not mix with each other in the marbling bath. They retain their clear colors and don't get muddied. In trying to duplicate this look on the computer, I have discovered that using the Displace filter with a variety of custom-made displacement maps successfully reproduces the clear colors in traditional marbling.

If you wanted to create a traditional piece of marbled paper, using inks, you would first prepare a bath for the inks. This bath is a water-based solution, called a *size*, that contains a thickening agent. Into this solution, you would drop colors of ink, forming *stones*, which are the basis of the marble.

The next step is to create the *getgel*, a Turkish word meaning "to and fro." You create the getgel by dragging a large rake through the dye bath, back and forth and up and down. The final step is to create a *nonpareil*. You do this with a comb that has finely-spaced teeth. From this base, you can create many different patterns. After your pattern is set, you carefully place the paper to be marbled on the size, allow it to absorb the inks, remove and wash it, and hang it up to dry.

Your process on the computer involves much less chance of getting wet, but it follows a similar path. You create the stones, the getgel, and then the nonpareil. I then show you how to create a traditional fountain pattern. I've made most of the displacement maps for you, but I will show you how to create your own and how to vary the patterns that you produce.

Making Maps

A good craftsperson keeps tools close by and always has the right tools for the job. Thus, you begin this project by building the first of the eight displacement maps that you'll need. Each map is based on a black-to-white or gray-to-white gradient. You begin by creating the gradient that you need.

1 Choose the Gradient tool. You don't need an image open for this step. Click the Gradient Sample icon on the Options Bar to open the Gradient Editor. Start by selecting the Black, White gradient.

You are building a specific gradient here, but you need to do this only one time. No matter what marbling pattern you use, only four variations on this basic gradient are actually practical.

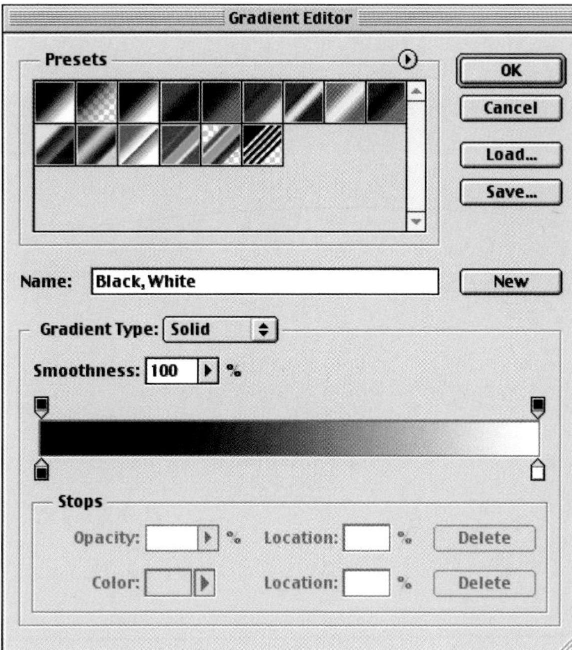

Open the Gradient Editor and use the Black, White gradient.

2 Leave a color stop at 10, 20, 30, 40, 50, 60, 70, 80, and 90% on the Gradient Bar.

In the next step, you set each color stop to the correct color. I have found that it's easier, however, to create the stops first.

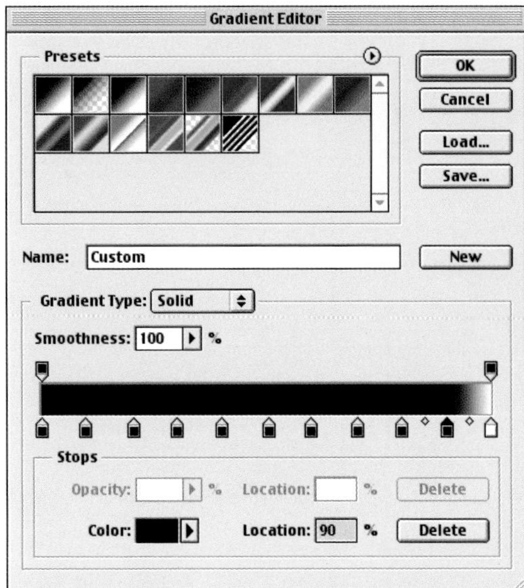

Leave color stops at 10% increments.

3 Double-click each color stop in turn and change the Brightness value in the Color Picker to the following values (you are setting only the B: control in the H: S: B: section of the Color Picker):

0 percent color stop: 0

10 percent color stop: 1

20 percent color stop: 4

30 percent color stop: 9

40 percent color stop: 16

50 percent color stop: 25

60 percent color stop: 36

70 percent color stop: 49

80 percent color stop: 64

90 percent color stop: 81

100 percent color stop: 100

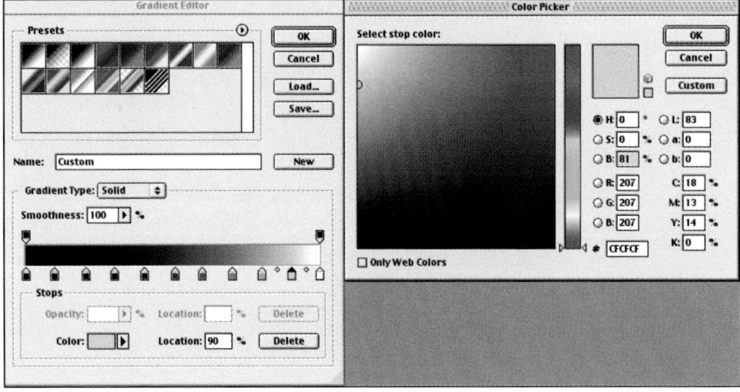

Assign the numbers 0, 1, 4, 9, 16, 25, 36, 49, 64, 81, and 100 to the Brightness value of each color stop in turn.

If you are at all mathematically inclined, you'll notice that these values are the squares of the numbers from 0 to 10. This sequence of colors is needed to make a gradient that produces a scallop in the displacement map rather than a sawtooth pattern, which would occur if you used a simple black-to-white gradient.

Picture two sticks that are spaced apart evenly. If you drag the sticks through the marble size, you would see that you drag the inks near the sticks much farther than you do the inks that are in the area between the sticks. This gradient does exactly the same thing. Because the Brightness setting works on a 0–100 numbering scheme instead of on the RGB 0–255 scheme, it makes a perfect setting to use to control the gradient colors.

4 Type **Black Quadratic** as the name for the gradient and click the New button to add this gradient to the presets.

5 The Gradient Editor should still be open. This time, select the Black Quadratic as your starting point. Double-click each color stop and subtract the Brightness setting from 100. This gives you the following list of brightness settings:

0 percent color stop: 100

10 percent color stop: 99

20 percent color stop: 96

30 percent color stop: 91

40 percent color stop: 84

50 percent color stop: 75

60 percent color stop: 64

70 percent color stop: 51

80 percent color stop: 36

90 percent color stop: 19

100 percent color stop: 0

This sequence creates the reverse gradient, which pulls the displacement up more strongly than it pulls it down. This gradient is the direct opposite of the Black Quadratic gradient.

6 Name the gradient **White Quadratic** and click the New button to add the preset to the menu.

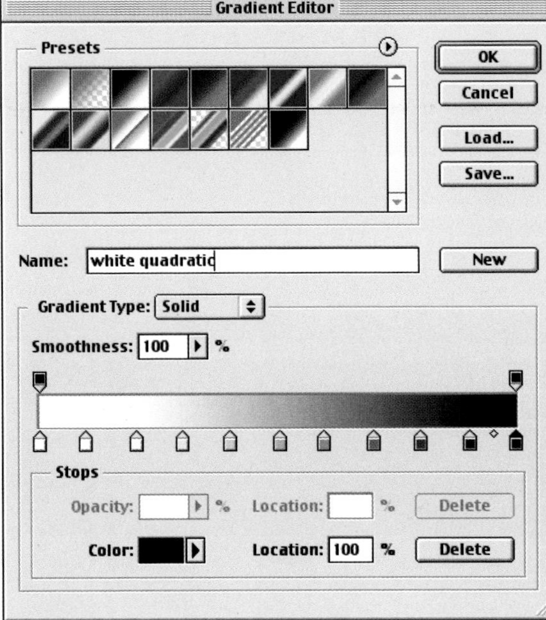

Create a new gradient preset named White Quadratic with each Color Stop's Brightness value set to 100 minus the corresponding value found in the Black Quadratic preset.

7 Create a new image that is 301 pixels wide and 20 pixels high, at 300 ppi, in RGB Color mode, and with a white background.

This is the start of the map that you will use for the first displacement. It is only half (plus 1 pixel) the size that you need. If you make your own marbling tools, this file is the start of a tool that is 2 inches wide on a 300-ppi image.

Your first "rake" is generally a 2-inch rake, so if you were planning to work on a 72-ppi image, you would create your first "half" file, 73 pixels wide by 20 pixels high. (The height doesn't matter, but at 20 pixels, you can at least see what is happening.)

8 Choose the Gradient tool and the White Quadratic gradient. Drag the gradient cursor from the left side of the image to the right side with the Shift key pressed to constrain the gradient to the horizontal. You should stop about 1 pixel from the right edge.

You might want to double-click the Hand tool to make this image as large as possible on your monitor. Check the Info palette to make sure that your starting value in the image on the left is RGB 255, 255, 255 and that your ending value on the right is RGB 0, 0, 0. You need to shorten the area covered by the drag to ensure that you end with black.

9 Drag the Background layer to the Create a new layer icon at the bottom of the Layers palette to duplicate the layer. Choose Image > Canvas Size. Anchor on the center-left and change the Width to 600 pixels. Don't check the Relative box.

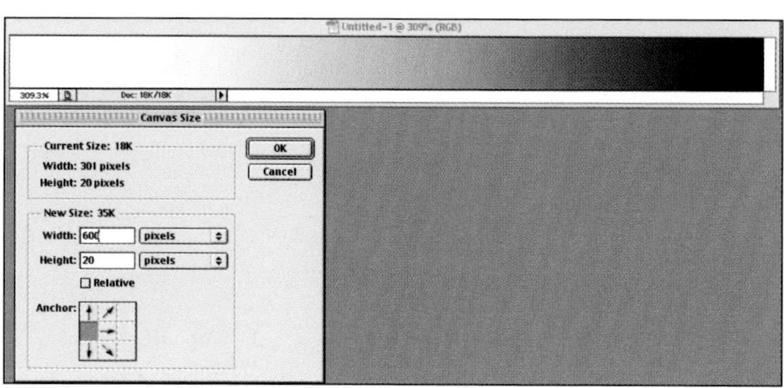

Use the Canvas Size command to make your image 600 pixels wide.

This gives you an image that will be 2 inches wide at 300 ppi. If you were working at 72 ppi, you would add 71 pixels to the canvas to get a size of 144 pixels. You need to duplicate the Background layer before you increase the canvas size so that you don't have to make a selection to create the other half of the gradient.

10 Make Background Copy active. Choose Edit>Free Transform (Ctrl+T/Cmd+T). Click the icon between the X and Y fields on the Options Bar and change the X: field to 300. Before you confirm the transformation, choose Edit > Transform > Flip Horizontal. Then click the checkmark.

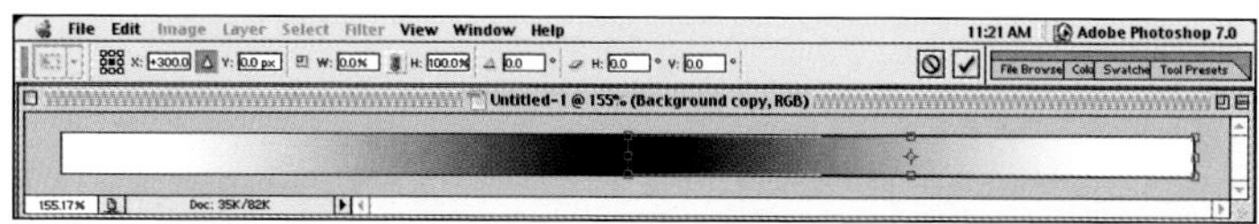

Choose Edit > Free Transform, move Background Copy 300 pixels to the right, and flip it horizontally.

Although these instructions seem finicky, by creating your original file at 1 pixel larger than half the needed size, and then moving the duplicate layer 1 inch (300 pixels instead of 301 pixels), you keep from repeating either the black or the white pixel at the ends of the gradient. This makes for a better pattern and a better displacement map.

11 Flatten the image. Choose Filter > Other > Offset with these settings:

Horizontal: 300 pixels right

Vertical: 0 pixels down

Undefined Areas: Wrap Around

In this image, the black pixels are the equivalent to the rake that drags the paint down. You want the black pixels to be on the edges of the image. The Offset filter is the easiest way to get this to happen.

12 Choose Edit > Define Pattern and name the pattern **2inch300ppiRake**.

13 Create a new image 1800×1200 pixels at 300 ppi, RGB Color mode, and with a white background.

This will become the first displacement map. It is the same size as the marbling you will create (6×4 inches at 300 ppi). Always make your maps the same size as the marble.

14 Choose Edit > Fill, and fill with the 2inch300ppiRake pattern that you just created. Save the image as **map1.psd**.

You need to save the image as a Photoshop file (.psd); if you don't, the Displace filter will not be able to use the file.

Cast the First Stone...

All marbling starts with stones. These are the colors that you select to give the color feel to the marble. You should pick a palette with five or six colors that are distinctively different. They should not be close to one another in value, and you should include white and black in the mix for contrast.

Although you could use a photo as your stones image, I don't recommend it. If you do, you run the risk of getting a muddy marble. You can control the amount of blending that you get in colors by creating dots of various sizes. There is not really any way to simulate in Photoshop the actual effect of dropping liquid ink onto a medium that spreads out. Though you could try to create stones in Painter's Blobs, but they still don't really push the "ink" aside.

The colors that you choose and the size of the dots make a huge difference in your results. In the example shown here, you can see the different results that you can get using the same displacement maps but with different stones images. Notice the sharply different color areas in the two images that use the same colors. The larger blobs of color create much more dramatic color areas in the final marble.

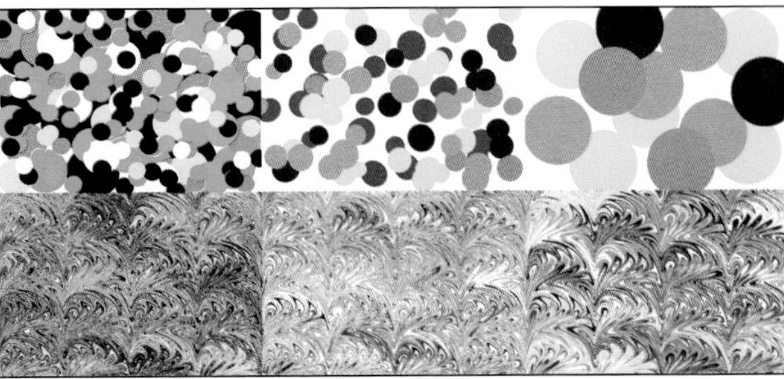

The size of the color blobs as well as the colors that you select make a difference in your final result.

In this project, you use a stones image that I created so that you can match your results against mine. (Of course, if you prefer to do your own thing, just create an image 1800 pixels wide by 1200 pixels high and paint blobs of color on it using the standard hard paintbrushes. I prefer not to use the Pencil tool for this, but the colors look much better in the final marbled image if you stick to a hardness setting of 100% on the brush tip.)

1. Open the image mutedstones.psd from the CD that accompanies this book.
2. Duplicate the image (Image > Duplicate > OK). You'll work in this image for the rest of the project.

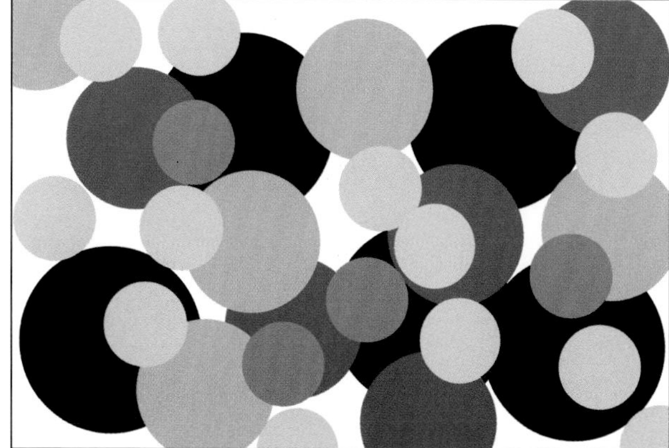

Open the image mutedstones.psd.

CREATING A GETGEL

A getgel is the first "mixing" that helps to prepare the marbling bath for more intricate patterns. The term is pronounced with the same "g" sound in both syllables. It is the "g" sound of "get"—not the sound of a "j." In this section of the project, you create this getgel using four displacement maps—the one that you created and maps 2–4 from the accompanying CD.

1. Working in the duplicate of the stones image, choose Filter > Distort > Displace and use these settings:

   Horizontal Scale: 0%

   Vertical Scale: 200%

   Displacement Map: Stretch To Fit

   Undefined Areas: Wrap Around

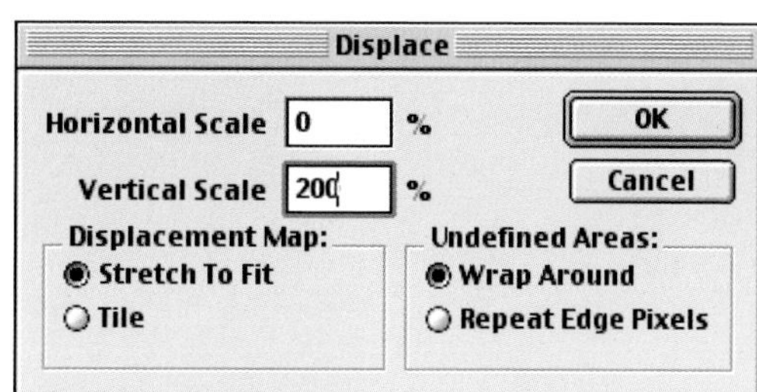

Use the Map1.psd displacement map to move the pixels in the stones image.

2 Click OK. When the Choose a displacement map dialog box appears, choose map1.psd, which you created earlier.

You can see how map1.psd pushes the areas with black pixels down, and the white pixels form a scallop shape.

Note: The Horizontal and Vertical scale values that I am giving you are appropriate for the size of the image. These values will not always be the ones to use. The Horizontal and Vertical scale percentages are not linked to your file size. Although it sounds as if these should be proportional, they aren't. If you set the Scale to 100%, the black pixels in the displacement map will move the corresponding pixels 128 pixels down or to the right, and white pixels will move 128 pixels up or to the left. Therefore, a 50% scale can move pixels a maximum of 64 pixels, and a 200% scale moves pixels a maximum of 256 pixels. Because 256 pixels might be too much movement for a small image or too little movement for a really large image, you will need to play with the scale values each time you change the image size to make sure that they work as intended.

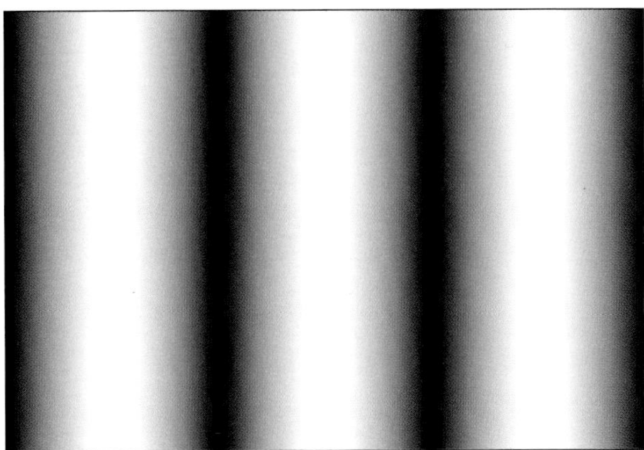

3 Choose Filter > Distort > Displace and use these settings:

Horizontal Scale: 0%

Vertical Scale: 200%

Displacement Map: Stretch To Fit

Undefined Areas: Wrap Around

Click OK. When the Choose a displacement map dialog box appears, choose map2.psd from the accompanying CD.

map2.psd uses a map that was made the same way you created map1.psd. However, it uses the Black Quadratic gradient and does not offset the gradient at all. This forces the map to displace up and between the "pulling" of the previous displacement map.

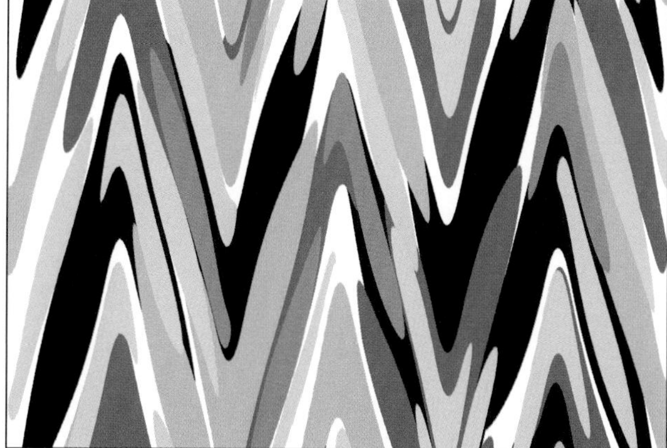

Offset the image using the same setting, but with map2.psd as the displacement map.

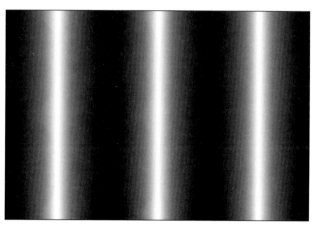

4 Choose Filter > Distort > Displace and use these settings:

Horizontal Scale: 200%

Vertical Scale: 0%

Displacement Map: Stretch To Fit

Undefined Areas: Wrap Around

Click OK. When the Choose a displacement map dialog box appears, choose map3.psd from the accompanying CD.

map3 uses map1 as its basis. This map pulls strongly to the right. I created it by rotating a copy of map1 90° clockwise (Image > Rotate Canvas > 90° CW). I then applied the Image > Image Size command with Constrain Proportions unchecked, and resized to 6 inches square. Finally, I chose Image > Canvas Size and anchor in the center-top square. Then, I set the height to 1200 pixels.

Offset the image 200% horizontally with map3.psd as the displacement map.

5 Choose Filter > Distort > Displace and use these settings:

Horizontal Scale: 200%

Vertical Scale: 0%

Displacement Map: Stretch To Fit

Undefined Areas: Wrap Around

Click OK. When the Choose a displacement map dialog box appears, choose map4.psd from the accompanying CD.

map4 uses map2 as its basis. This map pulls strongly to the left. I created it exactly as I created map3.psd. This completes the getgel.

Offset the image 200% horizontally with map4.psd as the displacement map.

Creating the Nonpareil

The getgel does the basic color mixing and the nonpareil creates the first pattern that can be used on its own. You would probably never want to stop with just the getgel; it isn't really very interesting. The nonpareil pattern, however, is both a stop "along the way" and a pretty pattern in its own right. The nonpareil is formed by stroking the getgel from top to bottom with a comb whose teeth are set ⅛ inch apart.

1 Choose Filter > Blur > Gaussian Blur and choose a blur radius of 1 pixel.

This tiny blur softens the jagged edges that the getgel has created. If you make your marble smaller, remember to reduce the blur Radius value as well.

2 Choose Filter > Distort > Displace and use these settings:

Horizontal Scale: 0%

Vertical Scale: 50%

Displacement Map: Stretch To Fit

Undefined Areas: Wrap Around

Tip: On an image of this size, a vertical setting of 25% also works well. It stretches much less, but it also gets much less jagged. It is another option for you to explore.

3 Click OK. When the Choose a displacement map dialog box appears, choose map5.psd from the accompanying CD.

To create the nonpareil displacement map, you would start back with the White Quadratic gradient and repeat the instructions in the "Making Maps" section. The only difference is the size of the image. To create a displacement with ⅛-inch teeth at 300 ppi, you need to create a tiny pattern that is 37 or 38 pixels wide.

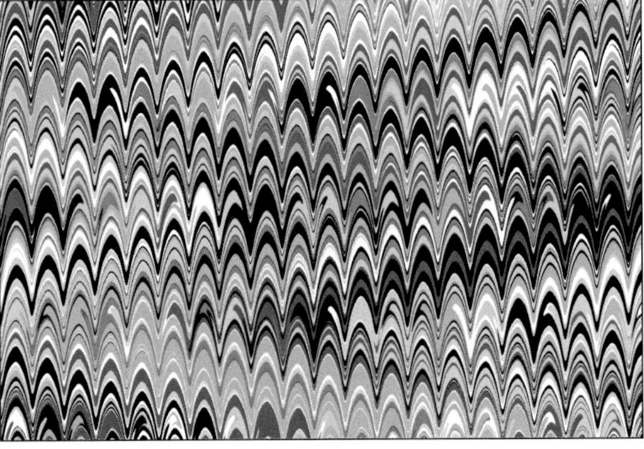

Offset the image 50% vertically with map5.psd as the displacement map.

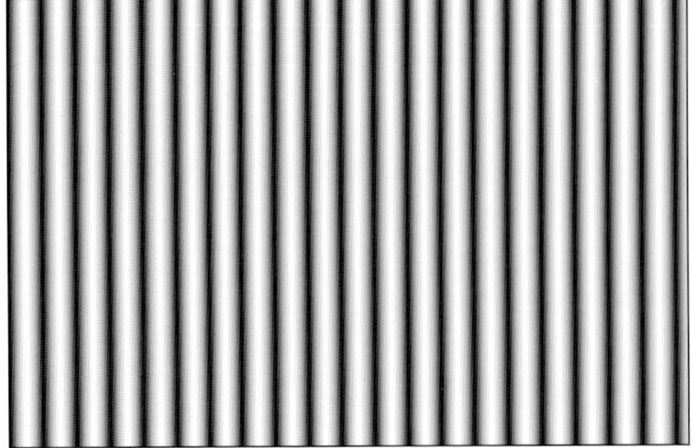

4 Choose Filter > Distort > Displace and use these settings:

Horizontal Scale: 10%

Vertical Scale: 10%

Displacement Map: Stretch To Fit

Undefined Areas: Wrap Around

Click OK. When the Choose a displacement map dialog box appears, choose map6.psd from the accompanying CD.

The only reason for this step is to add a little bit of "hand jitter" into the marble pattern. To this point, it has been straight and mathematically correct. No artist can really keep a rake on that straight a line. Therefore, I created map6, a seriously blurred version of a grayscale stones image at the nonpareil stage. You don't really even have to recreate this map. Just tile it over a smaller image or stretch it to fit a larger image. You can also create a copy and resize it as needed. You can always add a Gaussian Blur to it if it pixellates when you resize it.

Creating the Dutch Pattern

The Dutch pattern is another traditional marbling pattern that is created from the nonpareil. To create the Dutch pattern, you drag a 1-inch rake from left to right across a nonpareil.

1 Choose Filter > Distort > Displace and use these settings:

Horizontal Scale: 100%

Vertical Scale: 0%

Displacement Map: Stretch To Fit

Undefined Areas: Wrap Around

2 Click OK. When the Choose a displacement map dialog box appears, choose map7.psd from the accompanying CD.

To recreate map7 for a different resolution, you would need to follow the "Making Maps" section of this chapter using the Black Quadratic gradient as the basis of an image that was 1 inch wide when doubled (72 pixels at 72 ppi). The gradient also needs to be offset so that the white is at each end of the defined pattern. To make it easier to create the map, rotate the gradient image 90 degrees before you define the pattern. That way, the map is automatically a horizontal map.

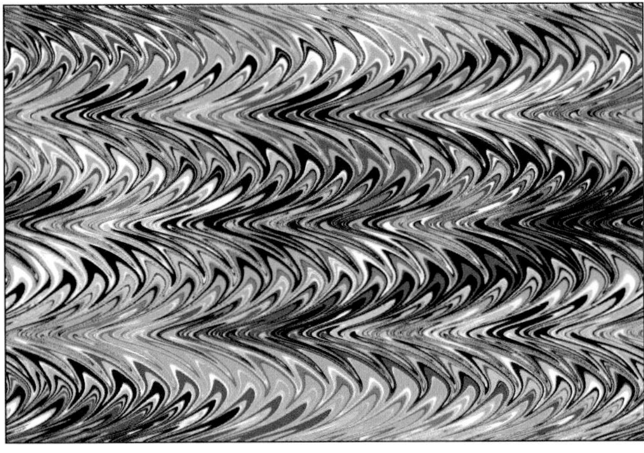

Offset the image 100% horizontally with map7.psd as the displacement map.

Creating the Fountain Pattern

The Fountain pattern is another traditional marbling pattern. It is created from the Dutch pattern. To create the Fountain pattern, you drag a 1.5-inch rake from top to bottom across a Dutch pattern.

1 Choose Filter > Distort > Displace and use these settings:

Horizontal Scale: 0%

Vertical Scale: 200%

Displacement Map: Stretch To Fit

Undefined Areas: Wrap Around

2 Click OK. When the Choose a displacement map dialog box appears, choose map8.psd from the accompanying CD.

This map is quite different from the maps you have used so far. To create it, I started with am image that was filled with neutral gray (RGB 128, 128, 128). This color does not displace at all. I added 10-pixel wide black lines at 1.5-inch intervals across the image. (You would use every 108 pixels if you were working at 72 ppi.) I then blurred the image at about 44 pixels. This produces a map that pulls down only. There is no matching upward pull on it.

If you find that the jaggedness of the image is distracting, you can reduce the image 50 percent or more. Most of the jaggies will smooth out. This is a much more successful strategy than the result because the blur only makes the marble look out of focus.

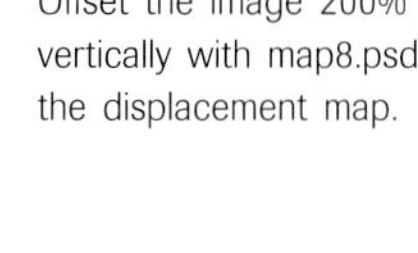

Offset the image 200% vertically with map8.psd as the displacement map.

Modifications

The variations on this technique could fill their own book. In this first set of images, I put the completed marble into the Liquify filter. In both examples, I used a 150-pixel brush with a Brush Pressure of 50 and a Turbulent Jitter of 1. In the top example, I took a nonpareil pattern into Liquify and pulled small circles clockwise across the top, counterclockwise across the center, and clockwise across the bottom. In the bottom example, I took a Dutch pattern into Liquify and pulled from right to left across the center of each previous "pull" as if I were offsetting the rake. However, I waved the brush slightly as I pulled.

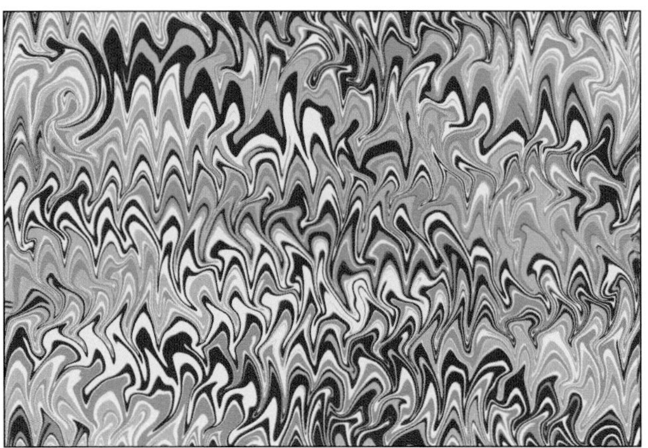

You can create freeform or wavy lines on a marbled surface in the Liquify filter.

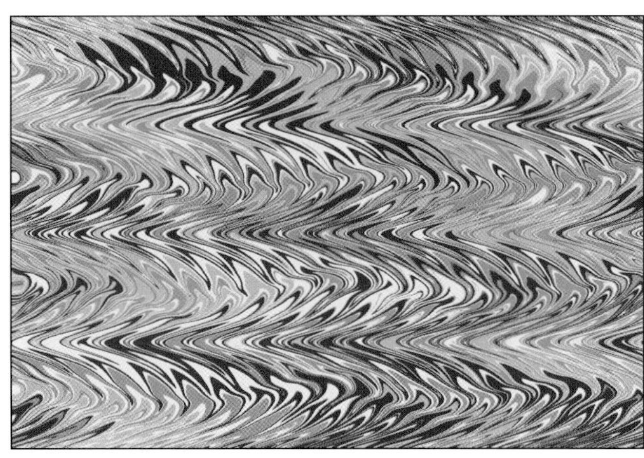

The second modification shows how to make a wavy curve in your displacement map. I started with map3.psd and inverted it. I then rotated the canvas 90 degrees clockwise and applied the Filter > Distort > Shear filter with the settings shown here. I then rotated the cans back 90 degrees counterclockwise to create the S1.psd map on the accompanying CD.

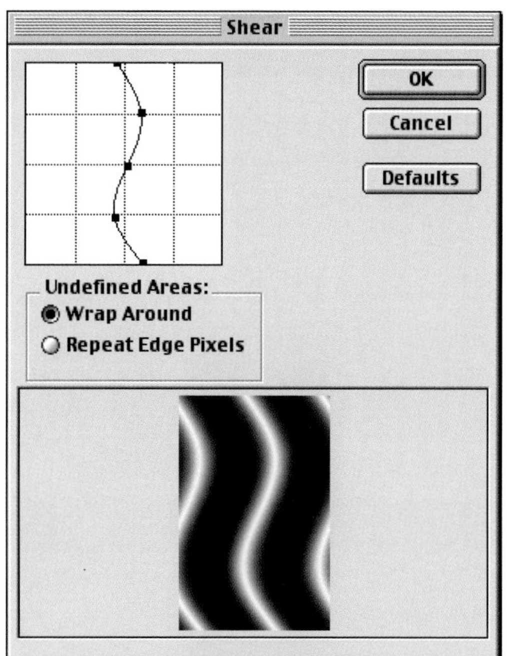

Rotate an inverted copy of map3 90 degrees clockwise, use the Shear filter, and then rotate it 90 degrees counter-clockwise.

To make the image shown here, which uses the S1.psd map, you can create a getgel and blur the image. You then displace it using halfinch1.psd at a vertical scale of 50% followed by the Displace filter using halfinch2.psd at a vertical scale of 50. Finish this with the Displace filter using S1.psd at a horizontal scale of 100.

Use S1.psd to create a Waved Chevron pattern.

In the third modification, you can make a pattern of gradient tubes. You just select areas from one of the maps you made or use black, white and white, and black gradients of various sizes. You then create a map and use the Liquify filter, or any other facility that you want, to create a displacement map. This technique was invented by Chris Setlock, an artist and a former student of mine, after he saw my marbling technique. He used the Polar Coordinates filter to create the 50-pixel pattern on a displacement map and then used Liquify to swirl it.

Filter a section of a gradient tube, use it as a pattern, and then Liquify it to create an interesting displacement map.

Depending on which image you then displace, you can get very different and dramatic results. The accompanying CD contains several displacement maps for you to try. In the first example shown, the Nonpareil stage was displaced at a vertical scale of 40 and a horizontal scale of 10. In the second example, the Fountain stage was displaced both vertically and horizontally 25%. The map was applied in Stretch To Fit mode in both examples.

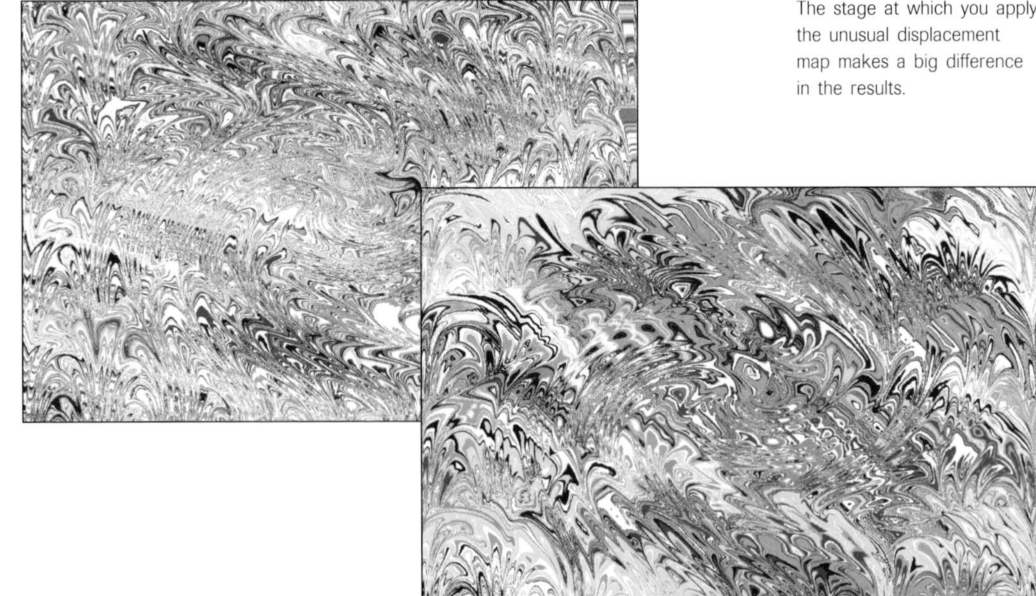

The stage at which you apply the unusual displacement map makes a big difference in the results.

You can also combine various marbling results using Blend modes. The first image overlays two patterns from two different color combinations using Normal mode but 48% opacity. The second example uses two different stages in marbling from the same Stones image. However, it then blends using Multiply mode and lowers the opacity of both layers over a white background.

You can combine the output from different marbling experiments using Blend modes and opacity changes.

Finally, you can also use the marbled image as the top layer in a series of clipping groups. Shown here is an example and the Layers palette that produced it. The dog is from the Art Parts clipart collection.

You can also create clipping groups using the marbled image as the top layer.

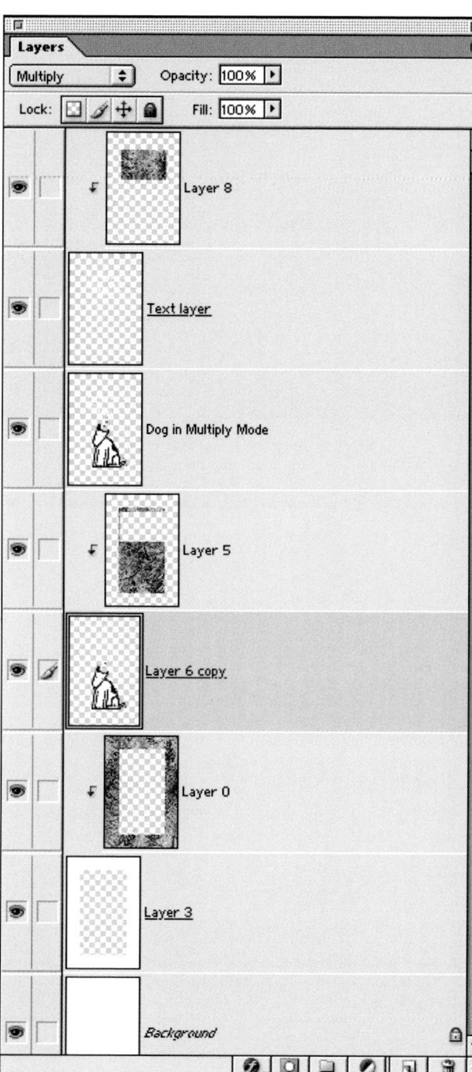

"Consistency is the last resort of the unimaginative."

—OSCAR WILDE

LIQUID PAINTING

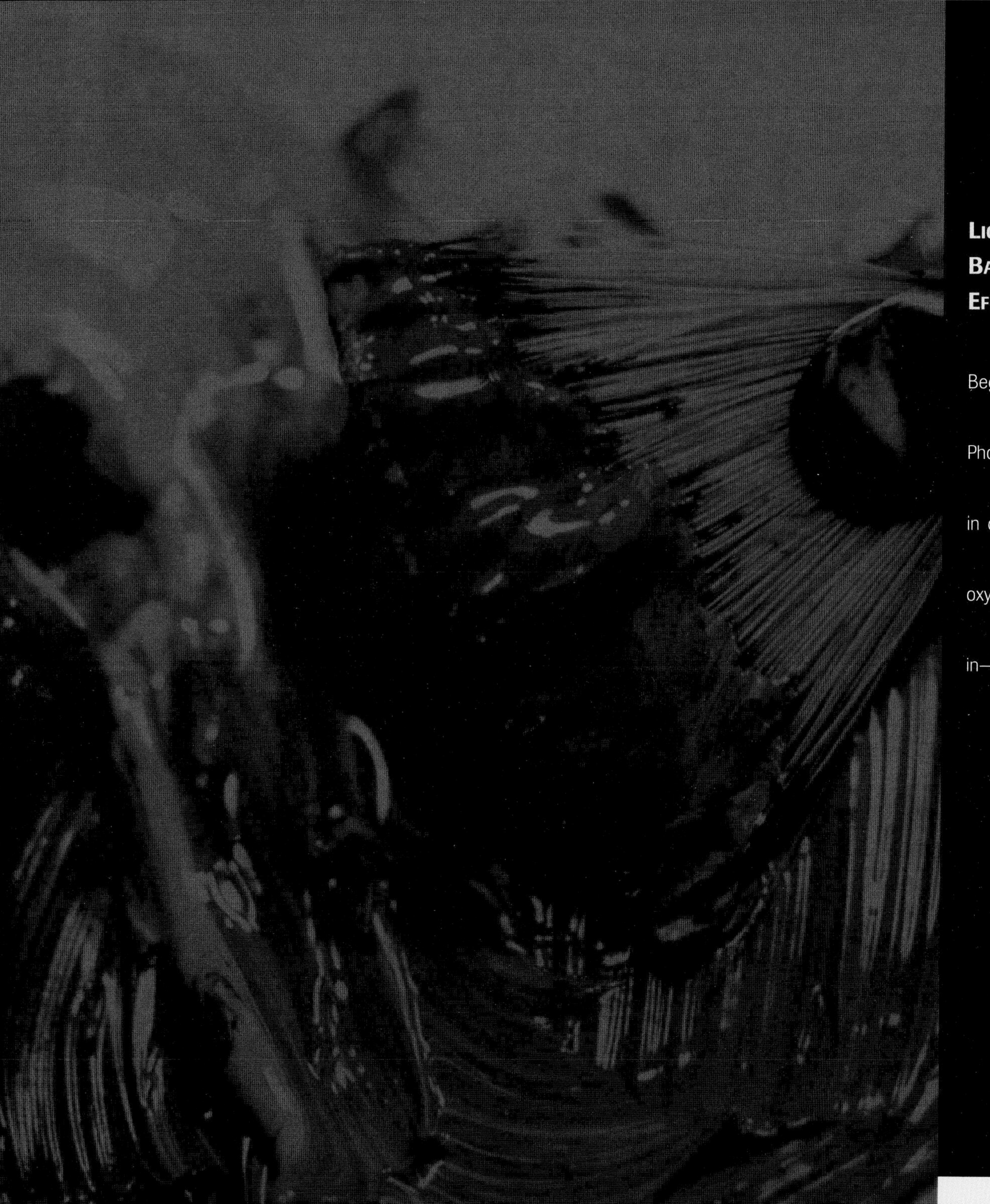

Liquify Your Assets for Luscious Backgrounds and Fluid Abstract Effects

Beginning with some gradient fills, you can use Photoshop's improved Liquify tools to engage in controlled chaos. If you can handle the oxymoron suggested by that phrase, come on in—the liquid's fine!

Project 6

Liquid Painting

By Rhoda Grossman

Getting Started

Most of Photoshop's commands and effects are precise and predictable. You can adjust sliders, enable check boxes, enter settings, and click OK to see the inevitable, and repeatable, results. Liquify offers the opportunity for some unpredictability.

On the other hand, the more you understand how the various Liquify tools behave, the more control you can develop. A black-and-white checkerboard fill can serve as the basis for some practice.

1 Open the Checkers.tif file from the CD-ROM and apply Filter > Liquify.

2 Use the Warp tool with a Brush Size of about 65 pixels at 50% Brush Pressure. Drag from left to right through the top row of squares.

Tip: You can make a straight drag by clicking the left-most square, holding down the Shift key, and clicking the extreme right square.

3 Use the Turbulence tool with the same settings on the next row of checkers.

Clearly, the Warp tool created more serious distortion than the Turbulence tool did. Next you'll try the Twirl tools.

4 Move down to the next row. Choose the Twirl Clockwise tool and hold your mouse button down or press your stylus in place where the first and second square meet. No movement or stroking is required, or desired.

The longer you press the pen or hold the mouse button, the stronger the effect. The sample shows four distortions for each Twirl tool, with each held from one to four seconds.

Skip the Pucker and Bloat tools for now. They work best on images with more tonal variation.

5 This time use the Shift Pixels tool. Drag horizontally along the edge where the next two rows meet.

Sure enough, the edge has shifted. If you dragged from left to right, the pixels shift up; from right to left, they shift down.

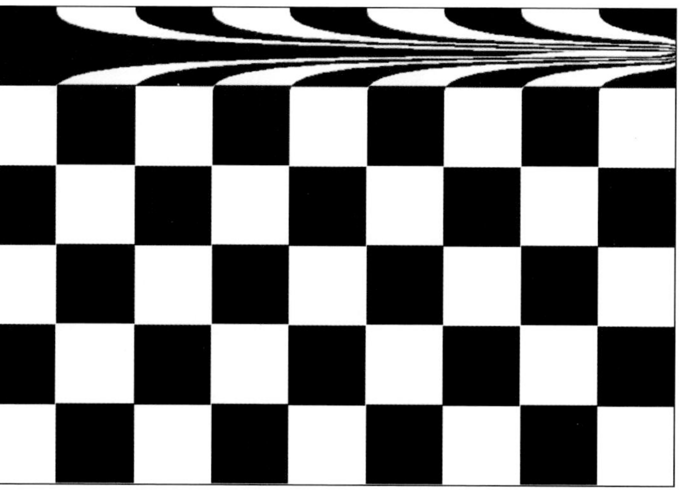

Drag the Warp tool through the top row.

Drag the Turbulence tool through the second row and use Twirl effects on the third row.

6 Finally, try the Reflection tool. This tool seems to operate along the same lines as a funhouse mirror. Place your cursor at the intersection of four squares and make a clockwise circle with a 64-pixel brush. Move to the next clean intersection, increase Brush Size to 120 pixels, and use the same motion. Repeat with a 200-pixel brush.

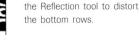

Use the Shift Pixels tool and the Reflection tool to distort the bottom rows.

You can achieve the illusion of 3D depth with the Reflection tool. The sample shows the effect of two shallow, downward curves dragged horizontally with a 100-pixel brush. The next sample was done with a 150-pixel brush, using three steeper, upward curves.

Create depth effects with a series of curved strokes.

Close the checkerboard file. There's no need to save your Liquify practice image, unless you want to keep it for reference.

The Source Gradient

A combination of gradient fills and fades provides the beginning for a rippling satin background. You can skip this part if you like and use the gradient images provided in the source folder on the *Photoshop 7 Magic* CD-ROM.

1 Make a new file that is 4.5 inches square at 300 ppi.

2 Choose the Gradient tool and the Yellow, Violet, Orange, Blue preset. Use the Diamond Gradient style and the Normal mode, and then drag diagonally from the lower-right corner of the image to the upper-left.

3 Enable Rulers (Ctrl+R/Cmd+R). Drag a horizontal guide to the 3-inch mark. Drag a vertical guide to the 1.5-inch mark and another to the 2-inch mark. These guides will help you place the next gradient accurately.

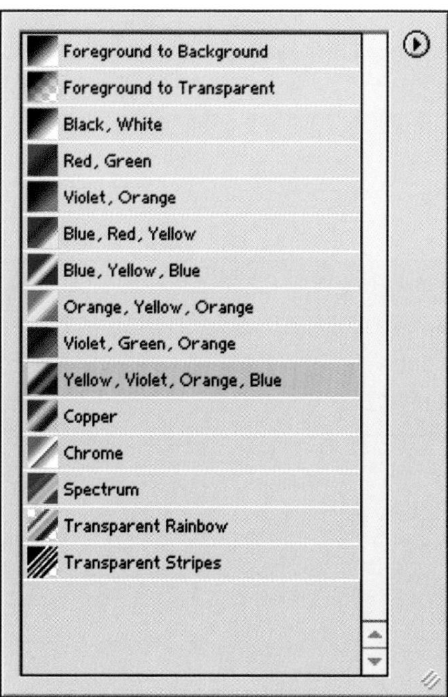

Choose the Yellow, Violet, Orange, Blue Gradient preset.

Drag a diagonal diamond gradient.

4 Use the same gradient settings and drag from the top of the 1.5-inch vertical guide to the point where the 2-inch vertical guide intersects the horizontal guide.

The second gradient completely obliterates the first one. You fix it in the next step.

Drag a second diamond gradient.

5 Use Edit > Fade Gradient at 40% in Normal mode. Use the View menu to clear the guides.

The two gradients blend together. One more fill-and-fade sequence will give us more complexity and smoother blends.

Fade the second diamond gradient.

6 Continue with the same gradient color preset, but switch to the Radial style. Begin the drag at a point 1 inch from the right edge and 1.5 inches from the top. Drag horizontally to the left edge. Use guides again, or just eyeball it. Constrain your drag to a perfect horizontal with the Shift key. Fade to 40%, using Overlay mode this time.

You now have an image with smooth variations in shape and luminosity. There is considerable range in hue and the colors are highly saturated. If you want to work with vibrant color, skip the next step and go directly to the Liquify process. I prefer to restrict the color variation and reduce color purity (saturation) to achieve a more realistic satin effect.

7 Choose a Gradient preset from the Pastels Library and drag a gradient in Color mode. The example uses the Brown, Tan, Beige preset with a diagonal drag in Linear style.

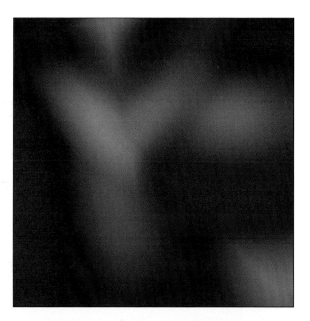

Drag and fade a radial gradient.

Another way to reduce color is with Image > Adjustments > Desaturate. You then use Edit > Fade to bring back some subtle color.

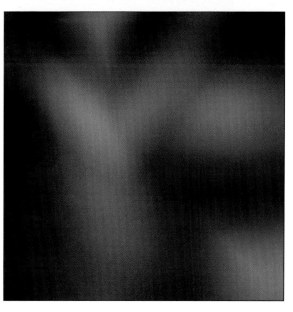

Simplify or soften color variation.

Get Gooey

Each Liquify tool has an assigned behavior, such as Twirl, Bloat, or Warp. Note, however, that results are not automatic; they depend on your brush strokes. I'll recommend tools and settings and show you my progress. But even if we begin with the same source image and follow the same steps in developing an image, results will vary.

Continue working with the gradient combination you just made or open GradBrown.tif from the resource folder on the book's CD-ROM.

1 Choose Filter > Liquify. Use the Warp tool with a 1-inch brush. (If your image is at 300 ppi, use a 300-pixel brush; at 72 ppi, use a 72-pixel brush; and so on.) Drag various curving strokes to suggest the look of draped fabric. When you are satisfied with this stage, click OK and save the image.

Note: You can undo the effects using the keyboard (Ctrl+Z/Cmd+Z), but not with the Edit menu, which is unavailable while you work in Liquify. There appears to be an unlimited number of undo levels (I got up to 26, and then got bored), but there is no Redo option! Incidentally, when Liquify was introduced in version 6, it had the classic single Undo option and a Redo option, using the keyboard to toggle.

The Reconstruct tool is like Undo on steroids! You can bring back the previous state (before invoking Liquify) with your choice of eight styles. Reconstruction can be done gradually, even with a mouse! Simply holding down the mouse button or the stylus, without moving it, increases the effect in the designated style: Rigid, Smooth, Loose, and so on.

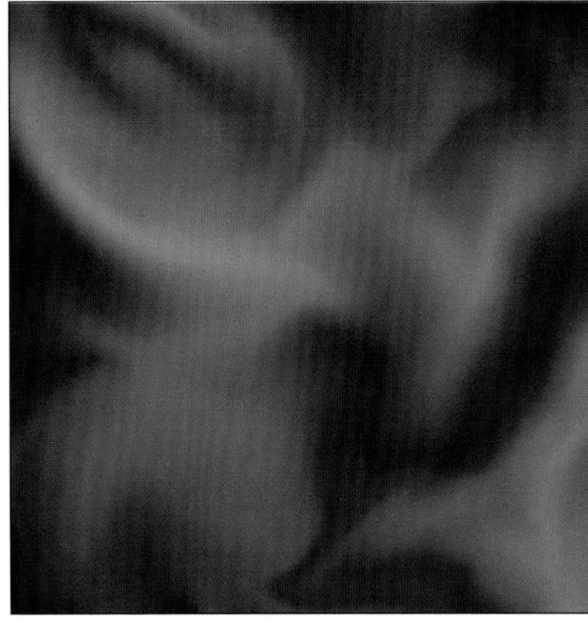

Apply Liquify effects with the Warp tool.

2 Apply Liquify again and work with the Reflection tool.

It works great for adding crisper folds and silky highlights.

At this stage you can continue developing the image in a number of directions. We'll enhance the satin look and then pursue a more surreal image. Be sure to save this version for some later variations.

Parts of my image don't quite support the illusion of silky fabric. Pucker and Bloat (also known as Pinch and Bulge, for you Painter users) can help. First practice a bit. Pucker makes an area smaller, and you can guess what Bloat does. "P & B" work much like the Twirl tools—the longer you apply them, even without much movement, the greater the effect.

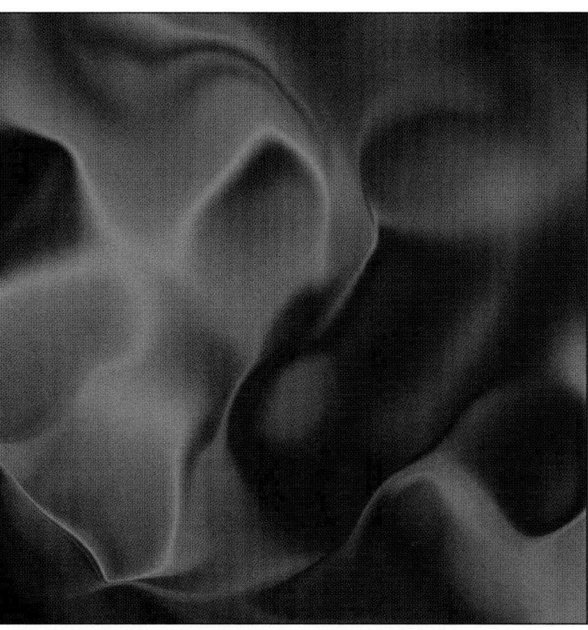

Apply more Liquify effects with the Reflection tool.

3 Return once more to the Liquify environment to touch up any problem areas with Pucker and Bloat. Use a 200-pixel brush. Switch to other tools as needed.

For greater realism, reduce hue variation again.

4 Use the Eyedropper tool to sample a medium brown from the image. Or use these RGB values in the Color Picker: R 133, G 91, and B 36.

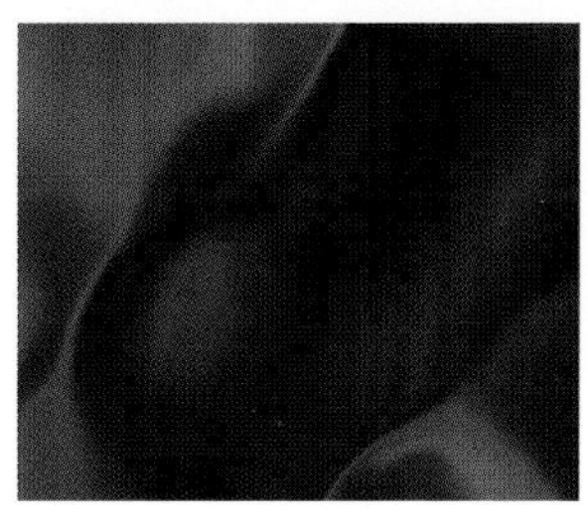

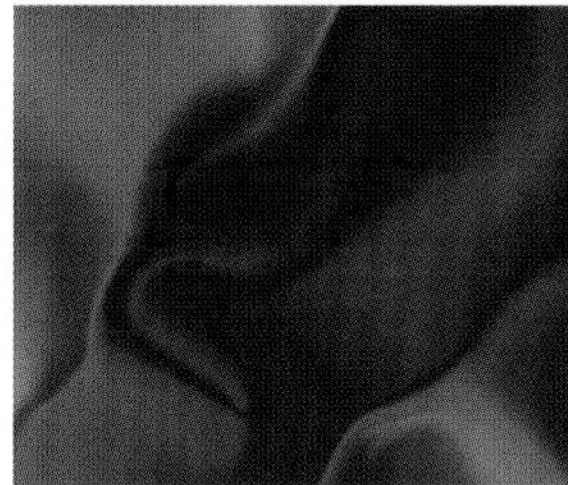

Before (left) and after Pucker and Bloat effects.

5 Use Edit > Fill, using foreground color in Color mode at about 40% opacity.

6 The entire image could use more highlights. Use Image > Adjust > Levels. Reduce the 255 Input Level to about 205, or drag the white triangle to the left until you like the result.

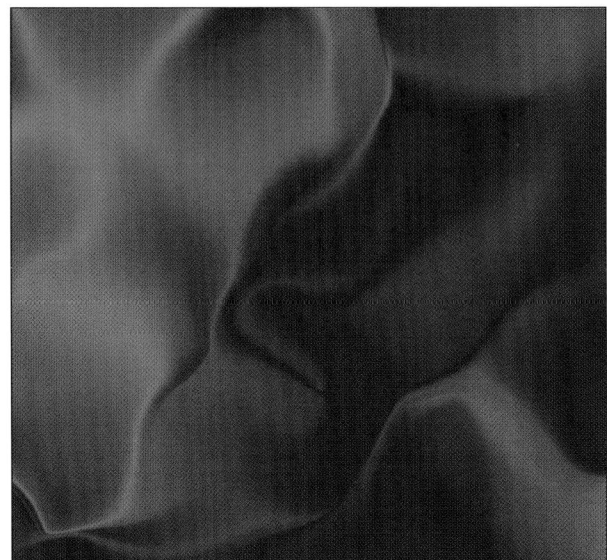

Decrease hue variation.

7 The area I worked on with Pucker and Bloat is still a bit too dark. If you have a similar problem, select it with the Lasso tool and apply a 20-pixel feather. Use Levels to brighten the selection.

8 There is a greenish cast to the selection now, so use Image > Adjustments > Color Balance to increase red and yellow slightly.

Tip: Adjustments to Color Balance are frequently necessary after Levels adjustments. In Project 4, "Painting from Photos," you'll find Phil Williams' handy recipe for an action that automatically presents you with the Levels dialog and then the Color Balance dialog, all with the click of your designated function key.

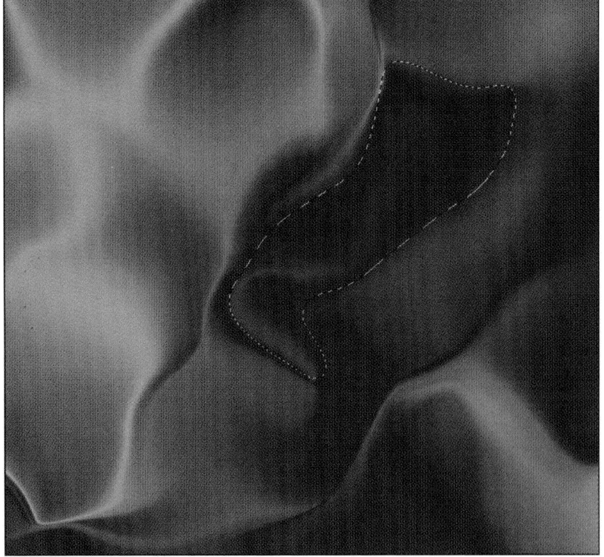

Make feathered selections of areas needing more adjustments.

9 A few strokes here and there with the Blur tool, and you've got a lovely and sensuous background.

This lustrous satin can make a stunning backdrop for displaying scanned objects such as jewelry, coins, or sculptures.

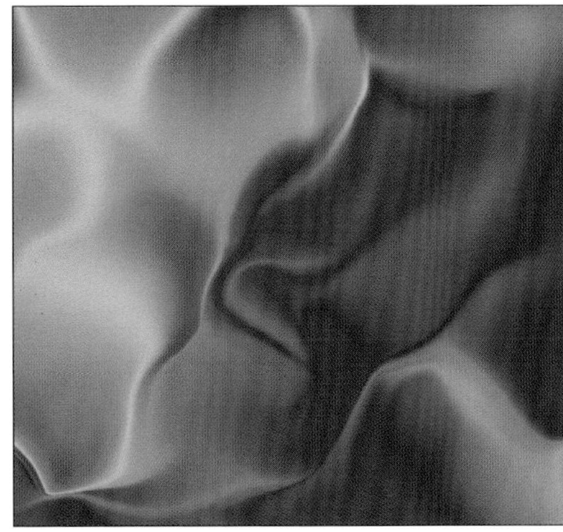

Adjust Levels and Color Balance for the selected area.

SURREAL FANTASY

Realistic effects are not considered in this variation. Experimentation is encouraged. The practice you did with the checkerboard image will come in handy here. You'll twist and twirl, blob and curl, freeze and thaw. Go ahead—have some fun!

1 Open the Liquified image you saved earlier, after Step 2. If you didn't save it, use SURREAL.tif from the source folder on the accompanying CD-ROM.

2 Apply Image > Adjustments > Auto Levels.

It increases the value range dramatically, creating some spectacular highlights. It also enhances hue variation.

Apply Auto Levels for dramatic results.

3 For an even more intriguing effect, use Edit > Fade Auto Levels using Pin Light mode, keeping the slider at 100%.

Pin Light is one of Photoshop's new Blending modes.

Fade Auto Levels using Pin Light mode.

4 Return to Liquify and create several spirals with the Twirl tools. Change the brush size frequently and use different lengths of time for variety in the twirl's curliness.

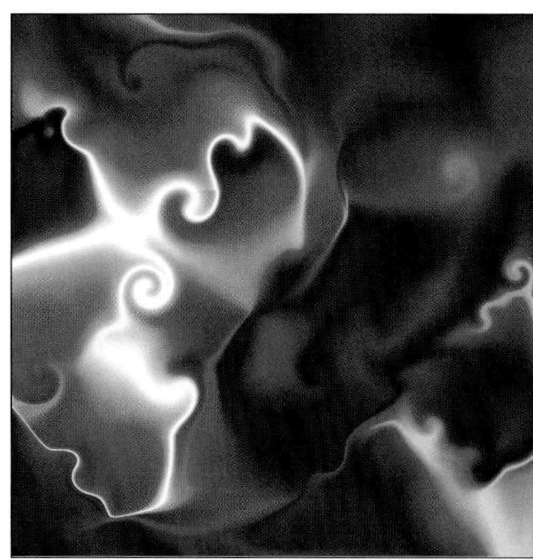

Get curly with the Twirl tools.

5 Examine the image. Is there an area that is especially promising? Paint over it with the Freeze tool so that it will be protected while you continue working.

Use the Freeze and Thaw tools throughout the development of your image. It's another way to control the chaos a bit.

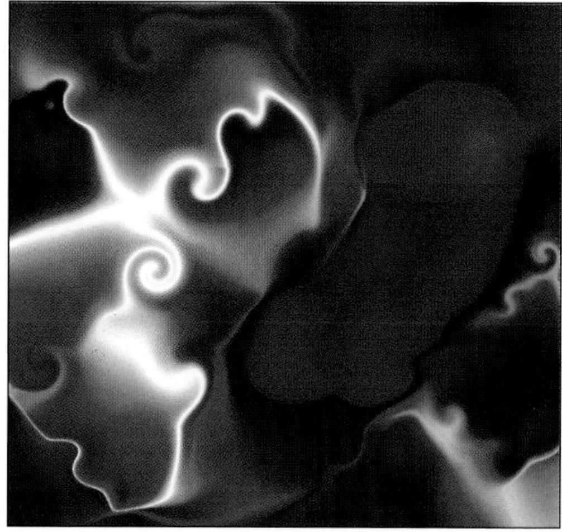

Freeze any areas that you want to protect.

6 Switch to the Reflection tool and continue working. Use roughly circular strokes and attempt to make some globular shapes.

Note: Globules can be made by applying circular strokes on an area where different colors or values meet. Take another look at the Reflection tool effects on the checkerboard practice file you made earlier. When you drag the Reflection tool around on the border between two different colors, one of the colors can jump across the border.

Add globules with the Reflection tool.

Go with the Flow

When you feel that enough interesting shapes or visual ideas have been provided with the Liquify techniques, work on the image in Photoshop's standard environment, where every feature and command is available. Some of the directions you might consider at this point include the following:

- Exploring variations
- Zoom-and-crop simplification

We'll combine both choices. The image at this stage is an especially good source for a series of layered variations that require little more than changing Blending modes.

1. Choose the Rectangular Marquee tool and set the Style to Fixed Aspect Ratio. Enter **1** into the Width and Height fields. Your rectangular selections will be constrained to perfect squares of any size.

   Constraining the aspect ratio of your rectangle enables you to use the zoom-and-crop maneuver without distorting your layers in later steps.

2. Zoom in on the image until only a small area fills your screen. If you're working with the 4.5-inch square at 300 ppi used here, 200% magnification is ideal.

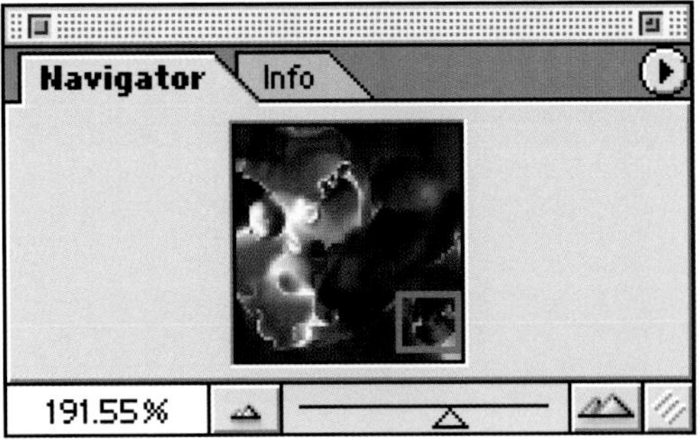

Zoom in on a small area of the image.

3 Use the Hand tool to scroll freely around the image. When you find a composition you like, make a square selection and copy and paste it to a new file. Make three such image fragments.

Okay—so it's zoom-and-copy-and-paste, but zoom-and-crop sounds better.

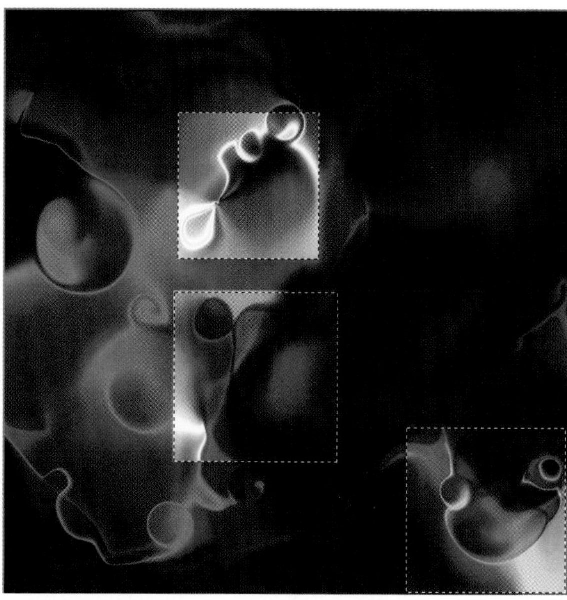

Make square selections of three image fragments.

4 Resize all three images to the same pixel dimensions. Combine them into one layered image that is wide enough to enable the layers to be side by side with some white space between them.

You have just made a triptych. The three elements should make an effective combination because they are fragments of the same liquid painting. This can be the end of the project, or you can explore additional ways to combine the three elements.

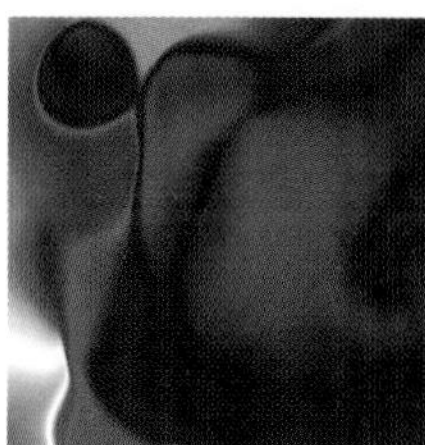

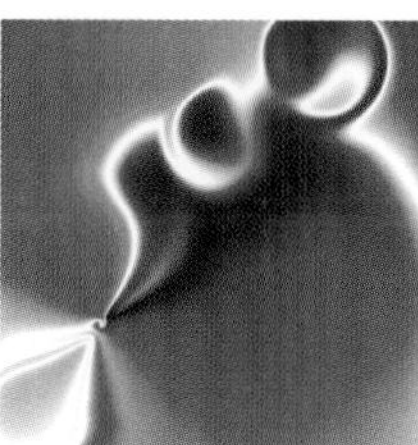

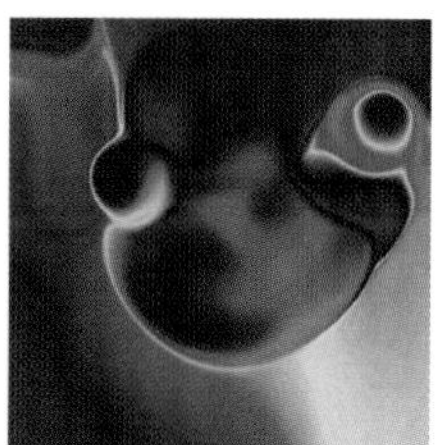

Make a triptych of the image elements.

5 Ctrl-click/Cmd-click one of the layers. Ctrl+J/Cmd+J to make another layer via copy.

6 Position this new copy exactly over one of the other two layers. Use the Shift key to constrain movement to the horizontal.

7 Change the Blending mode. Some modes are likely to be too harsh, unless you reduce the opacity of the layer.

Shown from left to right:

- Top layer: Linear light at 42% opacity
- Middle layer: Difference at 100%
- Top layer: Luminosity at 100%
- Middle layer: Linear light at 75%
- Top layer: Soft Light at 100%
- Middle layer: Hard Light 60%

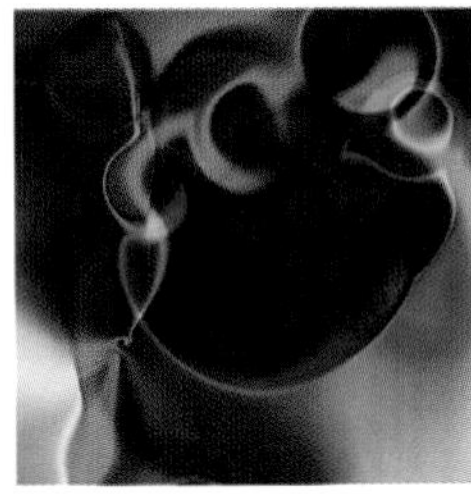

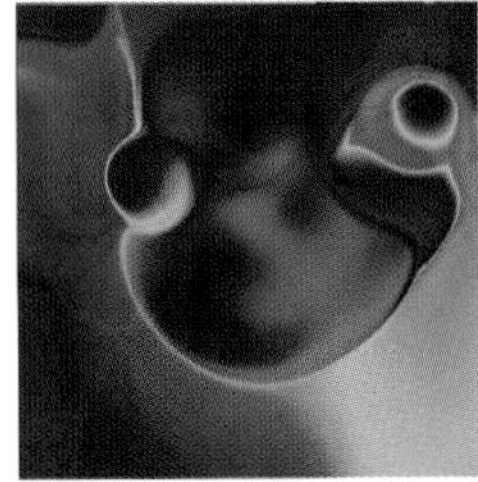

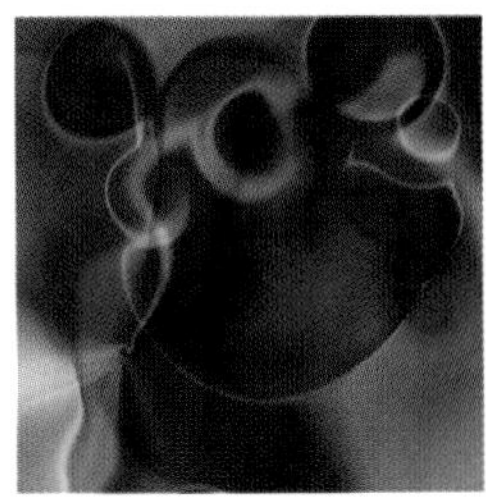

Explore several combinations of Blending mode and opacity.

8 Make a triple stack of layers so that all combinations are possible.

Modifications

There's a quick (and repeatable) way to achieve surreal effects when you begin with a liquified satin image.

1 Open the SURREAL.tif file again, or revert to its original state.

2 Use the Levels adjustment to change the white point from 255 to 180. This brightens the image by increasing highlights.

3 Choose Filter > Distort > Polar Coordinates, using the Polar to Rectangular option.

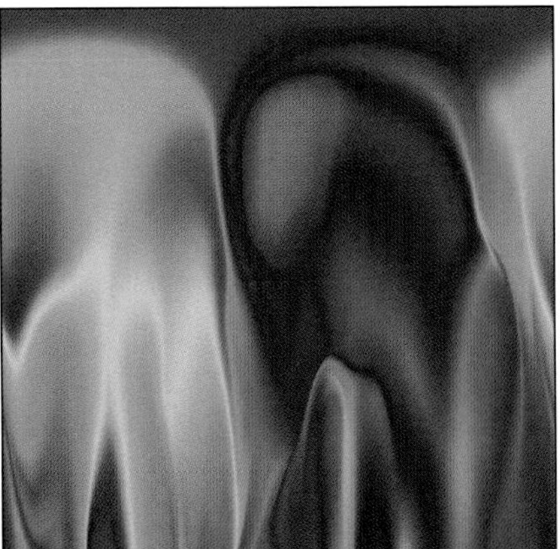

Apply Polar Coordinates to the brightened source image.

4 Fade the filter effect, using Lighten mode at 100%.

5 Repeat the filter-and-fade process. Ctrl+F/Cmd+F is the keyboard shortcut for repeating the previous filter.

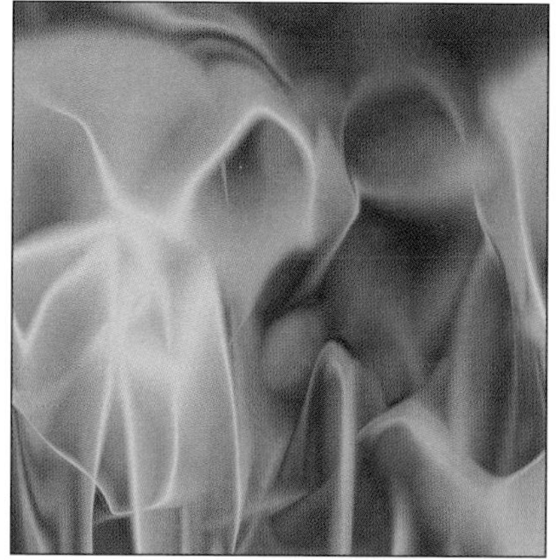

Fade Polar Coordinates, using Lighten mode.

6 Apply Auto Levels.

The left side of the image is a little washed out at this stage. We can fix that with a gradient fill.

7 Use the Eyedropper tool to sample a bright blue from the image, or enter these RGB settings: R 150, G 224, and B 244.

Apply Auto Levels after the second round of distortions.

8 Choose the Gradient tool with the Linear Style and the Foreground to Transparent preset. Change the mode to Difference and Opacity to 60%. Drag horizontally from the left edge to the center of the image.

This modification is a detailed image with a variety of organic forms and depth effects interacting in complex ways.

Enhance the left side of the image with a gradient fill.

"He who controls the past commands the future. He who commands the future conquers the past."

—GEORGE ORWELL

LENTICULAR PRINTING

Creating Depth and Motion

Lenticular printing is one discipline in what is more properly know as illusion arts. Holograms are another facet of this discipline. In Lenticular printing, the Lenticular material creates an illusion of movement, of distance, or of depth. You make a Lenticular print by placing an interlaced image. This image is cut and reassembled in vertical strips behind a sheet of plastic with a series of parallel lens or lenticules embossed into one surface. Then the lenses are aligned with the image, and the viewer sees only one frame at a time. As the viewing angle changes, each image is seen in a planned sequence, creating the illusion of movement, depth, or animation.

Project 7

Lenticular Printing

by Dorothy Simpson Krause
and Sherry London

Getting Started

I created a Lenticular portrait by resizing and aligning vintage photographs of a child, a young woman, and an elderly woman in Photoshop. The image that you are going to use here was originally part of a collage, from my series "Going Home." I transformed the image named "Bits and Pieces" into a Lenticular print. I used this piece again as "Generations" in part of the Sacred and Mundane series. (This version is the chapter opening image.) The two-inch square Lenticular portrait is centered in an old ceiling tile. The portrait has also been made into a two-inch square pin. I will speak more about the actual printing process later in this project.

Note: The level of the commands that the reader should know are not always consistent. As an example: the Image > Crop tool is specifically called out, but Image > Image Size is only inferred. A strict, descriptive layer naming convention would make the project much clearer. At different times a specific layer is referred to as Old Woman, old woman, and Top layer, while its actual name is Layer 0. This applies to two different exercises.

In this section of the project, you start by building the original image composite. To create a convincing flip from one portrait to the next, you need to start by cropping, resizing, and aligning the images. In a portrait such as this, the key is to make all three images align on the eyes of the various subjects.

The "Bits and Pieces" image.

1. Open **Child.tif**, **youngwoman.tif**, and **oldwoman.tif** from the accompanying CD.

   These three scans have not been retouched. They are raw scans.

2. Crop the Young Woman and Old Woman images to remove the frames. Either use the Crop tool or the Rectangular Marquee tool and the Image > Crop command.

   By removing the frames, you can get an accurate pixel count of the usable image width in the next step.

3. Check the file sizes (pixel count) for each image. Write down the image widths.

Open the Child.tif, young-woman.tif, and oldwoman.tif images.

Although your specific pixel count will differ from mine depending on the pixels that were cropped, the Old Woman image is the smallest. You can make your final composite only as wide as the smallest starting image.

4. Resize the Young Woman and Child images to the same width as the Old Woman image by choosing Image > Image Size; Resample Image and Constrain Proportions must both be checked.

5. Make the Old Woman image active. Choose Image > Duplicate > OK. Close the original Old Woman image and work in the copy.

6. Drag the Young Woman and Child images into the Old Woman Copy image with the Shift key pressed to register the alignment.

   The Old Woman Copy image is the longest of the three and so gives you the most amount of space in which to work.

7. To arrange the layers in chronological order, double-click the Background layer to make Layer 0. Arrange the layers so that the child is on the bottom and the old woman is on the top.

   This arrangement is a natural way for me to work and really has little effect on the final composite.

8. Make Layer 1 active and turn off the eye icon on Layer 0. Reduce the opacity of the Young Woman layer to about 45 percent. Drag the Young Woman layer so that her left eye is in the same location as the left eye of the child.

Arrange the layers so that the old woman is on the top and the child is on the bottom.

Actually, you are aligning the *right* eyes, but as you look at the image, the eyes are on your left. The opacity of 45 percent should give you enough of both images to be able to line them up.

Tip: I find this easiest to do if I zoom all the way in on the eyes.

9 Make Layer 0 active and turn the Opacity down to about 50 percent. Move the image until the eye aligns with the previous layers.

Tip: If you are having trouble doing this at all, go back to the Child layer and use the Elliptical Marquee tool to make a selection of the child's right eyeball (the one on your left). Save the selection as a channel and then invert the channel. Make the RGB composite channel active but turn on the eye to the Alpha 1 channel. The pupil shows up as solid red, making it easy to align the other two layers.

10 Look at the Layers palette to find the layer with the smallest height. (It is the Child layer.) Load the transparency of the layer and choose Image > Crop.

Your image is now at its correct height. However, in the next step, you need to check the width, which can be somewhat trickier.

11 Set the Opacity on all layers back to 100%. Turn off and on the eyes on the various layers to see if all the layers have filled the current image width. The Old Woman layer does not quite encompass the entire width, but the other two layers do. Load the transparency of the Old Woman layer and choose Crop.

This gives your composite the final dimensions.

12 Save the image as **COMPOSITE1.psd**.

Crop the composite to the layer that is the smallest in height.

Creating an Animated GIF

A Lenticular print can show motion, depth, and sequence, and it can flip between two or more static images. This image, as you can see from the layers that you composited, flips between the three images.

One way that I like to preview my image is to create an animated GIF. Building an animated GIF image helps me to visualize what will happen when the image is placed under the Lenticular material.

In this section of the project, you turn a color-corrected version of the composite into an animated GIF image that uses morphing (the calculation of in-between images) in ImageReady to simulate the flipping that occurs when the image is printed and bonded to the Lenticular surface.

1. Open the image smallportrait.psd from the accompanying CD-ROM.

   This image has already been color-corrected. Because the purpose of this technique is output and not the color-correction process itself, I thought it would be less time-consuming for you to start this section with a corrected file.

2. Choose Image > Image Size and reduce the image to 4 inches wide at 72 ppi. Save the image as **ANIMATION.PSD** and close the image. Open it again in ImageReady.

   The image size is set to print a 2-inch image at 720 ppi. This would make a huge animated GIF and is totally unsuitable. After you have created a tweened GIF animation, you no longer can edit the file in Photoshop, so it makes more sense to close it and reopen it. You won't be taking it back into Photoshop anyway.

Tip: Change the ppi setting in the Image Size command, and then enter the dimensions. If you do it this way, you need to set the dimension to 4 inches only once.

3 Turn off the Eye icons on Layer 1 and Layer 2. Look at the Animation palette. You will see only one frame, and it contains the image of the young child.

You create animation in ImageReady in layers and place each frame in a different layer or combination of layers.

4 Choose New Frame from the Animation palette pop-up menu, and then turn on the eye to the left of Layer 1 in the Layers palette. Turn off the eye to the Background layer.

It makes more sense to select New Frame before you change the status of the existing layers. If you don't do so, you'll have to go back and reset Frame 1 to the correct layer again.

5 Choose New Frame again and this time, turn on the eye for Layer 2 and turn off the eye for Layer 1.

You now have three frames.

6 Click Frame 1 to select it. Choose Tween from the side pop-out menu on the Animation palette. Use these settings:

Tween With: Next Frame

Frames to Add: 2

Layers: All Layers

Parameters: Position, Opacity, Effects

These settings create a tween that has two steps to go from the image of the child to the image of the young woman.

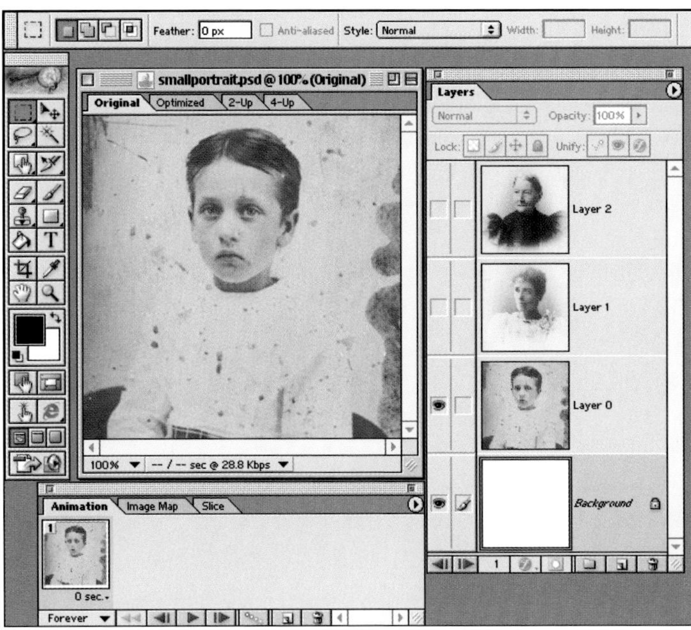

Turn off the Eye icons on the top two layers.

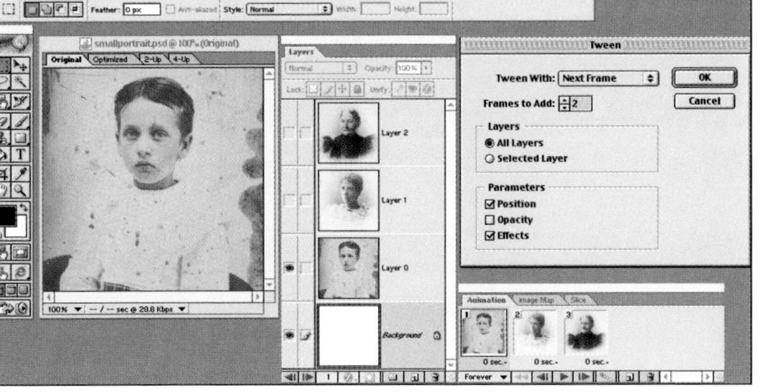

Select the Tween command and use these settings.

7 Click what is now Frame 4 to select it. (Frame 4 is the solid image of the young woman.) Press the Shift key and click Frame 5 as well. Choose Tween and use the same settings as before.

Two more frames are added between the young and old women.

8 Click Frame 1 again. Choose Tween. Use the same settings for everything, except for the Tween With. For that, choose Last Frame.

You now have nine frames and have added the two new frames to the end of animation after the old woman.

9 Click under each frame to set the timing. Set Frames 1, 4, and 7 to 1 play for 1 second each. Set the remaining frames to play for 0.5 seconds. Set the animation to play Forever. Click the Play button in the Animation palette to preview the animation.

The shorter setting on the tweened frames makes the transitions smoother.

10 In the Optimize palette, use these settings:

Format: Gif format

Lossy: 0

Color Reduction Algorithm: Perceptual

Colors: 256

Dither Algorithm: Diffusion

Dither: 100 percent

I want to see the image at the best possible settings to preview my motion, or flip. If you plan to post a GIF animation of your own to the web, you need to optimize much more than this. This animation would take well over two minutes to load on a 28.8K modem.

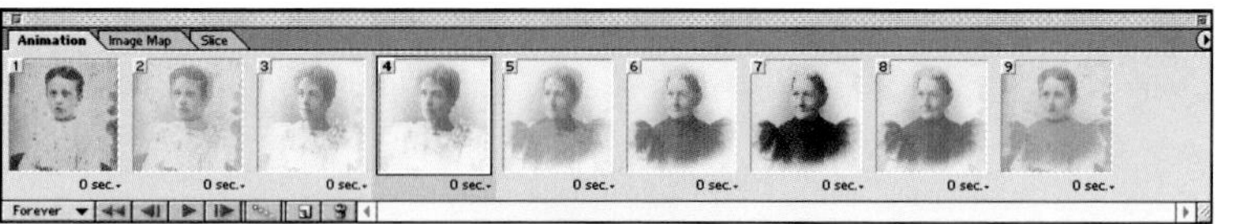

Create the last tween between the first and last frames.

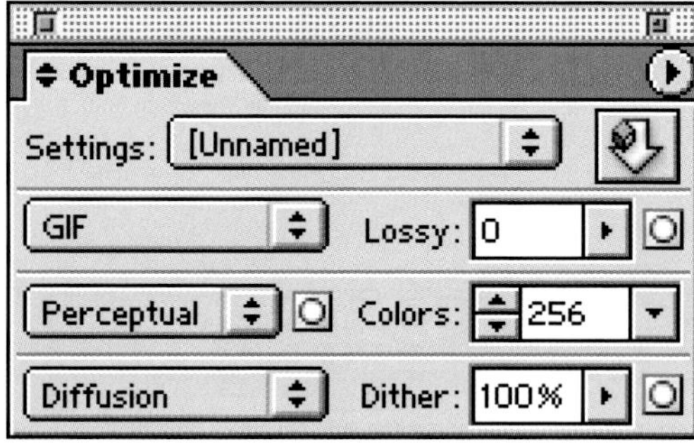

Choose these settings in the Optimize palette.

11 Choose File > Save Optimized As. Save it as **Animation.gif**. I didn't bother with saving HTML with it, but you may if you want. You can see Chapter 9, "Web Page Design in Photoshop and ImageReady," to learn more about the various output settings in ImageReady.

Preparing and Printing the Image

This technique is on Lenticular printing, but, so far, you have done everything *but* prepare the image for printing under a Lenticular lens. To remedy that, I detail my printing process for you next, and then Sherry London shows you how to create an interlaced image in Photoshop.

After I have the image prepared at the correct size and have worked out my motion or flip in ImageReady, I take the image into one of two special-purpose, Windows-only programs from Kutuzov (see **www.flipsigns.com**). The programs are called SuperFlip and 3D Genius. SuperFlip is used for motion or flipping, and 3D Genius can create 3D illusions that are visible without the use of special glasses.

SuperFlip creates an interlaced image that is made up of sequential strips from all three images. This is the image that I finally printed. I printed this image on a Kimoto white film using a Mutoh Falcon printer and a Wasatch RIP. Using a CODA laminator, the print was aligned to a 40-lenticule per inch (lpi) lens from MicroLens. It then was laminated. The three photographs, seen as a merging animation, create a sense of the aging process.

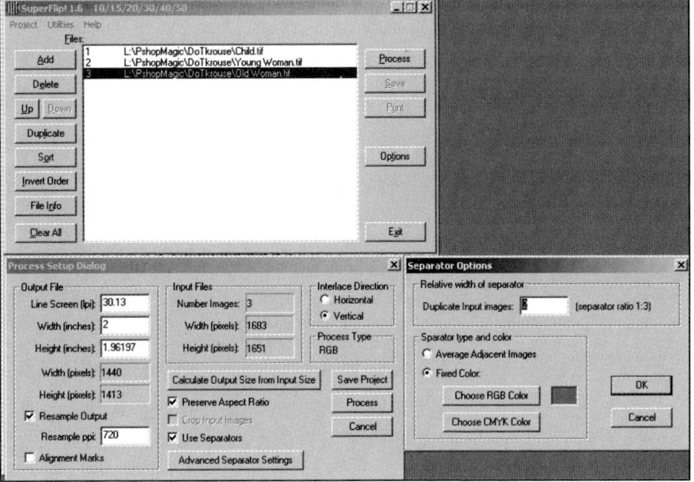

Place your image into SuperFlip.

Modifications

by Sherry London

Dorothy's techniques are wonderful, but the high-end output devices might leave you wondering if you could ever afford to experiment with this technique. Mac users might wonder if they could even attempt the process with software designed only for Windows. The exciting answer is that you can try this technique yourself for very little cost by using a technique in Photoshop that I will show you.

If you have an inkjet printer that will output at 720 ppi or greater, that's a good enough entry point to this very exciting medium. After I show you how to create your own interlaced image in Photoshop (the process is not as sophisticated as creating it in SuperFlip, but it *is* readily available), I will give you contact information to pursue this topic further.

Begin by constructing the interlaced image.

1. Open the portrait.psd image from the accompanying CD in Photoshop.

2. Add a Layer Mask to Layers 0, 1, and 2. To do so, just click the Add Layer Mask icon while each layer is active.

   Don't put anything in the mask just yet.

3. Create a new file that is 3 pixels high by 24 pixels wide.

   In this file, you create three different patterns—one for each layer mask.

4. Enlarge the small pattern file as much as possible and select the 1-pixel pencil with black as your foreground color. Draw the following patterns:

   Row 3 (bottom row): 16 black, 6 white, and 2 black

   Row 2 (middle row): 8 black, 6 white, and 10 black

   Row 1 (top row): 6 black and 18 white

Note: How did I get the number 24? When you create an interlaced image, the images that you want to interlace are cut into strips. At least one strip from each image has to fit exactly under one lenticule. I obtained a sample pack of lens from MicroLens that were 30.13 lpi (lenticules per inch). The formula for determining how many pixels fit under one lenticule is printer resolution ÷ lens count. In this case, 720° 30.13=23.9 pixels. Because we cannot print a half pixel, I chose 24 pixels as the number of pixels per lenticule. The images need to be interlaced in 24-pixel sandwiches.

It's easier to count if you work from Row 3 up. The patterns are based on 6 pixels, plus 2 pixels of separator for each image. The separator strips are not strictly necessary, but they reduce ghosting, which is a mixing of the images that does not give you a clean flip from one image to another.

5 Set the Fixed Size option of the Rectangular Marquee tool to 1 pixel high by 24 pixels wide. Select the first row and choose Edit > Define Pattern. Name the pattern **Strip1x24**. Create the **Strip2x24** pattern from Row 2 and the **Strip3x24** pattern from Row 3.

Draw the pattern for the mask in the small pattern file.

6 Fill the Layer Mask on Layer 0 with Strip1x24. Use Edit > Fill > With Pattern, 100 percent opacity, and Normal mode. Fill the Layer Mask for Layer 1 with Strip2x24 and the Layer Mask for Layer 2 with Strip3x24. Fill the Background layer with solid neutral gray (or pick a common color from the image).

The Layer Masks cut the image into long strips and interlace them.

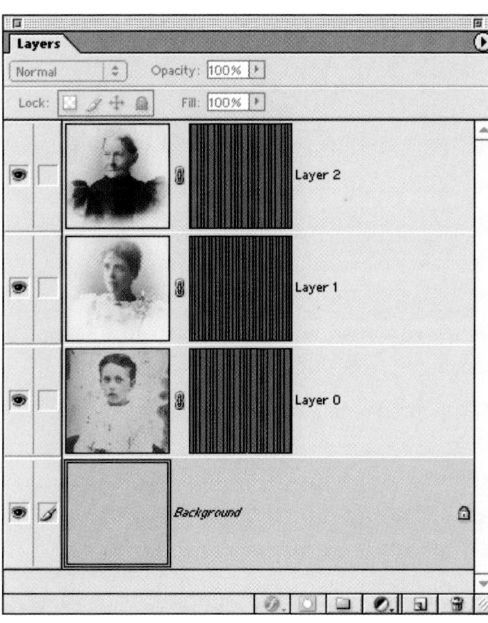

Fill each Layer Mask with the correct pattern.

7 Save the layered file. Then choose Image > Duplicate > Duplicate Merged Layers Only > OK.

This is the image that you will print. First, however, you need to compensate for that fractional pixel per lenticule.

8 Choose Image > Image Size, and then increase the image size by 200%. Choose Image > Image Size, and then reduce the image size by 50%.

This little step seems as if it changes nothing because when you are done, the image is the same as it was when you started. However, in the interpolation up and down, the strips have blurred along the edges and the problem of banding (missing a lenticule) has been reduced or eliminated.

Duplicate the interlaced image with merged layers only.

9 Choose File > Page Setup. If you have the option, make sure that you print at 720 or 1440 ppi, use photo glossy paper, and then set the print uality to Photo. Then print the image.

Your setting will differ, but shown here are my settings for the Epson 1200 printer.

10 If you have the Lenticular material, you can place the image under it for now. Hold it there and look at the flip to see that everything is working properly.

11 You can purchase the material with or without adhesive. If you get it with adhesive, you can pull off the tape, place the print, and push the entire setting firmly against a tabletop to set it. You can also take it to a professional laminator who will do a much better job on it.

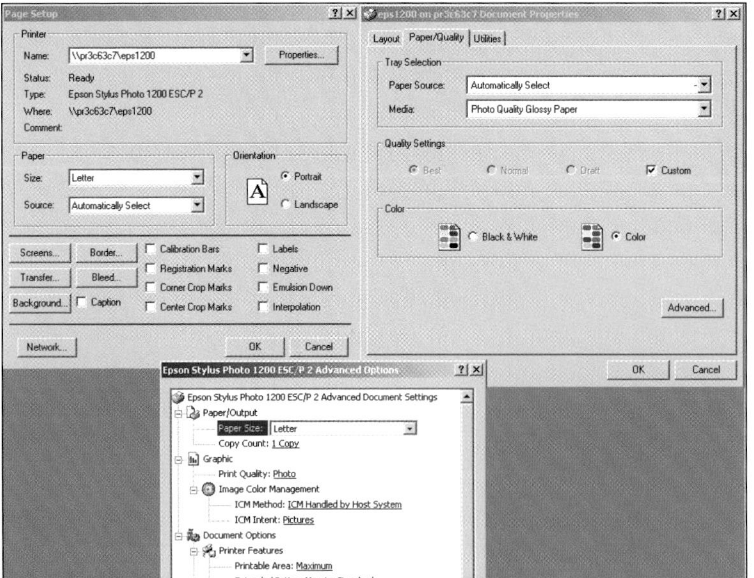

Set the page settings for your printer.

You can obtain the Lenticular material from MicroLens. Ask for either Jim Owens (**microlensjim@aol.com**) or Ken Conley at (704) 847-9234. They will be happy to help you and to answer any questions you might have. Although I figured out the technique of using Layer Masks to create the interlaced image, I could not have done it without the help of both Jim and Ken. Call them. They will answer any questions and supply you with samples as well. You can also obtain the SuperFlip program from them. It comes free with a five-pack of lens material (which can be purchased for under $100).

You can also speak to Tom Mark at Kutuzov. Kutuzov is a group of illusion artists in Las Vegas, and the group is named for the one-eyed general who could not see 3D. The goal of Kutuzov is to teach and to prevent the illusion arts from dying out. Their aim is to teach at least two people in each country about these techniques. You can obtain SuperFlip from them just by asking for help. You can reach Tom Mark at **kutuzov@inermind.net** or at (702) 384-0568. You will find him fascinating to speak with.

You can use Lenticular printing for anything from decorative jewelry to business cards to outdoor billboards. You can also do some incredible 3D projects. For instance, you can create a primitive 3D interlacing in Photoshop by altering the position of copies of the *same* image or by taking multiple photos of the same image from a variety of camera angles. The 3D butterfly postcard that was done by Tom Mark using 3D Genius is one of the most impressive 3D effects I've seen. You can see other examples (flat, of course) at **www.flipsigns.com/sales.htm**.

If you want to see what motion looks like, I have included on the accompanying CD-ROM two animated GIF images done by Dorothy Simpson Krause. They were done for her "Primordial Fear" image, which moves across the surface of a Lenticular print.

This butterfly image, designed by Tom Mark in 3D Genius and viewed on the Lenticular surface, exhibits incredible 3D imagery.

CREATING ART NOUVEAU WEB ELEMENTS

"Give me a lever long enough and a fulcrum on which to place it, and I shall move the world."

—ARCHIMEDE

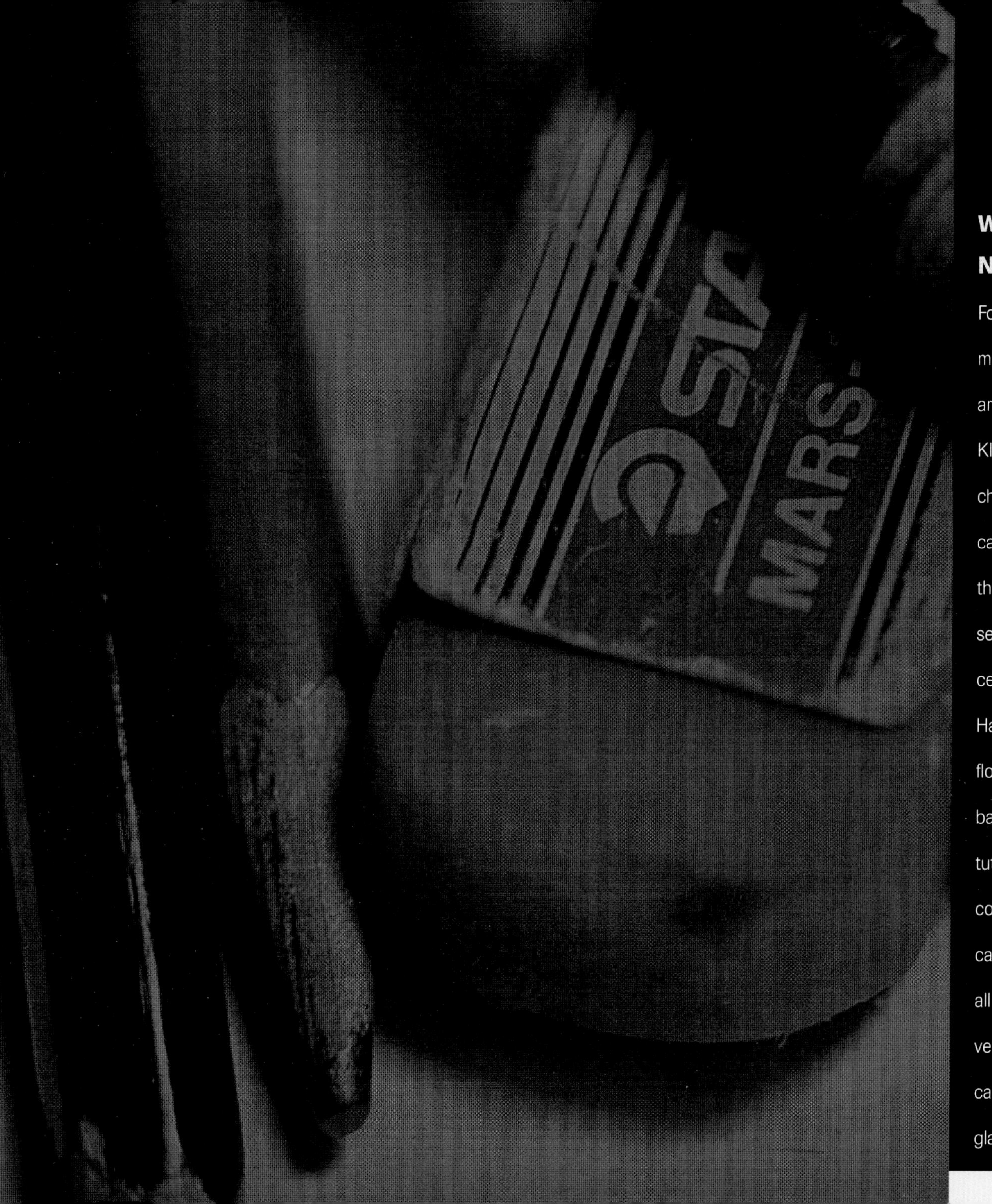

Web Elements with an Art Noveau Flair

For years, artists have admired the work of the masters of the Art Nouveau period. These artists include Alphonse Mucha and Gustave Klimt. Although the Art Nouveau period is characterized by its rich ornamental asymmetrical style, the true essence of the period is in the flowing curves, the delicate lines, and the seemingly uninterrupted flow of each magnificent piece.

Have you ever wondered how they got those flowing lines and dancing curves so perfectly balanced in Art Nouveau posters and ads? This tutorial guides you through designing detailed, complex images that flow with those same delicate lines and curves. The best part is that it's all from one basic drawing. With the help of a very cool, third-party plug-in (BladePro), you'll capture an almost magical look and the feel of glassy metal.

Project 8

Creating Art Nouveau Web Elements

by Kelly Loomis

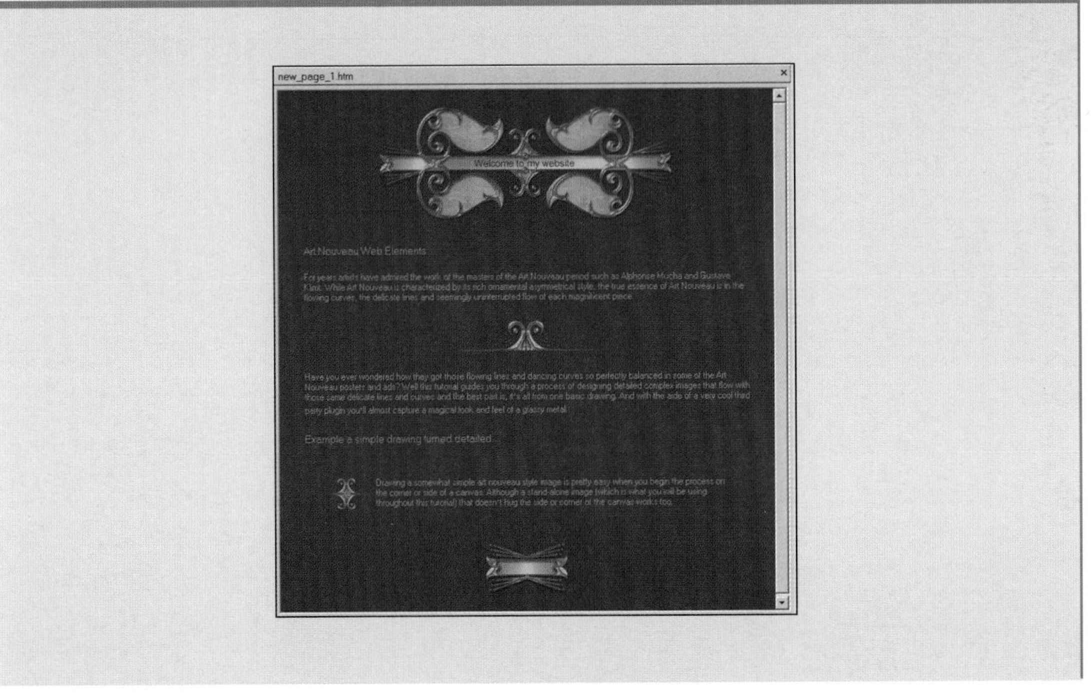

Getting Started

Drawing a somewhat simple Art Nouveau style image is fairly easy when you begin the process on the corner or side of a canvas. A stand-alone image, which is what you will be using throughout this project, also works well, even though it doesn't hug the side or corner of the canvas.

You can create a variety of designs just by flipping, rotating, and cutting and pasting sections of your original doodle. The following images show you that you can create everything you need to make Art Nouveau images, functional buttons, and page titles for the web from one basic starting point.

These two examples show how you can take the same element and develop numerous other elements from it.

In this project, you work with a single element that I have designed, which is the starting image from the previous examples. However, before we start, I thought you might like to know how I created the example. I usually start with a pen and ink sketch that I scan into the computer. Depending on the complexity of the image, I either take the scan into Illustrator or into Flash.

I like that Flash can "paint" vector images. After I auto-trace the image, I can clean it up in Flash easily. My starting image is much larger than the small piece that you see here because it is so much easier to work large and get the lovely flowing curves that are so typical of Art Nouveau. When I start my work in Flash, I save the image as an Illustrator image and then take it into Adobe Illustrator for final tweaking.

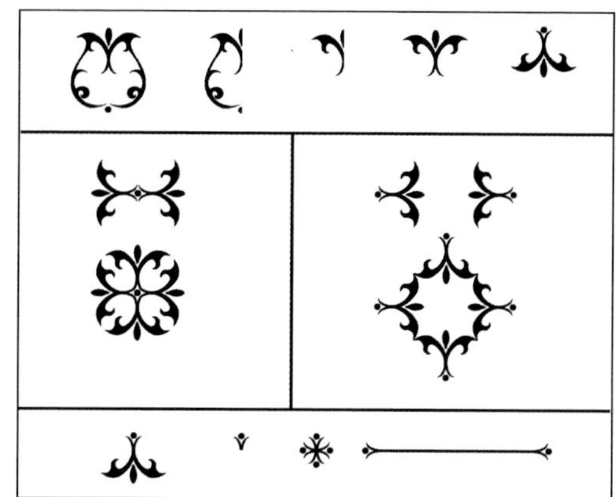

Tip: I always make the placed file a few pixels smaller than the image into which I am placing it. This gives room for the object to anti-alias without getting cut off. If you simply accept the suggested size, you lose the soft edge where the object touches the boundaries of your image.

Flash saves straight lines as strokes rather than as filled objects, and strokes do not automatically scale when you make an object smaller. Therefore, after I have opened my image in Illustrator, I ungroup the image and look for strokes. The Object > Expand command changes the strokes into filled objects. When I group the object again, everything scales perfectly. At this point, I save the object as an Illustrator file. In Photoshop, I create a new file at my desired working size. This is always much smaller than the Illustrator file. I choose File > Place to place the image into Photoshop. Then I rasterize it.

If you don't have Flash or Illustrator, you can scan your drawing and select it in Photoshop. Then change the selection into a working path and tweak the shape using Photoshop's Pen tools. Creating a smooth object is harder to do in Photoshop than it is in Illustrator, but you can do it all in Photoshop if you have no other option. You can then save the finished object as a shape (Edit > Define Custom Shape), which you can resize at will.

Installing SuperBladePro

SuperBladePro is the newest version of Lloyd Burchill's acclaimed SuperBlade filter. SuperBladePro is an amazing filter. It has incredible possibilities for creating jeweled surfaces, and it gives you almost unparalleled control over your final results. This is a "filter with a following." An entire web ring of sites is devoted to SuperBladePro and its presets. I could not get the results I want without it.

To complete the project as written, you need to download a free demo of the filter from the FlamingPear web site (**www.flamingpear.com**) or install it from the CD that accompanies this book. You will need to locate your plug-ins or alternate plug-ins folder. (If you are feeling lazy, you can load my filtered version, but you will be missing out on trying an incredible filter.) Install the filter now; you then can work through the project without having to quit Photoshop to install the filter.

Tip: You can set an alternate plug-ins folder by selecting it in the Edit > Preferences > Plug-Ins and Scratch Disks preference. I always put my third-party filters in a separate folder because it makes it much easier to upgrade, update, or reinstall Photoshop when necessary. With your third-party plug-ins stored safely outside the Photoshop folder, you can't accidentally lose them.

After you have installed the SuperBladePro demo filter, copy the following files from the accompanying CD to the Environments and Textures folder of the SuperBladePro plug-in:

- Mac: Blade1.pct, Blade2.pct, and SBP_preset_Mac.q5q
- Windows: Blade1.bmp, Blade2.bmp, and SBP_preset_Win.q5q

Creating the Main Image

In this part of the project, you open the starting image, and then flip and rotate it to create the start of the main web element.

1. Open the image nouvmain300.psd from the accompanying CD.

   This image has a white Background layer and is set to 300 ppi.

2. Choose Image > Duplicate > OK to create a copy of the starting file. Close the original.

3. Choose Image > Rotate Canvas > 90° CW.

   This sets the correct orientation for this example.

4 Set your Background color to white. Choose Image > Canvas Size. Anchor it in the center-top square and change the Height field to 200%.

Don't check the Relative check box. Click OK.

5 Duplicate Layer 1 by dragging it to the Create New Layer icon. Choose Edit > Transform > Flip Vertical. Choose Edit > Free Transform (Ctrl+T/Cmd+T). Click the triangle icon between the X and Y positions on the Options Bar to make the transform relative, and change the Y: position to 100. You want the two objects to just touch one another. If they don't, click back in the bounding box and then press the down-arrow or up-arrow button until the transformation box is correctly positioned. (In this example, 102 relative pixels is the correct amount.) Click the check mark to complete the transformation.

By using the Free Transform command to alter the Y: position, you keep the two objects aligned.

6 Choose Layer > Merge Down (Ctrl+E/Cmd+E).

7 Choose Image > Canvas Size and anchor the image in the center-left square. Change the Width to 200%. Don't check the Relative check box.

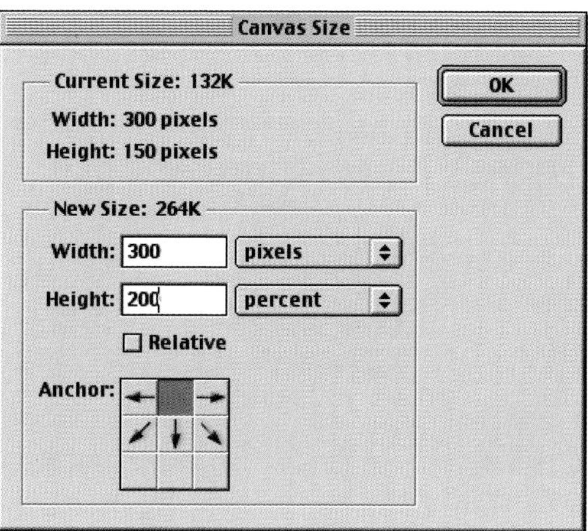

Double the height of the canvas.

Use the Free Transform command to shift the Y: position 102 relative pixels. (The image is shown at 300% magnification.)

8 Duplicate Layer 1 by dragging the layer to the New Layer icon in the Layers palette. Choose Edit > Transform > Flip Horizontal. Choose the Move tool, keep the Shift key pressed, and carefully drag the layer to the right until the small circles overlap in the center. Merge the layers down.

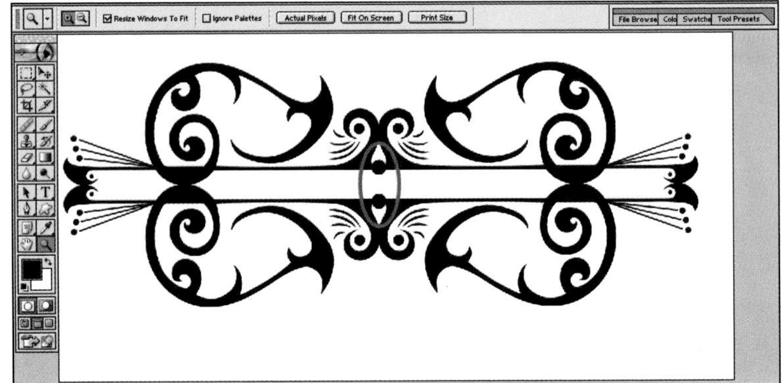

Duplicate Layer 1, flip it horizontally, and drag it to the right until the small circles (shown here circled in red) overlap.

9 Duplicate Layer 1 again. Double-click the layer name in the Layers palette and change the name to **Distorted**. Drag the layer below Layer 1 and turn off the eye to hide this layer. Make Layer 1 active.

Photoshop 7 enables you to alter the layer name in the Layers palette itself (no dialog box pops out) just by double-clicking it. You'll use this layer as a tool later in the development stages.

Applying the SuperBladePro Filter

Now it's time to use SuperBladePro to add color and texture to the sketch that you have transformed.

1 Press D to set the colors back to the default of black and white. Make Layer 1 active. Press Shift+Ctrl+Backspace/Shift+Cmd+Delete to fill the shape with white.

Holding the Shift key as you fill the shape preserves the transparency of the layer. Although the layer looks solid white, it isn't (if you've done this right). If you turn off the visibility of the Background layer, you'll see that you have filled only the black shape on the layer, not the entire layer.

Tip: Filling the image without making a selection but while preserving transparency is the only way to retain the anti-aliased edge on the shape and still cover the original black pixels with white.

2 Select the layer's nontransparent pixels by Ctrl-clicking/Cmd-clicking the layer name in the Layers palette.

You need to have a selection when you apply the SuperBladePro filter.

3 Choose Filter > FlamingPear > SuperBladePro. Click the Load Preset button. When the dialog box appears, click the Load Preset button. Navigate to the Environments and Textures folder inside the SuperBladePro folder and select the SPB_Preset_Mac.q5q preset for the Mac and the SPB_Preset_Win.q5q preset for Windows. All the settings are changed by the preset.

If you receive an error message that the filter cannot locate the Environment Map, click Cancel. Cancel back to the Filter dialog box. Then click the Environment Map picture and choose the Blade1.pct (Mac) or Blade1.bmp (Windows) image. All the settings will be correct. Click OK to apply the filter. The image shown here identifies the location of both the Load Preset button and the Environment Map button. In addition, it shows all the correct settings that will appear.

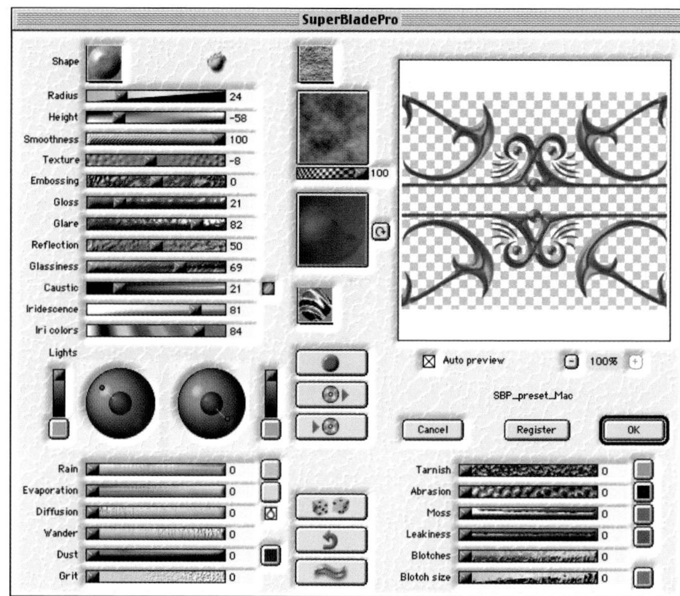

Click the Load Preset button to load the copied preset into SuperBladePro.

Note: You can create realistic textures using SuperBladePro. Be sure to spend some time playing with the various options. The Environment Map that you use when you create the texture makes a huge difference in your results when you are looking for that perfect texture. I will spend a solid day just trying out combinations until I find exactly the right one. I have included another Environment Map on the CD. It is Blade2.bmp or Blade2.pct.

4 Choose Filter > Blur > Gaussian Blur and use a Radius of 0.4 pixels. Deselect.

This smooths some of the sharpness in the filter.

Filling in the Gaps

In this section, you create your own gradient preset to fill in some of the empty areas on the shape.

1 Select the Gradient tool and open the Gradient Editor. Choose the Black, White gradient preset. Set both Opacity Stops to 100%. Double-click the bottom-left Color Stop (location 0%) and change the color to RGB 111, 107, 183. Click the far-right Color Stop (location 100%) and change the RGB to 107, 225, 255. Name your new preset **Nouveau** and click New to add it to the Gradient presets list.

The colors that I have chosen for the gradient were originally sampled from the filtered image. If you are working with your own example, you can sample any two colors that you like from your object.

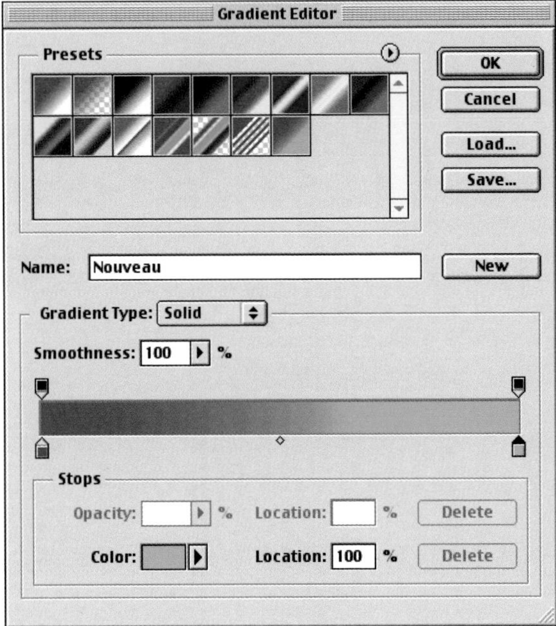

Create a new gradient preset.

2 Make the Background layer active and add a new layer just above the Background layer. Name this new layer **Gradfills**. Choose the Magic Wand tool and set the following:

Tolerance: 0

Anti-aliased: Checked

Contiguous: Checked

Use All Layers: Checked

Leave the Gradfills layer active.

You need to select some specific areas to fill with the Nouveau gradient preset. In the next step, you see which selections you need to make. When you are finished making the gradients, choose Select > Deselect.

3 For each area in the following list, use the Magic Wand tool to select the area. Choose Select > Modify > Expand 2 pixels, and then drag the Gradient cursor in the direction indicated:

Area 1: Drag top-left to bottom-right.

Area 2: Drag top-right to bottom-left.

Area 3: Drag from the center of the right side, as shown, and then just slightly to the right and down. Make sure that you place the cursor in the same location as the red arrow on the image.

Area 4: Drag top-left to bottom-right.

Area 5: Drag bottom-right to top-left.

You need to expand the selection because the Magic Wand tool at 0 doesn't select behind the anti-aliased edges of the object. You have the room to expand the selection because the active layer is underneath the filtered object and the overlap will be hidden. Because you have selected the Use All Layers option on the Magic Wand tool, you can click to pick up the correct area even though there is nothing on the active layer.

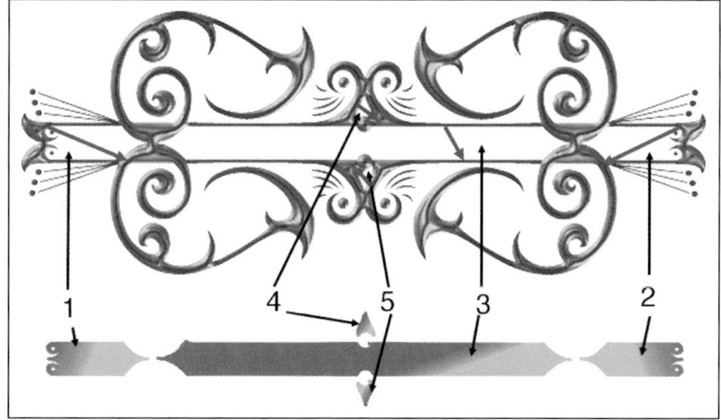

Follow the red lines on the image to place your cursor for the gradients on the Gradfills layer. The black lines show the numbers that refer to the list; they also show the finished area of fill.

In Search of Color

Selecting the perfect background color is as important as selecting the perfect frame for a conventional piece of artwork. In this section, you select a color to go behind the object and to act as the background color for your web page. By using a Color Fill layer to hold this background color, you gain the flexibility to change your project at any time during the developmental stages. Keeping your options open means that the final image can look very different in Step 10 than it did in Step 4, but you don't need to start over or lose any time to make the changes.

1 Make the Background layer active. Choose Layer > New Fill Layer > Solid Color. In the dialog box, set the Color to None, the Mode to Normal, and the Opacity to 100%. Make sure that Group With Previous Layer is unchecked. Name the layer **Color Fill BG**. In the Color Picker, change the RGB to 32, 29, 96.

If you later need to change the color in the Color Fill layer, all you need to do is double-click the Layer thumbnail (not the Mask thumbnail) to reopen the Color Picker. You can also choose Layer > Change Layer Content.

Note: I used the Eyedropper tool to sample various colors from the image until I found the one I liked best.

Preparing a Texture Element

In this section, you use the Edit > Transform commands to alter the basic ornament to create a design that you'll use to texture a selection for some of the curved leaves in the ornament. You start by distorting the design you already created in the Distorted layer. Although these next few steps might be a bit time-consuming, you'll see how they add a beautiful touch to the overall look and feel of the image.

1. Ctrl-click/right-click the Distorted layer name in the Layers palette, and then choose Duplicate Layer from the pop-up menu. Choose New in the Document pop-up in the Destination area of the dialog box, and then name the new file **WhirlyGig**.

   You don't need to make the layer visible to copy it to a new image.

2. Work in the new image. Choose Edit > Transform > Distort. On the Options Bar, change the Width to 40% and click the check mark to execute the transformation.

   Make sure that you don't click the link between the Width and Height to preserve the aspect ratio. You want to change only the width. You are making the width approximately the same size as the height to create a symmetrical design element.

3. Duplicate the layer by dragging it to the Create New Layer icon at the bottom of the Layers palette. Choose Edit > Transform > Rotate 90° CW.

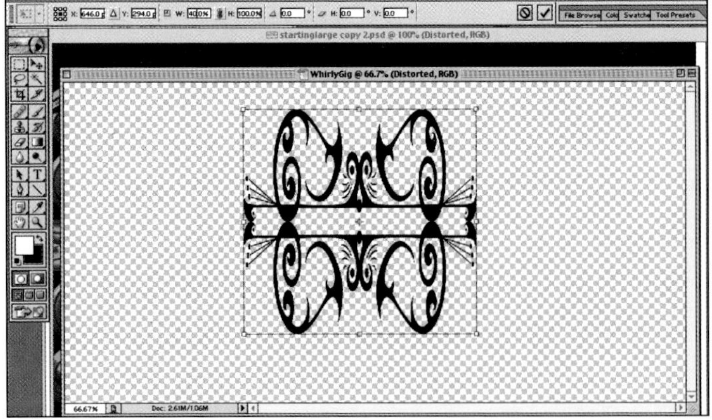

Choose Edit > Transform > Distort and, on the Options Bar, change the Width of the object to 40%.

4. Click the Lock Transparent Pixels check box in the Layers palette. Using the Gradient tool with the Nouveau preset, drag across the shape in the layer from the top-left to the bottom-right.

5. Make the original layer active and check the Lock Transparent Pixels check box. Using the Gradient tool with the Nouveau preset, drag across the shape in the layer from the bottom-left to the top-right. Choose Layer > Merge Visible to merge the two layers into one.

6. In the merged layer, choose Edit > Transform > Scale. On the Options Bar, click the link icon between the Height and Width fields to preserve the Aspect Ratio. Change the Width and Height to 50%, and then click the check mark icon on the Options Bar to execute the transformation.

7. Drag the Rectangular Marquee tool around the scaled object and choose Image > Crop. Save the file as **WhirlyGig.psd**.

Note: You can also use this file as you are developing other web elements to coordinate with the current one.

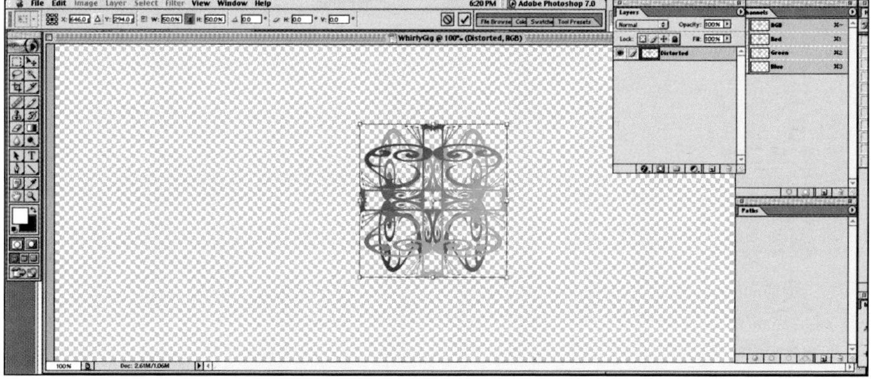

Scale the contents of the merged layer by 50%.

Creating the Texture

In this section, you use the WhirlyGig texture element to add texture to a selection. You'll learn how to finesse the selection by creating a guideline to keep the Magic Wand tool from selecting too much, and you'll apply the texture with the Clone Stamp tool.

1. Make the Color Fill BG layer active. Add a new layer. Double-click the layer name and name it **Decor**.

   By making the Color Fill BG layer active first, you automatically add the new layer in the correct position.

2 Choose the Pencil tool with the Hard Round 1-pixel brush. Make white your foreground color. Look carefully at the image shown here to see where you should draw two lines.

The two lines that you draw keep the Magic Wand tool from selecting the entire background of the image. You are closing off the areas of the lower-left leaf to make an enclosed shape.

Using the Pencil tool, continue the lines in the lower-left leaf shape to create an enclosed element.

3 Choose the Magic Wand tool. It should still be set to the following:

Tolerance: 0

Anti-alias: On

Contiguous: On

Use All Layers: On

Click inside the enclosed shape. Choose Select > Modify > Expand by 2 pixels.

By expanding the selection by 2 pixels, you place image edges underneath the existing ornament so that you will have no gaps. You also include your extra pencil lines in the selection where they will be covered in the next step. The selection should not extend into the dark blue background except where it is just over the two pencil lines that you drew.

4 Choose the Gradient tool and use the Nouveau preset. Begin from the top-left and drag the cursor to the bottom-right in the selection on the Decor layer. Leave the selection active. Notice that the white line to close the selection is now covered by the gradient.

5 Arrange your workspace so that you can see both the WhirlyGig image and the web element that you have been designing. Make the WhirlyGig image active.

6 Select the Clone Stamp tool. Click the Brushes palette icon at the far right side of the Options palette to reveal the Brushes palette. If the palette does not show the same options as the image shown here, click the Brush Tip Shape entry to alter the focus of the dialog box. Select the 1 Soft Round 100 Pixels brush and alter the diameter of the brush until it covers the entire WhirlyGig object (it should be between 150 and 170 pixels).

Because the brush is soft, it covers more than the preview shows.

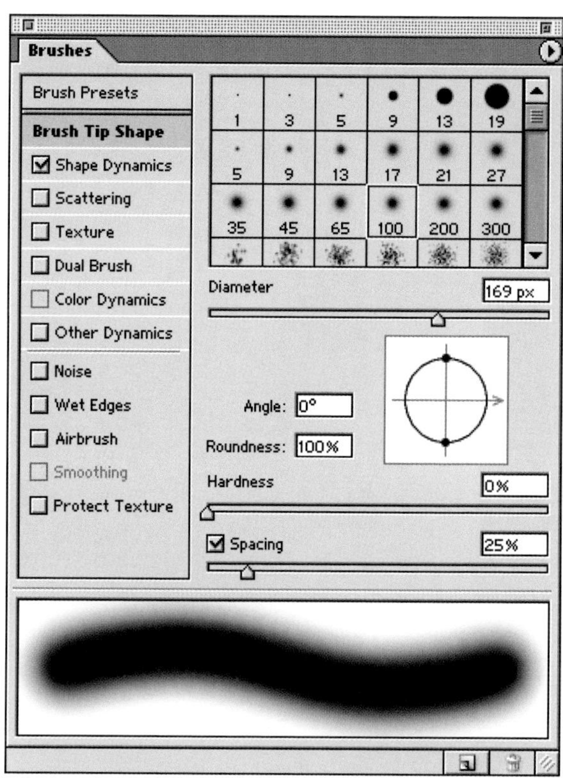

Create a 169-pixel soft brush for the Clone Stamp tool.

7 Hold down the Alt/Option key and click with the Clone Stamp tool in the center of the WhirlyGig object.

This sets the "copy from" point for the Clone Stamp tool.

8 Make the nouvmain image active and click once, or possibly twice, in the center of the selection. Deselect when you are done painting.

Be careful—you do not want the texture too dark. The idea is that it should look a bit washed out or transparent. The applied gradient and Clone Stamp complement and add an almost whimsical touch to the overall look of the image. The selection marquee keeps the Clone Stamp tool from painting outside the shape.

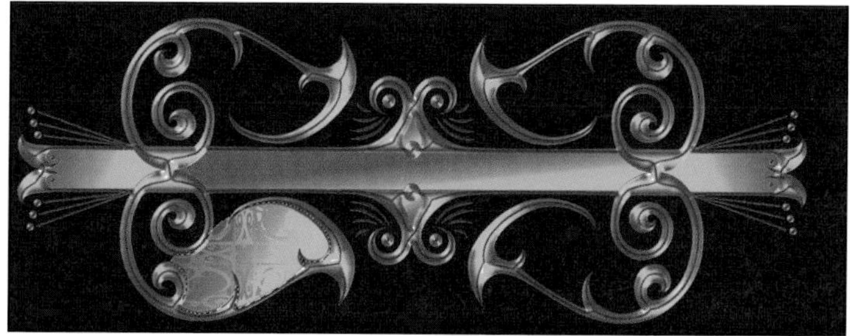

Click in the center of the selection to stamp a light version of the texture onto the gradient.

Duplicating the Textures

In this part of the project, you learn some tricks for duplicating the texture that you just created and placing it into the correct positions for the other leaf elements.

1. Turn off the eye for the Layer 1 and Gradfills layers (the visibility for the Distorted layer should already be off). If you see any white guidelines around the outside of the texture shape, zoom in and use the Eraser tool to carefully remove them. Turn the visibility of the Layer 1 and Gradfills layers back on.

2. Drag the Decor layer to the New Layer icon at the bottom of the Layers palette to duplicate it.

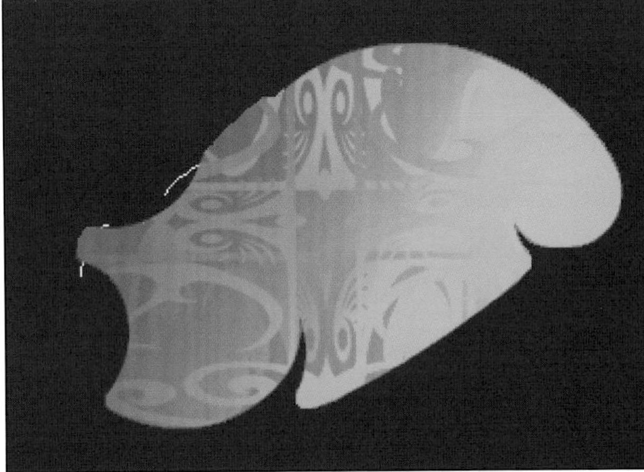

Use the Eraser tool to remove any stray white pixels from around the texture shape.

3. Choose the Paintbrush tool with the Hard Round 3 pixels brush. You can leave white as your foreground color. The Decor copy layer is active. Paint a small spot of white on the Decor layer at the highest point on the top-left leaf, as shown.

   Your next step is to flip the layer vertically. When you flip a layer, the center of the opaque pixels on the layer is automatically used as the center point for the transformation. By placing a dot at the highest point of the top shape, you ensure that the texture object lands in the correct location when you flip it. You are changing the center of its opaque pixels by painting the white dot. The dot, of course, is not visible when you paint it, and it will be covered by the main shape when you flip the object as well.

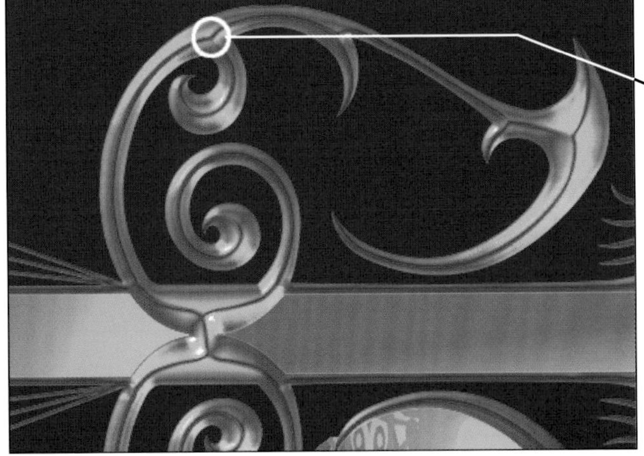

Paint a dot at the highest point on the top-left element.

Note: If you want to be precise about this (and taking the time now means that you are less likely to need to do major repairs in the next section of the project), you can reduce the opacity on Layer 1 until you see how far under the metal frame the texture layer extends. Making sure that the Decor copy layer is active, you can then place your dot at the matching location under the top leaf element. Then bring Layer 1 back to 100% opacity and make the Decor copy layer active again.

4 Choose Edit > Transform > Flip Vertical. Merge down the layers.

If you need to, move the texture into the correct place before you merge the layers. Note that you really should not need to move the flipped object at all if you placed the dot in the correct place in Step 3.

5 Duplicate the Decor layer. Choose Edit > Free Transform. Move the center point of the bounding box until it is exactly in the center of the main object (between the two dots). Keep the Shift key pressed as you move the center point. Place your cursor outside the bounding box near the top-left corner and rotate the object 180 degrees. You can also type **180** into the Rotate field on the Options Bar. Click the check mark to complete the transformation.

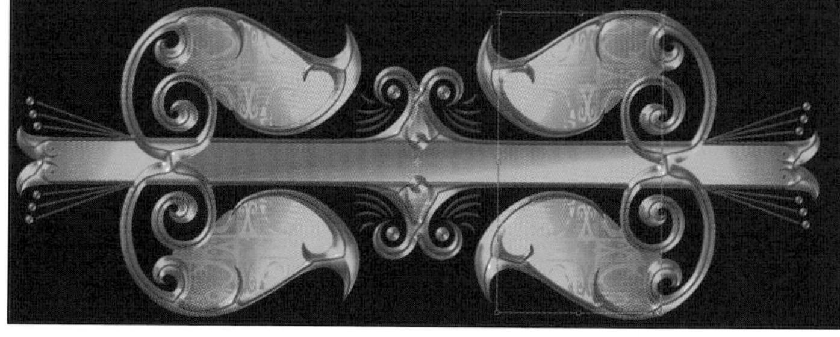

Move the center point of the Free Transform bounding box to the center of the object and rotate the object 180 degrees.

Although you could just flip the layer horizontally, I like this method for making sure that the object lands in the correct location without having to manually place it there. Keeping the Shift key pressed as you move the center point of the bounding box keeps the center point constrained horizontally. That way, you need only judge the vertical center, and that is easy to do on a symmetrical design such as this one.

6 Merge the layer down into the Decor layer below.

DETAILS, DETAILS, DETAILS

If you're anything like me, you know that details really matter. Thus, the beautiful transformations of the last section need a bit of fine-tuning. If you look carefully at the image, you'll see that the metal of the main object doesn't create a complete frame for the texture objects you just placed under it.

In this part of the project, you copy a section of the metal frame and fix the main object so that it looks as if the leaves were closed shapes from the beginning. You will use a combination of Liquify, the Clone Stamp tool, and cut, paste, and rotate to alter the image.

I realize that you could have extended the frame before the project began, but often as you design, something occurs to you that was not obvious at the start. If it can be fixed at this stage of the process, that's better than starting over. Even so, this is undoubtedly the most painstaking part of the entire process.

Note: There are many possible ways to fix the gap in the metal frame. I prefer to work so that no change is permanent and so that I can always revert back. For this reason, I like to use Layer Masks wherever possible so that I don't alter pixels in the image until I am sure that I like my results. Feel free to live dangerously if you like and take a shorter route to the finish post!

1. Duplicate Layer 1 by dragging it to the New Layer icon on the Layers palette. Rename Layer 1 as **ORIGINAL** and hide the layer by turning off the eye icon to the left of it. Make the Layer 1 copy layer active. For additional insurance, click the Create New Snapshot icon in the History palette to save this image state as a snapshot.

   The layer copy is your insurance that you can always get back to the original metal frame. The snapshot gives you the added protection of being able to revert to this point or to spin off a new copy from this image state.

2. Drag the Rectangular Marquee tool (or the Lasso tool) around the area shown here in red. This is on the lower-right leaf element of the metal frame. Choose Layer > New > Layer via Copy (Ctrl+J/Cmd+J).

   You'll use this copy in the next step to patch the gap in the frame.

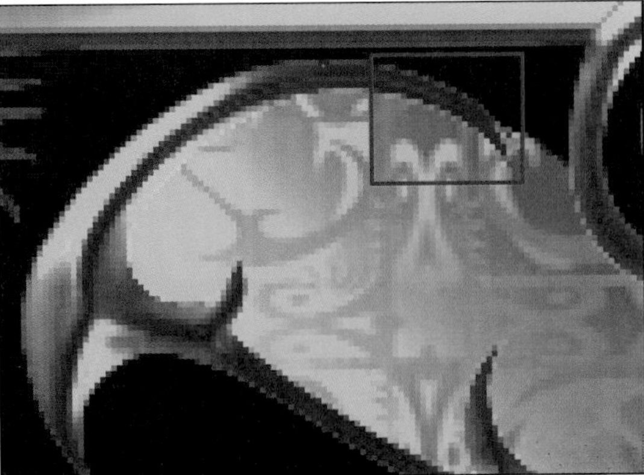

Create a selection around the tip of the metal frame and copy the selection to a new layer.

3 Using the Move tool, slide the copied metal frame tip so that the new tip closes the gap in the frame. Try to position the tip so that it also covers the edge of the texture object beneath it.

The image shown here gives the approximate location for the copied tip. In the next step, you fix the overlap so that the two pieces become one.

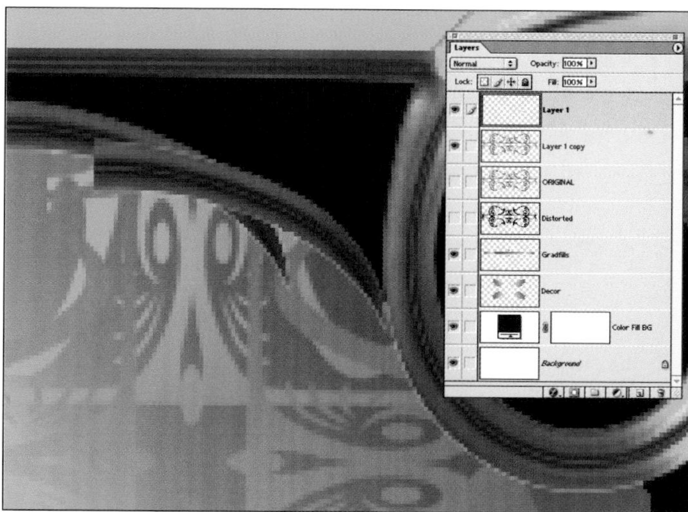

Move the copied tip so that it closes the gap.

4 Add a Layer Mask to Layer 1 (the copied tip layer). Working with a small paintbrush and black, carefully paint the Layer Mask to get as seamless a blend of the new tip into the original frame as you can.

The dark embossing line is the item that you are trying to make into a continuous line.

Blend the new tip (the area in red) into the original by painting into a Layer Mask.

5 Make the Layer 1 copy layer active and add a Layer Mask to that layer as well. Paint out the area of the original tip so that you have only one line. Then make Layer 1 (the copied tip layer) active and merge the two layers. In the dialog box that appears, choose Apply to apply the Layer Masks on both layers before merging.

You need to apply the masks to each layer so that the masks don't cancel out your changes. The only problem left with the merge is that the glorious curve has a flat spot on it. You'll turn to the Liquify command in the next step to fix that.

6 Choose Filter > Liquify and set the brush size to about 12. The Warp tool is the active tool as you enter the Liquify command. You can leave Brush Pressure at 50, but change the Turbulent Jitter setting to 1. Zoom into the image at about 800 percent and carefully place the brush over the flat spot on the curve. Then just drag the curve upward slightly until it forms a beautiful arch. Click OK.

It should take only one or two strokes to form the correct curve. Be careful not to disturb the pixels any more than necessary. If you need to move the brush, revert the image and choose a large brush instead. Notice that in Photoshop 7, the Liquify command has moved to the Filter menu.

7 Select the patched area of the frame using the Rectangular Marquee tool. Choose Layer > New > Layer via Copy. Duplicate this layer two more times (for a total of three layers).

You will use these patch layers to apply the new curve to the other portions of the frame. Although you'll need to get rid of the underlying curve, you won't need to adjust the copied curve again.

8 Using each patch layer in turn, flip one patch horizontally, another vertically, and the third 180 degrees as needed. Then drag them to one of the open areas on the frame. Use a Layer Mask for safety if you want, or the Eraser tool, to remove the unneeded portion of the original frame on the Layer 1 copy layer. Apply the next patch until all three patch layers are in position. Make the top layer active and merge each layer down until you merge the last patch into the Layer 1 copy layer. If you have used a Layer Mask on that layer, click Apply before you do the final merge.

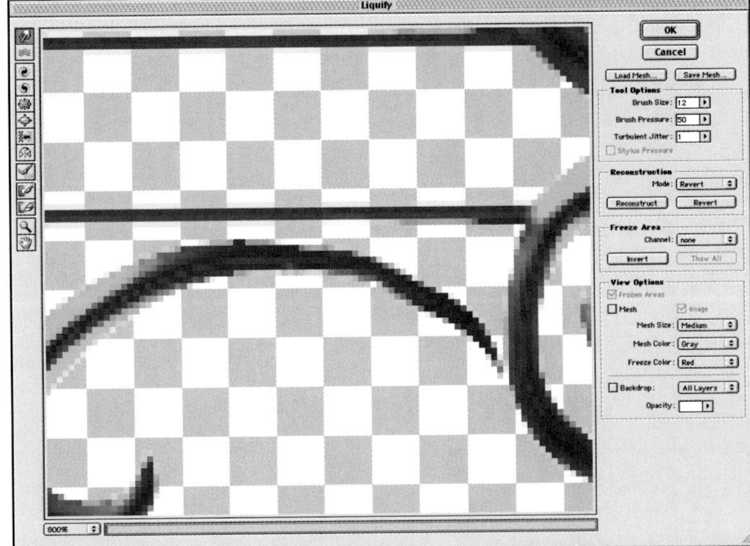

Use Liquify to restore a true curve to the frame.

You will need to flip one layer horizontally, one vertically, and one 180 degrees. You can align the layers that you flip by dragging them while pressing the Shift key. This won't work for the layer that you rotate 180 degrees, so you'll have to judge that one by eye.

Note: After you have applied all four patches, check the Décor layer carefully to see if any edge is exposed. If necessary, use the Clone Stamp tool or the Pencil tool to extend the texture so that the four patches again fit under the frame with no exposed blank space.

A Touch of Layer Styles

As you near the end of the process, you need to add some final touches. Photoshop's Layer Styles has a host of effects that you can use on any layer in the project.

1 Make the Décor layer active. Choose Layer > Layer Style > Inner Glow or click the "f" in the Layers palette. Change the settings as follows:

Structure:

Blend Mode: Normal

Opacity: 20%

Noise: 0%

Color: RGB 102, 0, 241

Elements:

Technique: Softer

Source: Edge

Choke: 0%

Size: 29 pixels

Quality:

Contour: Gaussian

Anti-aliased: Not checked

Range: 50%

Jitter: 0%

Although the effect is subtle, it adds a delicate highlight to the inner edge of the objects and blends beautifully with the rest of the layers.

2 Activate the Layer 1 copy layer. Choose Layer > Layer Style > Drop Shadow or click the "f" in the Layers palette. Change the settings as follows:

Structure:

Blend Mode: Normal

Color: RGB 0, 0, 0

Opacity: 60%

Angle: 120°

Use Global Light: Checked

Distance: 3 px

Spread: 3%

Size: 3 px

Quality:

Contour: Linear

Anti-aliased: Not checked

Noise: 0%

Layer Knocks Out Drop Shadow: Checked

This step adds a wonderful clarity to the Gradfills and Decor layers.

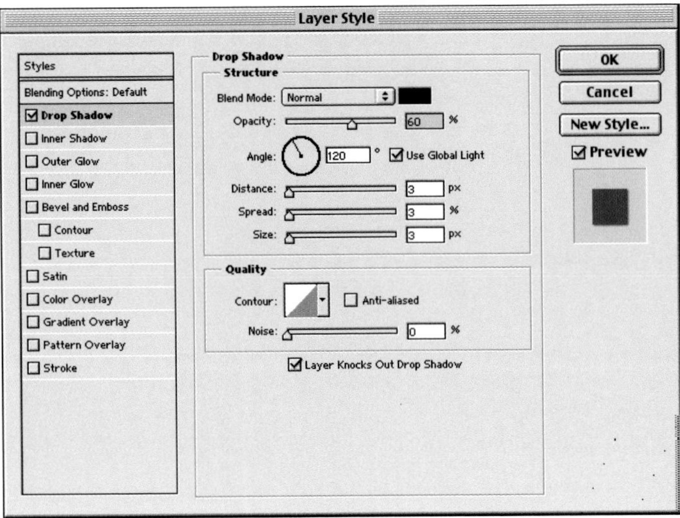

Add a Drop Shadow to the Layer 1 copy layer using these settings.

3 With the Layer 1 copy layer still active, choose Layer > Layer Style > Inner Shadow or click the "f" in the Layers palette entry and select Inner Shadow. Change the settings as follows:

Structure:

Blend Mode: Soft Light

Color: RGB 0, 0, 0

Opacity: 50%

Angle: 120°

Use Global Light: Checked

Distance: 5 px

Choke: 0%

Size: 5 px

Quality:

Contour: Linear

Anti-aliased: Not checked

Noise: 0%

The Inner Shadow effect blends with the top part of the active layer and darkens the metal.

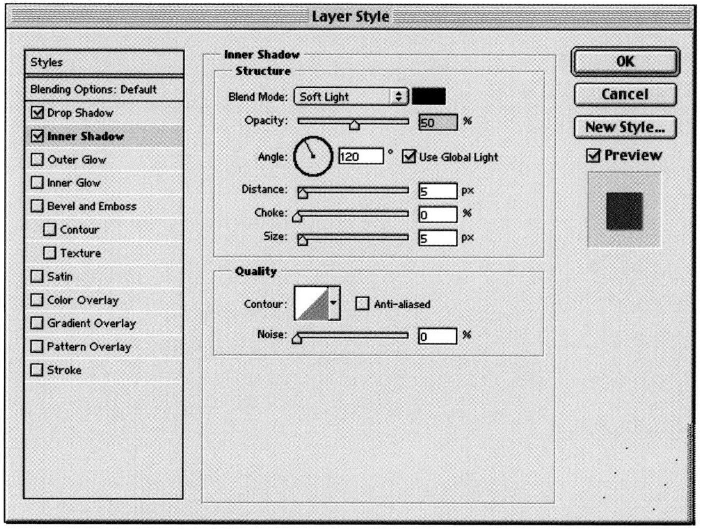

Add an Inner Shadow to the Layer 1 copy layer using these settings.

Note: Photoshop 7 has changed the way you open the Layer Styles dialog box. You can reopen the dialog box to alter settings by pressing Alt/Option and double-clicking the layer name in the Layers palette. You can also press Alt/Option and double-click the "f" icon on the Layers palette or the "f" in an Effects entry on the Layers palette.

Finishing Touches

At this point, the web element is finished. You can add text to it if you wish. I use the same color as the background for my text when it contrasts with the element. That's another way to tie the background and foreground together. Choose your font with care. Your font should match the look and feel of the web element and be legible on the web.

The only remaining task is to save this element for the web. Make sure that you first save a fully layered version of your work as a Photoshop (.psd) file. That way, you have all the layers available to you for modification should you want to use them for other web elements such as buttons, bars, navigation bars, and bullets. In the "Modifications" section of this project, I discuss a few of the elements.

1 Duplicate the image that you have saved as a .psd file. On the duplicate, use the Crop tool to crop the image close to the boundary of the web element. Make sure that you have entered no dimensions into the Crop Height or Crop Width fields.

Note: When you crop the image, be careful with the Drop Shadow effect that you applied to it. The background color of both the image and the web page need to have the same color as the image background. If you cut off any of the drop shadow, the element borders will be both obvious and ugly. Thus, be sure to leave some background color around the image.

2 Be sure these layers are visible: Text (if you have created any), Layer 1 copy, Gradfills, Decor, and Color Fill BG. Leave the Background, ORIGINAL, and Distorted layers invisible. Choose Layer > Flatten Image.

If the "Discard Hidden Layers?" warning appears, click OK.

Note: A flattened file is not required to save an image for the web. Photoshop is quite capable of flattening the image as it saves it in a web format. However, if you reduce the image in size, some of the Layer Styles don't resize along with the image. This can change the effects that you worked so hard to size correctly. Therefore, I always flatten my images before I resize them, if I have applied Layer Styles.

3 Choose Image > Image Size and reduce the image to 400 pixels wide, 72 ppi. Make sure that you check the Constrain Proportions and Resample Image options.

The web element as you designed it is too big for a web page.

4 Choose File > Save for Web. Here are the settings that I like to use:

JPEG High

JPEG

High

Progressive: Unchecked

ICC Profile: Unchecked

Optimized: Checked

Quality: 60

Blur: 0

Matte: Leave blank

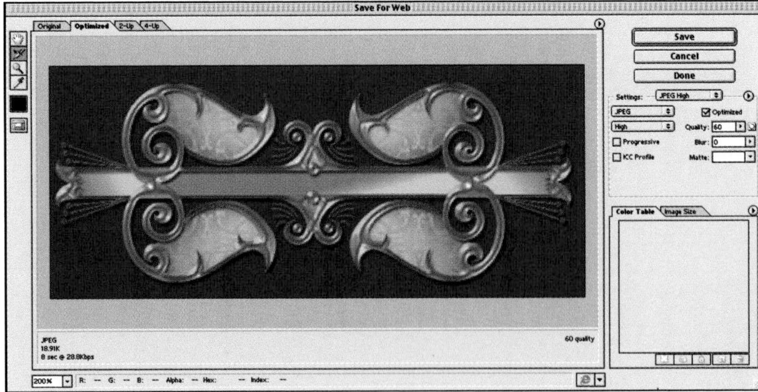

Save a flattened copy of your image for the web using the JPEG and High settings.

Modifications

You can use the techniques you've learned in this project in a variety of applications. You'll get significantly different results by applying different blend modes, changing the hues and values (Image > Adjustments), or opting not to use a third-party plug-in at all. Here are some of the other graphics I created from this project.

By using the layers from the main project, you can develop a spacer bar, a navigation bar, and link buttons to complete a web set for the Internet. Add your text and you're ready to go!

Create a complete web element set using rearrangements of the image you have just created.

Adding a gradient to the background and main design gave this image a completely different feel. From Layer Styles, I added a drop shadow with two different angle directions. I applied an Inner Glow and then changed the Hue and Saturation in the Decor layer. I used the Clone Stamp tool to paint directly on the main design in Layer 1 and vióla—I have a completely different look.

By changing the background color and gradient colors and applying the texture differently, you can totally alter the look of the image.

In this modification, I used the same gradient colors you used throughout this project. I then applied the Render > Difference Clouds and the Stylize > Solarize filters (in that order) to the Layer 1, Decor, and Gradfills layers. I used the Eyedropper tool to sample colors in the image to locate the perfect background color, and the effect is lovely.

I hope these techniques inspire you to experiment with Art Nouveau images or any graphical design where this technique can be applied. I also hope it inspires you to bring your art to the web.

Difference Clouds and Solarize change the appearance of the element in this modification.

WEB PAGE DESIGN IN PHOTOSHOP AND IMAGEREADY

"If being an egomaniac means I believe in what I do and in my art or music, then in that respect you can call me that… I believe in what I do, and I'll say it."

—JOHN LENNON

An Easy Way to Create a Web Site

I was getting ready to redesign my own web site and was faced with the challenge of how best to approach the task. I had considered the writings of a number of authors who all presented strong cases for doing things "their way." However, like most projects that you do for yourself, I felt it was time to set a deadline and press ahead. I was suffering from analysis paralysis.

Photoshop is my main tool as a working artist, and right there in front of me was the tool I needed. It had been there since version 5.5, though it was a tool I seldom used because the web is not my normal medium.

ImageReady, the Slice tool, the Slice Selection tool, and Layer Based Slices—all are waiting for the Photoshop user who needs to design web pages. Add styles to your tool box and you have the equipment for a truly professional looking site. I use Adobe GoLive for my actual site building, but creating all the pages first in Photoshop shortens my development cycle.

Project 9

Web Page Design in Photoshop and ImageReady

by Rob Barnes

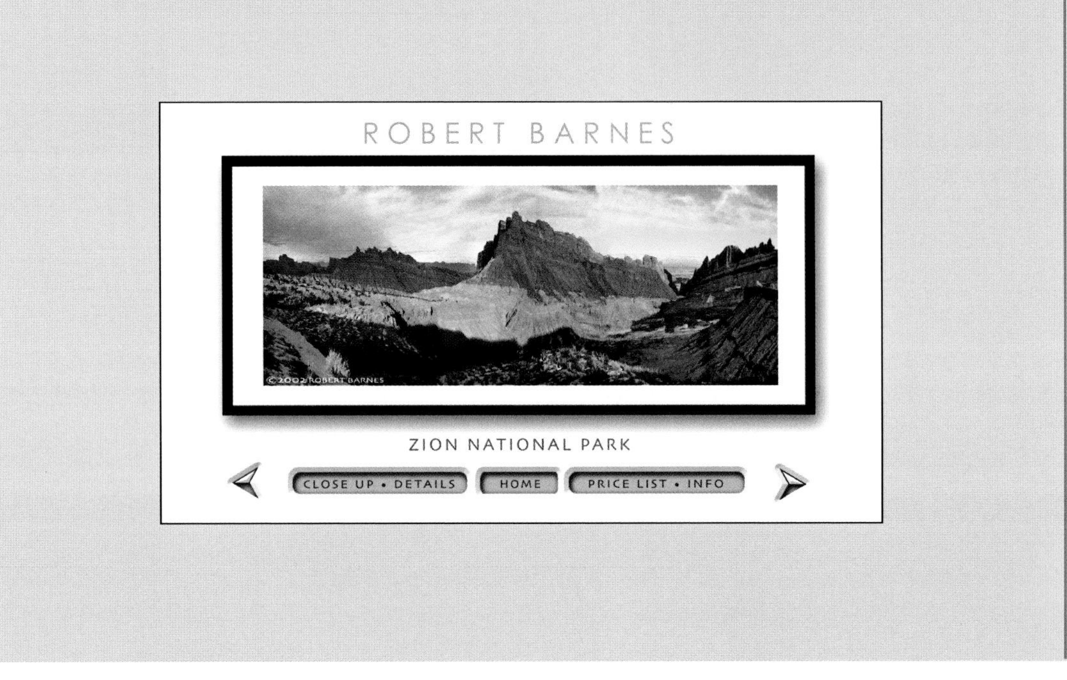

Getting Started

When I started designing the newest version of my online art gallery, I wanted a more efficient method for creating the web page. After a bit of reading and talking with my friends, I realized I had been overlooking the obvious every time I used Photoshop: slices work. The process boils down to this:

1. You design your web page and make sure that each element for the page is on its own layer.
2. Then, using a few simple commands, you divide the image into pieces (slices) that can have different attributes. Some slices—like my art work—are JPEGs. Some—like my buttons and labels—are GIFs. All are optimized and output to a file that is useable by Adobe GoLive or Dreamweaver.

In this project, you re-create one of the gallery pages on my web site. In the process, you learn how to use guides, set up a template document, create styled buttons, save styles, create rollovers, and export the final result to GoLive.

A Simple Page

I wanted a very simple page. I am an artist, and I wanted my art—not my web-design skills—to stand out. Therefore, all I wanted from the site design was a clean look, as if you were seeing images hung on the white walls of a gallery. I wanted the interface to be consistent, so that the navigational elements stayed the same for each page. I had taken a number of seminars on web design and read too many books. When I finally realized that the answer had been in Photoshop all along, the rest of the design process was easy.

I designed my home page first. The illustration shown here is my home page at **www.barnesgallery.com**. Feel free to drop in and visit the entire site. You'll see slices put to good use on almost every page.

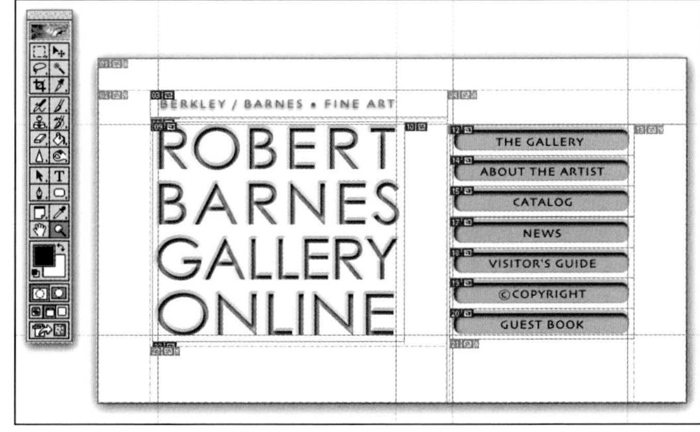

The home page at **www.barnesgallery.com**.

After I designed the home page, I knew I had the look I needed for the entire site. I was ready to develop the gallery pages. You can come along and re-create them with me.

1. Create a new image sized at 760×430 pixels in RGB Color mode at 72 ppi with a white background.

   This size page works well in a browser for a user who has an 800×600 screen. The white background easily adjusts to any size monitor.

2. Choose View > Rulers (Ctrl+R/Cmd+R) if your rulers are not on.

   Now you can begin to set guides that will help partition the space for your design elements. In the next step, you'll see a "no math" trick for finding the center of an image.

3 Zoom in on a small area near what you think is the center of the image. Choose the Rectangular Marquee tool and drag out a selection that is 2×2 pixels in size. Fill the selection with black or any color except white. Cut the selection to the clipboard (Ctrl+X/Cmd+X).

4 Double-click the Hand tool to make the image fit into the window. Paste in the selection from the clipboard (Ctrl+V/Cmd+V). Then drag a horizontal and a vertical guide from the rulers into the center of the 4-pixel square.

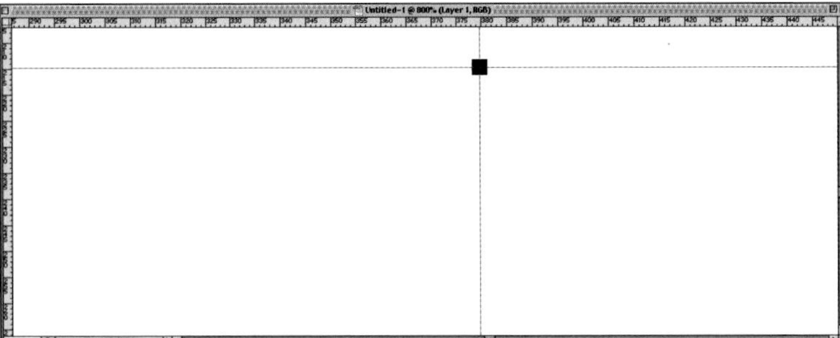

Drag a horizontal and vertical guide to the center of the black square (this is a zoomed-in view).

The selection automatically pastes itself into the exact center of the image as long as nothing else is selected and the entire image is visible. When you cut the selection, you also removed the selection marquee, so this places the small square exactly where you want it. The guides fit between the pixels.

5 Drag Layer 1 to the trash. You won't need it again.

6 Open the file Text.psd from the accompanying CD-ROM.

This file contains all my text elements. I used the Century Gothic and Skia fonts, both of which are standard fonts on the Mac. However, because some of you won't have these fonts, I rasterized the text so that you don't need the font to recreate this web site.

7 Make the ROBERT BARNES layer active in the text file. Hold the Shift key and drag the layer into the empty web page image. Keep the Shift key pressed as you drag the text toward the top of the image. Center it by eye between the 0-pixel tick mark and the 50-pixel tick marks on the side ruler.

The Shift key constrains the dropped text so that the center of the word hugs the center guide.

8 Drag another guide from the top ruler to the 55-pixel tick mark on the side vertical ruler.

You'll use this guide as the top of the gallery painting for the page. I tried to leave a visually pleasing balance here rather than measure and figure things in advance.

9 Open the file image.psd from the accompanying CD-ROM. Using the Move tool, hold the Shift key and drag Layer 1 into the web page. Keep the Shift key pressed as you drag the image up until it snaps to the upper horizontal guide.

The original of this image is over 6 feet wide. This is a digital painting done from a photograph.

Place the painting into the image. Center and snap it to the top guide.

10 Drag a guide to the bottom of the painting. Then drag a guide 55 pixels below that. Finally, drag a guide centered between the two new guides (at 28 pixels below the first new guide that you added in this step).

This sets the spacing for the text that identifies the image. You need to center the text (which you'll do in the next step) between the bottom of the painting and what will become the top of the buttons. The spacing of 55 pixels matches the space at the top of the image.

Create three equidistantly spaced guides from the bottom of the painting to match the spacing between the painting and top of the image.

11 Make the text image active. Drag the IMAGE TITLE BAR layer from the text image into the web page image, holding the Shift key as you drag. After you get it into the web page image, keep the Shift key pressed as you drag it to snap it to the middle of the three new guides.

Although you are snapping the baseline of the text to the guide, in the next step, I show you how to center the text on the guide itself.

12 Zoom in closely on the text. Press Ctrl+T/Cmd+T to transform the text. You don't want to change the text dimensions. All you want to do is drag the text so that the center marker snaps to the intersection of the two guides.

Because the center handle of the Free Transform command's bounding box is always the exact center of the object, it becomes easy to center the text on the guides. In the image shown here, I added a larger red circle so that you could see the center point more clearly.

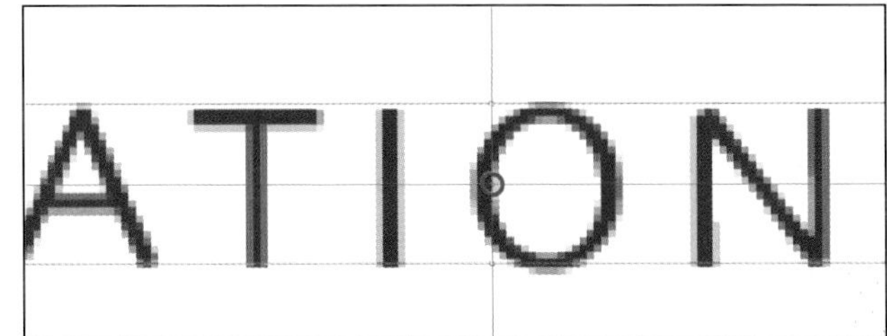

Drag the text without resizing or rotating it so that the center point in the bounding box hits the intersection of the two guides.

You've Got Style

I'm going to take you on a brief detour here before you create the buttons. Photoshop 7 has a neat new feature that enables you to apply a style at the same time that you create a shape. This means that you can decide on the effects you want to add to a button, save the effects as a style, and then create your button "to size" with the effects already in place.

I played around with a number of different effects before I discovered one that I really liked for my site. I have also included a set of styles (BARNESStyles.asl) on the accompanying CD. You can play with these as you like. They are the result of a lot of experimentation. I decided to use a white "blank" for my button because you can see it under the black text in the Normal state, and you can apply color changes to the button color to create Over and Down states.

1 Create a new file that is 100-pixels square, in RGB Color mode, 72 ppi, and has a white background.

This is the "play file" where you will define your style.

2 Choose the Rounded Rectangle tool from the Shape tools slot in the toolbox. Leave the default Radius of 10 pixels. Make sure that Style in the Options Bar is set to None. Change your foreground color to white and drag out a small shape.

Its size doesn't matter right now. This shape is just to choose the effects.

3 Choose Layer > Layer Style > Bevel and Emboss or select it from Add a layer style at the bottom of the Layers palette. In the Layer Style dialog box, set the following:

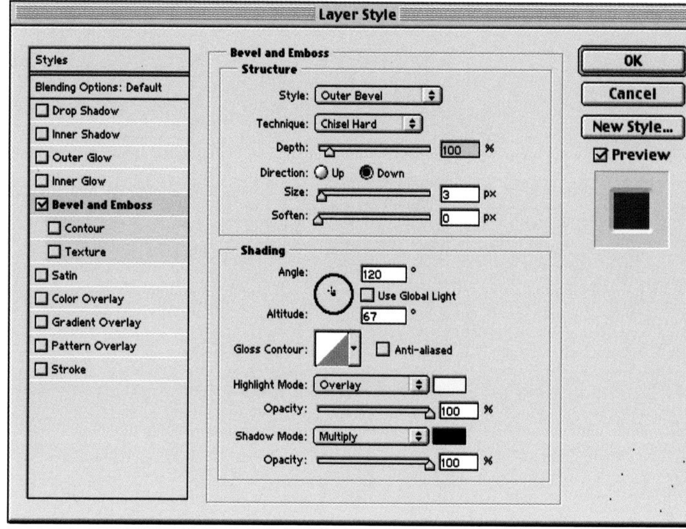

Apply a Bevel and Emboss Layer Style to the button using these settings.

Structure:

Style: Outer Bevel

Technique: Chisel Hard

Depth: 100%

Direction: Down

Size: 3 pixels

Soften: 0 pixels

Shading:

Angle: 120°

Use Global Light: Not checked

Altitude: 67°

Gloss Contour: Linear

Anti-aliased: Not checked

Highlight Mode: Overlay

Color: RGB at 253, 244, and 237

Opacity: 100%

Shadow Mode: Multiply

Color: RGB at 0, 0, and 0

Opacity: 100%

The bevel is the most critical part of the design process for a button. It sets the tone for any other effect that you apply.

4 Add an Inner Shadow Layer Style to the button using these settings:

Structure:

Blend Mode: Multiply

Color: RGB at 0, 0, and 0

Opacity: 85%

Angle: 120°

Use Global Light: Not checked

Distance: 3 pixels

Choke: 15%

Size: 6 pixels

Quality:

Contour: Linear

Anti-aliased: Not checked

Noise: 0%

These settings add some interest to the button face.

5 Apply a Color Overlay style to the button using these settings:

Blend Mode: Multiply

Color: RGB at 0, 0, and 0

Opacity: 25%

It is this setting that you'll change for each state. By setting the Opacity to 25%, you'll just gently shade the button with each new color. Don't click OK just yet.

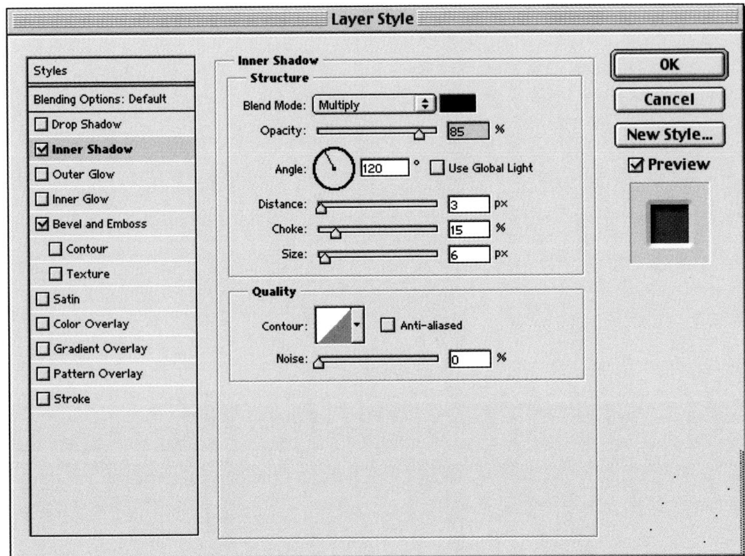

Apply an Inner Shadow Layer Style with these settings.

6 In the Layer Style dialog box, click the New Style button. In the dialog box that appears, name the style **MyWebButton** and check the Include Layer Effects and Include Layer Blending Options check boxes.

By including the current Layer Effects and the current Blend mode options, you preserve as much information as can be recorded in a style. This style does not, however, include the color of the button or the fact that is applied to a shape. You can close the button image; you won't need it again.

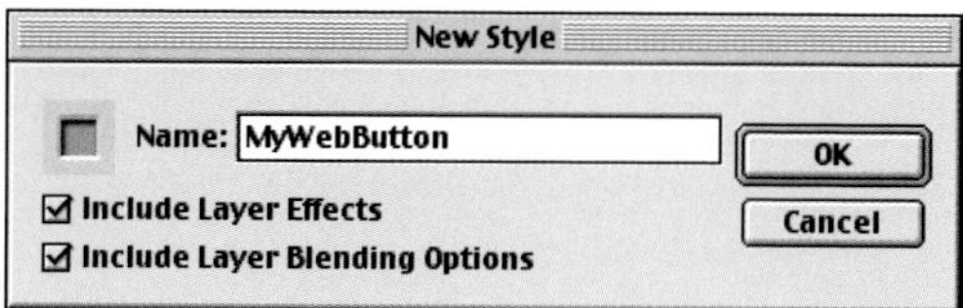

Name the style **MyWebButton** and check the Include Layer Effects and Include Layer Blending Options check boxes.

All Buttoned Up

In this section of the project, you create the buttons that enable you to navigate from one page to another. You learn how to place the text for the buttons, which I prefer to do before I actually create the buttons, and how to set the guides to help with the placement of the buttons. Each button actually consists of a button "blank" and the text that goes on top of it. You'll create the buttons and automatically apply the style you previously created.

1 Make the web page image active. Drag another guide from the top ruler to 23 pixels below the last horizontal guide that you set (pixel 398 along the side ruler).

This guide marks the center point of the buttons and button text. It is halfway between the previous guide and the bottom of the page.

2 Drag the HOME layer from the text file into the web page image, keeping the Shift key pressed as you drag. Then drag the word "HOME" downward, still with the Shift key pressed, until it snaps to the new guide.

Again, you are using the Shift key to keep the text centered and constrained.

3 Choose Edit > Free Transform (Ctrl+T/Cmd+T). As you did in the previous section, use the arrow keys to make the center point of the text snap to the intersection of the guides. Then commit the transformation.

4 Drag a guide from the side ruler to pixel 325 along the top ruler. Then drag another vertical guide to pixel 435 along the top ruler.

I got this placement of guides by first dragging a guide to the nearest "multiple of 5" to the left of the word "National." Having seen the placement of "HOME," I decided that the next button should stop about where "National" begins. There are 55 pixels between the start of "National" and the center of the image. Therefore, the second guide needs to be at 380+55, which is pixel 435.

Drag vertical guides to the 325 and 435 pixel marks along the top ruler.

5 Drag the CLOSE UP • DETAILS layer from the text file into the web page image. This time, don't keep the Shift key pressed. Instead, zoom in on the area near the HOME text where you want this text to go. Position it a bit to the left of the 325-pixel guide. The center of the text should snap to the guide. Then drag in the PRICE LIST • INFO text and place it to the right of the 435-pixel guide.

You'll fine tune the placement of the text after you have made the buttons.

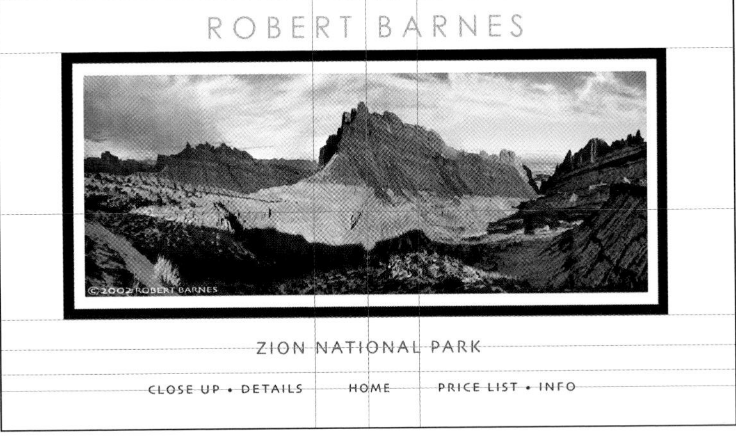

Drag the two long button text layers into the web page image.

6 The Rounded Rectangle tool should still be selected. Leave Radius set on the Options Bar to the default of 10 pixels. Click the Geometry options drop-down arrow to the right of various shape tools on the Options Bar and enter a fixed size of 184×22 pixels. Set the color to white and choose the MyWebButton style that you created in the previous section.

I figured this size out in advance by looking at the longest of the text boxes. It is easier for you to set the fixed size than it is to experiment, which is what you will need to do when you create your own pages.

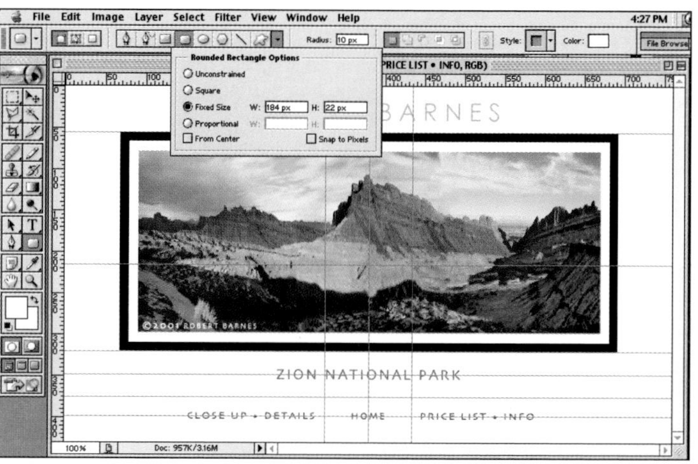

Set the Rounded Rectangle tool to a fixed size of 184×22 pixels.

7 Make the CLOSE UP • DETAILS layer active and create the button by clicking the intersection of the guides just above the PRICE LIST • INFO text. Switch to the Move tool, hold down the Shift key, and drag the shape down until it is bisected horizontally by the next lower guide.

At this point, the button is positioned directly under the PRICE LIST • INFO text.

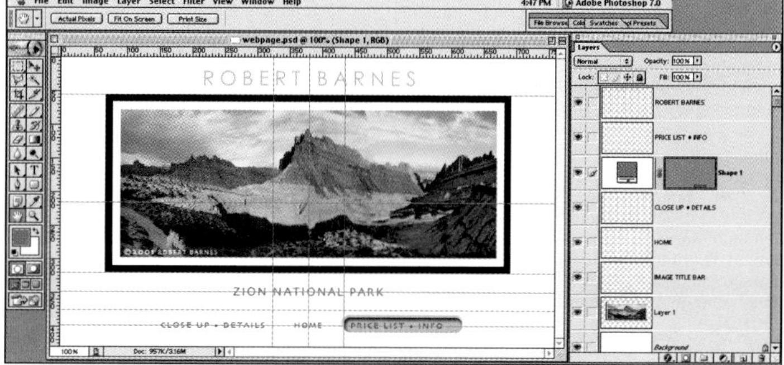

Create the first button under the PRICE LIST · INFO text.

8 Double-click the Shape 1 name in the Layers palette and change the name to RIGHT BUTTON. Drag the layer to the Create a new layer icon at the bottom of the Layers palette. Rename this duplicate layer as LEFT BUTTON and drag it below the CLOSE UP DETAILS layer. Use the Move tool and hold the Shift key as you move the LEFT BUTTON object to the left until it snaps to the vertical guide to the right of the words CLOSE UP DETAILS.

Now you have placed the second button.

9 Change the fixed size of the Rounded Rectangle tool to 81×22 pixels and check the From Center check box in the Rounded Rectangle options dialog box. Make the IMAGE TITLE BAR layer active. Click the intersection of the guides under the HOME button to place this button. Change the layer name to **HOME BUTTON**.

The From Center check box is a handy addition that enables you to click in the center of an object (if you know where it is) and leave a precisely sized shape.

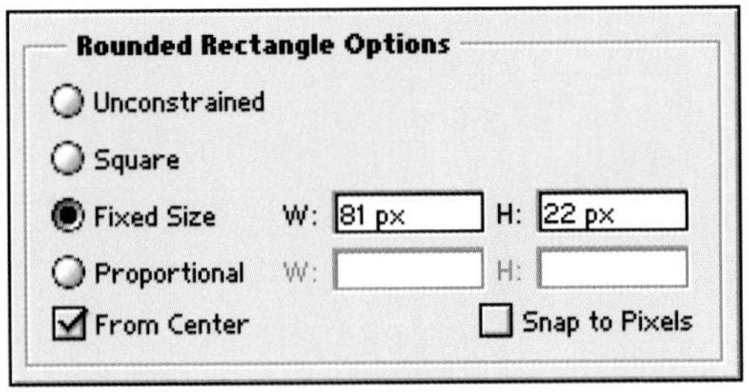

10 Drag two vertical guides from the side ruler and place them between the black border and the white matte of the painting on each side of the painting.

These guides indicate the ending positions of the last text elements that you will place—the Previous and Next arrows.

11 Make the PRICE LIST INFO layer of the image active. Drag in the LEFT ARROW layer from the text file and position it on the left side of the image, touching the leftmost guide. Click the MyWebButton style in the Styles palette. Do the same thing with the RIGHT ARROW layer and position it touching the rightmost guide.

The original font used was Webdings at 45 points.

12 Make the RIGHT BUTTON layer active and click the Lock Position icon above the Layer entries on the Layers palette. Click the Link icon area on the PRICE LIST INFO layer. Choose Layer > Align Linked > Horizontal Centers.

By locking the position of the button layer before you align the layers, you make sure that the button base, which is in the correct position, doesn't move.

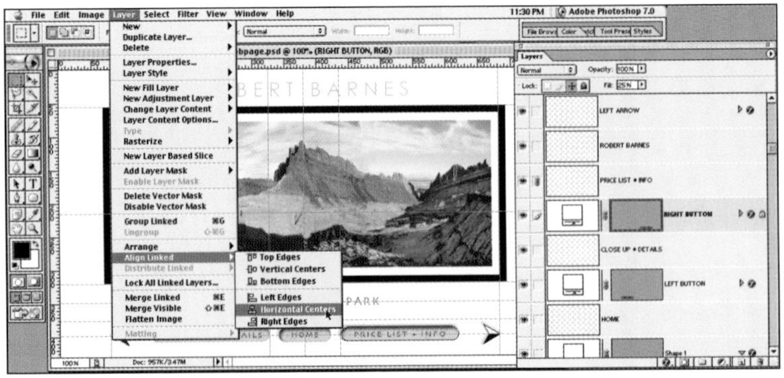

Rounded Rectangle Options

- Unconstrained
- Square
- Fixed Size W: 81 px H: 22 px
- Proportional W: H:
- From Center
- Snap to Pixels

Set the size of the HOME button to 81×22 pixels and check the From Center check box.

Lock the position of the RIGHT BUTTON layer and link it with its text. Then align the horizontal centers of the two layers.

13 Make the LEFT BUTTON layer active and click the Lock Position icon above the Layer entries on the Layers palette. Click the Link icon on the CLOSE UP • DETAILS layer. Choose Layer > Align Linked > Horizontal Centers.

You don't need to align the HOME layer and button because they should already both be centered.

14 Make Layer 1 active. Choose Drop Shadow from the Layer Style menu with the following settings:

Structure:

Blend Mode: Multiply

Color: RGB at 0, 0, and 0

Opacity: 53%

Angle: 120°

Use Global Light: Checked

Distance: 7 pixels

Spread: 0%

Size: 10 pixels

Quality:

Contour: Linear

Anti-aliased: Not Checked

Noise: 0%

Layer Knocks Out Drop Shadow: Checked

A Slice of Genius

At this point, you are ready to slice your web page. By slicing the graphics, you create separate areas for buttons or for other graphic elements.

You can create the slices in either Photoshop or ImageReady. I generally prefer to do it in Photoshop and then go into ImageReady to create the rollovers, which you can't do in Photoshop. You can create slices either by using the Slice tool or by telling Photoshop to make slices from existing layers.

You will create each needed slice by using the Layers method. Photoshop calls these slices User Slices and it creates autoslices to complete the page.

1. Choose View > Extras to hide the guides. Make the ROBERT BARNES layer active and choose Layer > New Layer Based Slice.

   The slice symbol appears around the layer. You can leave the guides showing if you prefer, but I think it just complicates things.

2. Select each of the following layers in turn and make them into layer-based slices:

   - Layer 1
   - IMAGE TITLE BAR
   - LEFT ARROW
   - LEFT BUTTON
   - HOME BUTTON
   - RIGHT BUTTON
   - RIGHT ARROW

   On the text and button layers, make sure that you select the button bases and not the accompanying text. The slicing will slice through the entire image and show whatever is in the slice boundaries, even if it is not on the same layer as the slice.

3. Save the image and click the bottom of the Toolbox to transfer into ImageReady.

   The image darkens and then transfers control into ImageReady, where you can see all the user slices defined in the Rollover palette.

Define the other layers as layer-based slices.

Rollover and Bark

You are ready to create the rollovers for the LEFT, RIGHT, and HOME buttons. These buttons provide the needed navigation. Although the page has the back and next icons as well, it isn't necessary to make them look different when the user rolls over them or clicks them.

The purpose of the rollover is visual confirmation of a user's actions. Although it is possible to link to another web page from a static image, common web usage advises that you define at least three states for most buttons. These states are the visual appearance of the button in the Normal condition (the mouse is not near the button), the Over state (the mouse is on top of the button), and the Down state (the user clicks the mouse to select that option).

ImageReady enables you to create styles that include rollovers. Because you want a consistent user interface, you will define the first rollover changes that you make as a style and then apply it to the other two buttons.

1. Choose View > Extras to hide the guides, and then View > Show > Slices to see the slices.

2. In the Rollovers palette, make the entry for the LEFT BUTTON active. Make the LEFT BUTTON layer active in the Layers palette as well.

   You need to know the slice number of the LEFT BUTTON because the Rollovers palette has no way of knowing which layer(s) are associated with the slice. In my image, it is slice 21.

3. Choose New Rollover State from the drop-down menu on the right side of the Rollovers palette. This automatically adds an Over state to the LEFT BUTTON slice.

   Notice the downward pointing arrow that now appears to the left of the webpage_21 slice on the Rollovers palette. This shows that the Over state is nested under that slice.

Note: I personally find this coordination a bit awkward. You need to be aware of three palettes as you define the rollovers: the Layers palette, because it contains the effects applied to the image; the Rollovers palette; and the Layer Options palette, because that is where you'll make the changes for each rollover state. However, when you realize that you need to watch and coordinate the three palettes, you begin to develop a rhythm.

4 Click the Color Overlay effect under the LEFT BUTTON entry in the Layers palette. The Layer Options palette changes to show the Color Overlay effect. Change Opacity to 25%. Click the color swatch and choose white (RGB at 255, 255, and 255) from the Color Picker.

You now have set the color of the button to white when the user rolls over the button in a browser.

5 Choose New Rollover State again from the side menu on the Rollovers palette. Then assign a 25% opacity and a color of RGB at 102, 204, and 204 to the Color Overlay effect.

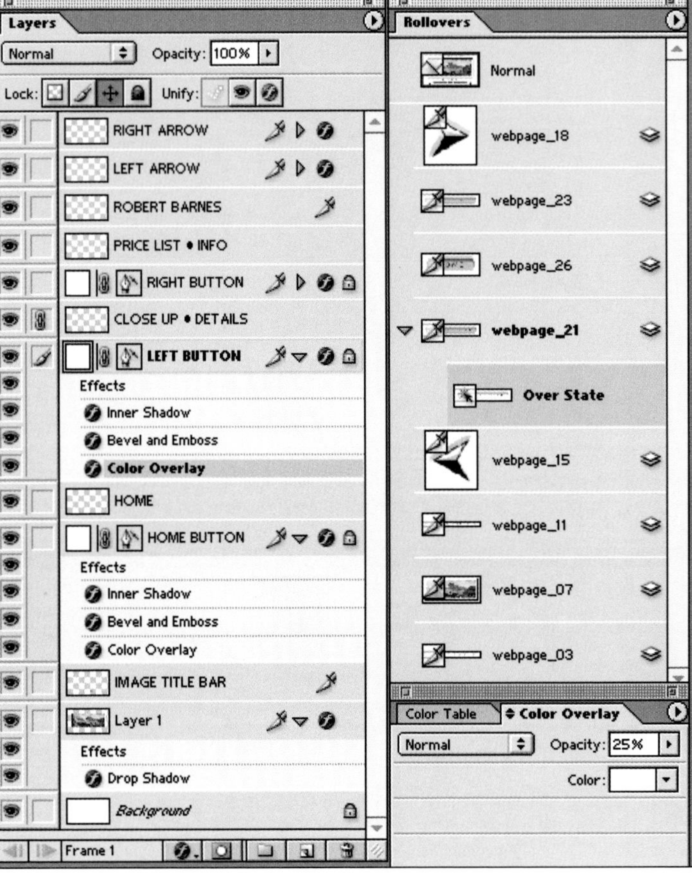

Assign a 25% white Color Overlay effect to this rollover.

6 Choose New Style from the side drop-down menu on the Styles palette. Name this style **MyWebPageRollover** and check all three check boxes to save the rollover state with the style.

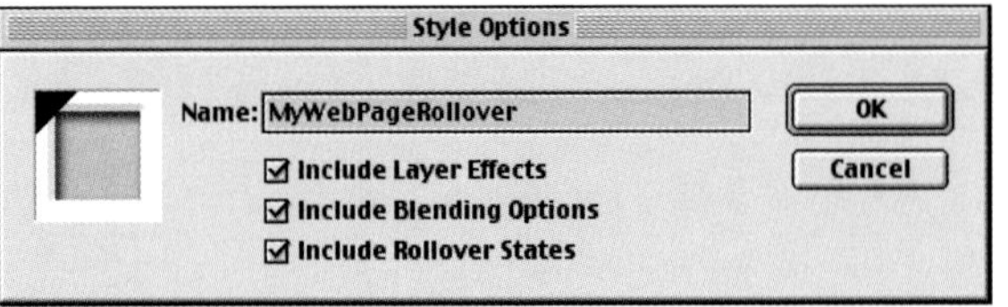

Save the style as **MyWebPageRollover** and include the rollovers.

You can tell if an ImageReady style has a rollover attached to it because it has a black arrowhead in the corner.

7 Make the RIGHT BUTTON layer active and click the associated web slice in the Rollovers palette (slice 23). Click the new style you created. Then repeat the same process with the HOME BUTTON layer and slice 26 (use the appropriate slices for your image if they differ from mine).

The saved style makes it very easy to create these two rollovers. Notice that the Rollovers palette shows the twisty arrow as soon as you apply the style.

8 Save the file.

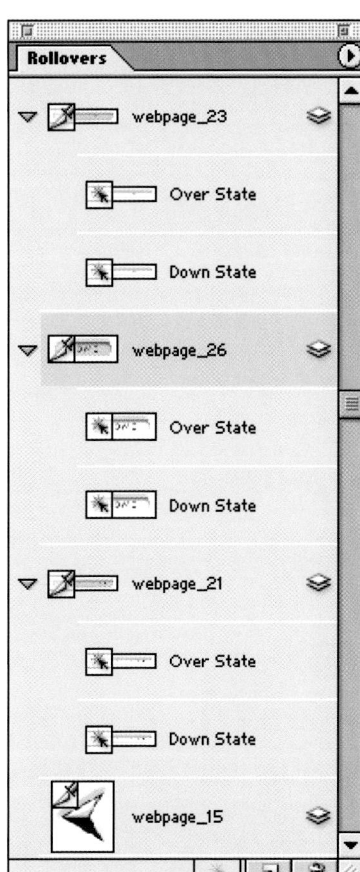

Apply the new rollover style to the other two button slices.

In the Export (and Optimization) Business

In this final section of the project, you optimize the settings for the web page in ImageReady and then export the page for the web. I'll show you how to change the autoslices that ImageReady created into No Image slices to improve download time. You'll see how you can optimize different slices to export as a GIF or JPEG. Finally, you'll see how to export the HTML and sliced files into GoLive.

1 Choose the Slice Select tool. Then choose Select > All Slices. Shift-click each slice that has a blue number to deselect it.

This is the easiest way to select all the autoslices that ImageReady created to "fill in the blanks" between the slices that you created (which are the user slices). The problem is that when left alone, each autoslice will generate an image to be put on the web page. You might want that, such as when you have a background pattern that you need to maintain. However, the blank areas in this page are just that—blank. There is absolutely no good reason to make a page download more slowly by generating white images. To prevent these slices from creating images, you need to select them first—which you have just done. In the next step, you will get rid of their images.

Select all the autoslices.

Note: In the Edit > Preferences > Slices dialog box, you can set the amount of dimming that occurs when a slice is not selected User Slices portion of the Color Adjustments region. The default is 20 percent. I like to keep this at 60 percent because I find that I can't see the contrast well enough otherwise. Selected slices are yellow. However, when you select all the slices and then try to deselect just the user slices, everything still looks as if it is surrounded in yellow and it is hard to determine what is not selected unless the dimming makes that very apparent.

2 Choose No Image from the Type drop-down list in the Slice palette.

This converts all the autoslices into No Image slices. These slices are now in blue because they are user slices, but they will no longer generate real GIF or JPG images. Instead, they will cause a transparent GIF image to be inserted into the HTML layer table for your page. They won't use any time to download.

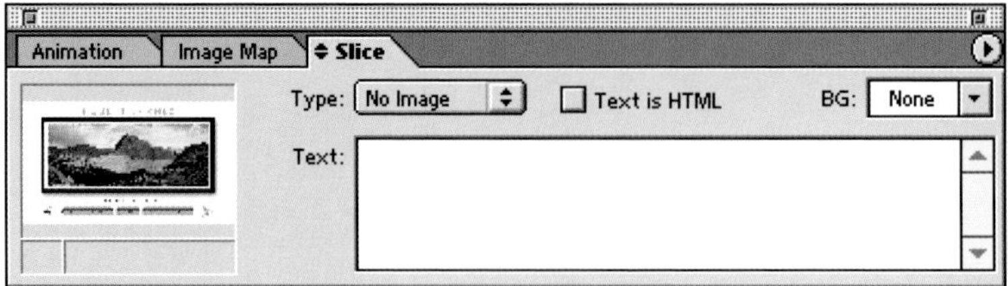

Change the selected slices to No Image slices.

3 Choose Select > Deselect Slices. Then use the Slice Select tool to select the large painting. In the Optimize palette (not the Optimized tab), select the JPEG High preset.

My artwork is my livelihood, so if any part of this page needs to look spectacular, this is it. To me, it is worth the extra file to have my artwork look good. This is the one area of the image that uses a JPG format. All the other slices can be saved as GIFs.

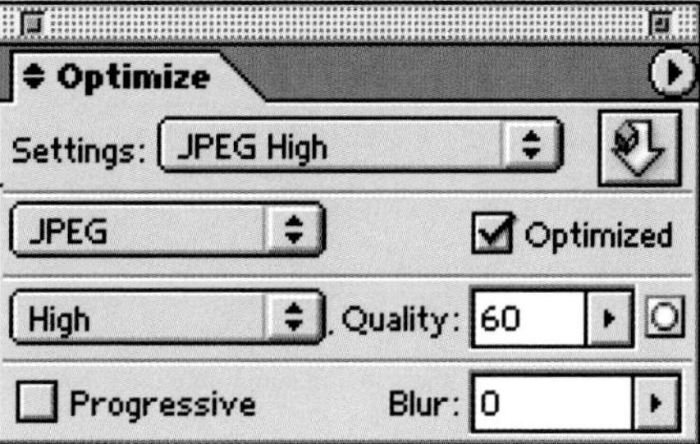

Assign the JPEG High preset to the painting.

4 Select the other images slices (there are seven of them). Assign the GIF 32 No Dither preset to them in the Optimize palette.

The GIF format is perfect for these slices. They have few colors and they all need to remain crisp and clear. The JPG format would mangle the colors, but GIF is just right.

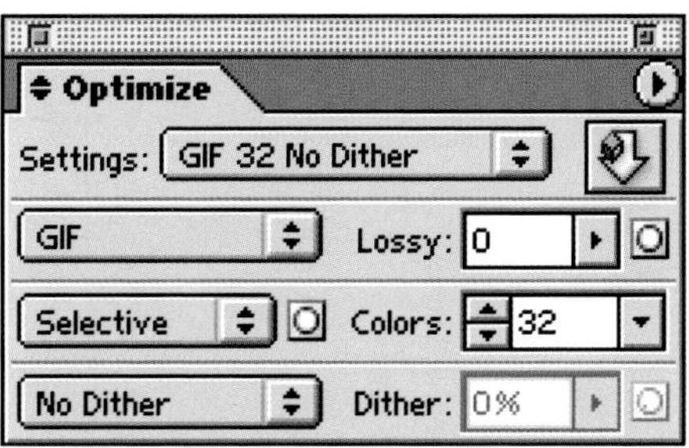

Assign the GIF 32 No Dither preset to the selected slices.

5 Choose File > Output Settings > HTML. On the first screen, change the settings to Include GoLive 5 (or Earlier) Code. Accept the other default settings. Click Next and accept all the defaults. You don't need the Image Map or Background settings. In the Saving Files setting, change the naming conventions to slice name+hyphen+rollover state. Set all the other boxes to none except for the final box, which should have .ext in lowercase text. Uncheck the Put Images in Folder check box.

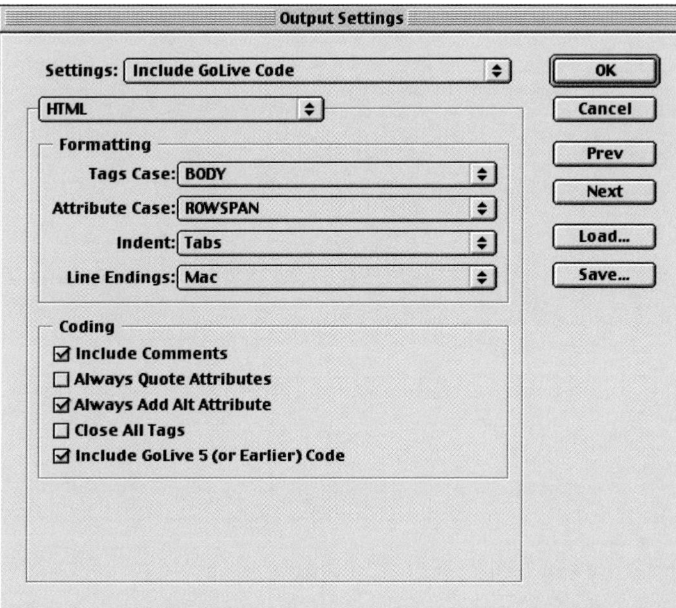

Choose File > Output Settings and use the settings as shown.

These settings are the basic default for saving files for use in GoLive (the Adobe web page authoring tool). Because you don't have any remote rollovers in this page, there is no reason to make the rollover names any longer than needed. In addition, GoLive will recognize the code written by ImageReady more easily if you make a folder and put both the images and the HTML code in it rather than write code that places the images into a different folder.

6 Make the Rollovers palette active and rename each slice by double-clicking the slice name, and then giving each slice a meaningful name.

It helps to rename the slices so that you can understand the HTML code that is generated.

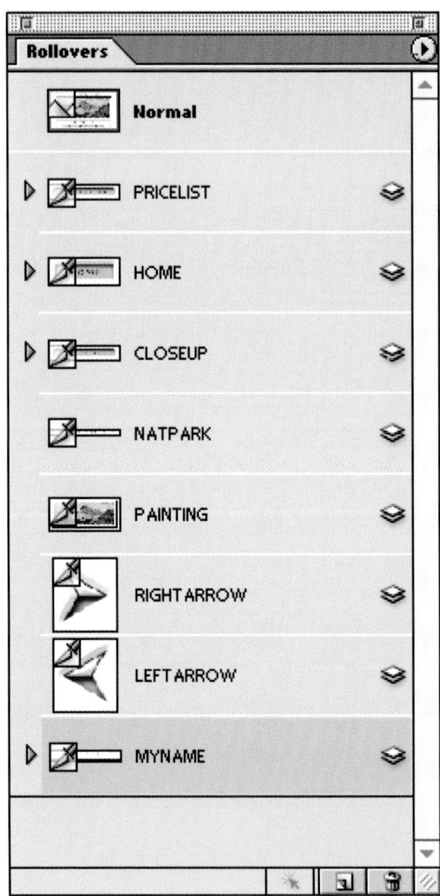

Rename each slice with a descriptive name.

7 Choose File > Save Optimized As. Create a new folder to hold the HTML and the images. Export the HTML, the images, and the slices.

In ImageReady, I did not enter a URL link for each button. I have a very large site and I find this much easier to do after all the pages are generated and placed in GoLive.

8 View the final HTML code in your browser to make sure that is displays correctly.

Remember that you did not include URLs; thus, the buttons will not work.

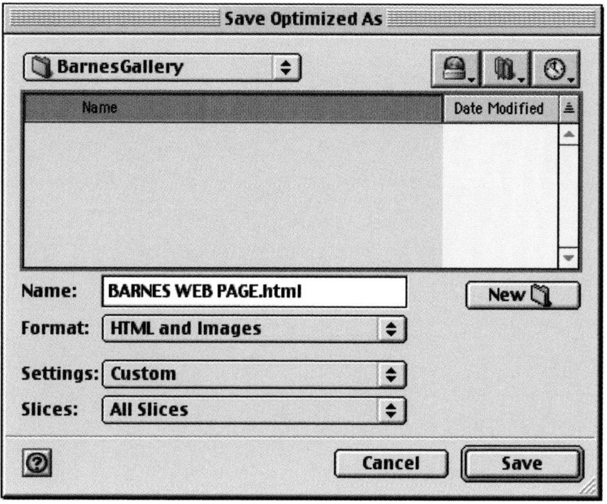

Save your optimized web page.

MODIFICATIONS

The best part of creating the web page this way is that I can drop in any of my paintings, change the image name, and immediately get a new page. I have no extra work to do.

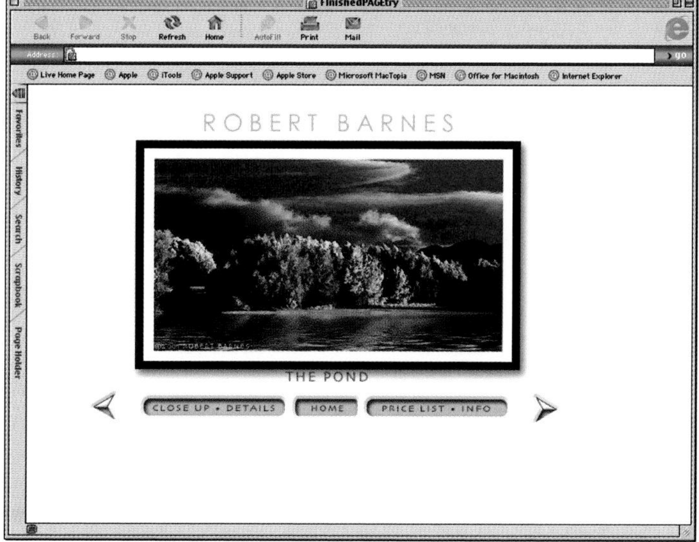

It's really easy to create additional pages.

CUSTOMIZING AND ALTERING ACTIONS

"If it keeps up, man will atrophy all his limbs but the push-button finger."

—FRANK LLOYD WRIGHT

Creating an Automatic Web Page Layout

Imagine that at some time in the past, you commissioned a Photoshop guru to create an action for you that would instantly generate a complete web page layout. This action creates the basic page, complete with colors and button links, a copyright notice, and a page title. All that's left for you to do is to supply the content and write the HTML code.

You've created simple actions before, but this complicated action really looks forbidding. However, your needs for page layout have changed and you want to make changes in the template as well. How can you do that and where should you begin?

Project 10

Customizing and Altering Actions

by Al Ward

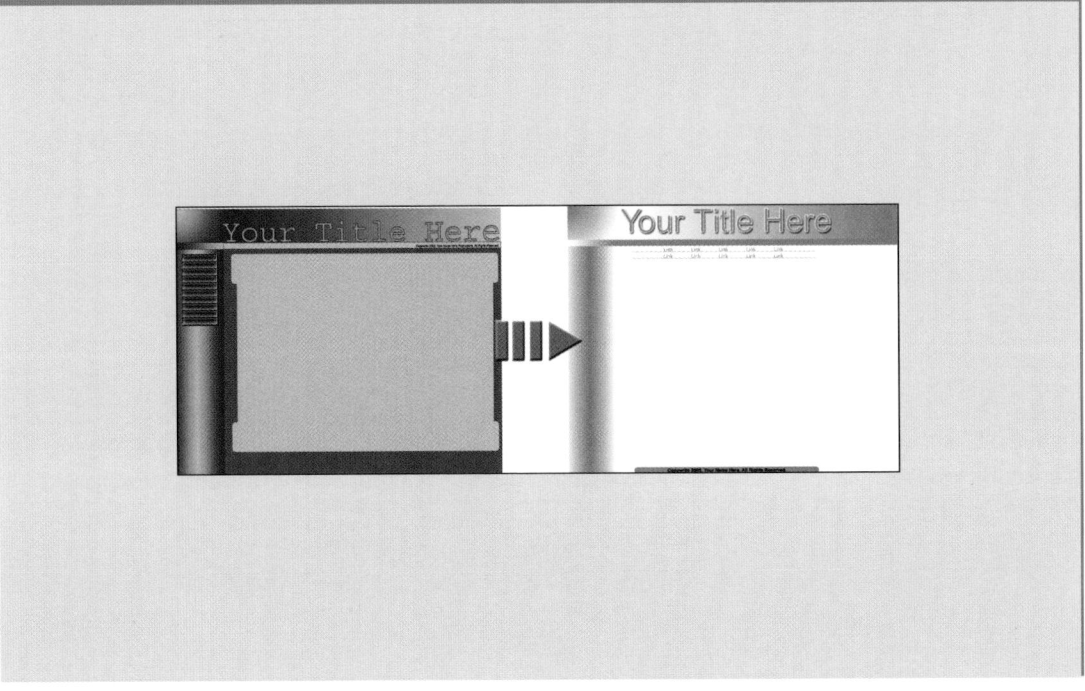

Getting Started

Actions are everywhere. You can find them all over the web. My own site, **www.actionfx.com**, specializes in actions, and Adobe sponsors their own Action Exchange as well. If you have a steady stream of action effects at your disposal, you really ought to know how to change the actions if they don't quite do what you want. In the process of changing an action, you can also learn how to write one of your own.

To work with this project, you need to load the action that I have created for you. Here's how:

1 Locate the WebPage.atn file on the accompanying CD-ROM.

Note: .atn is the extension that Photoshop gives to actions. As long as you have the correct extension on the file, the action is cross-platform. It doesn't matter whether it was created on a Mac or on a Windows computer; it plays on either system.

2. Make the Actions palette active. From the flyout menu, choose Load Actions. Navigate to the location of the WebPage.atn file on the accompanying CD and select it. Click Append.

   The action now is added to your Actions palette and is ready to use.

Introducing the Action

Fortunately for us, no event in an action is cast in stone. An action is only as smart as the steps followed during its creation; it's a recording, after all.

Photoshop enables users to edit actions by deleting, adding, or rearranging the order of commands. You can also change settings within the commands themselves to suit our current requirements. All it takes is a little ingenuity, a little experimentation, and a little practice working elbow-deep in the Actions palette.

Don't be daunted by what might appear to be an endless list of commands and settings that appear in the palette when in Edit mode. There are ways to isolate and change settings in the action without rewriting it from scratch.

Before you dive into changing the web page action, take a look at what it does.

1. Find the WebPage.atn action set in the Actions palette. Click the arrow to the left of the set to expand it, and then click the Webpage Layout action entry underneath to select it. Make sure that you are not clicking the folder. Press the Play Selection button at the bottom of the Actions palette. You can close the generated web page after you have looked at it and the action has finished playing.

   The Play Selection button is the third icon from the left along the bottom of the Actions palette, and it looks like an arrowhead. The action starts by creating a new document, and it plays until it has created a web page. It creates the same web page every time it plays—on any copy of Photoshop on which it is loaded.

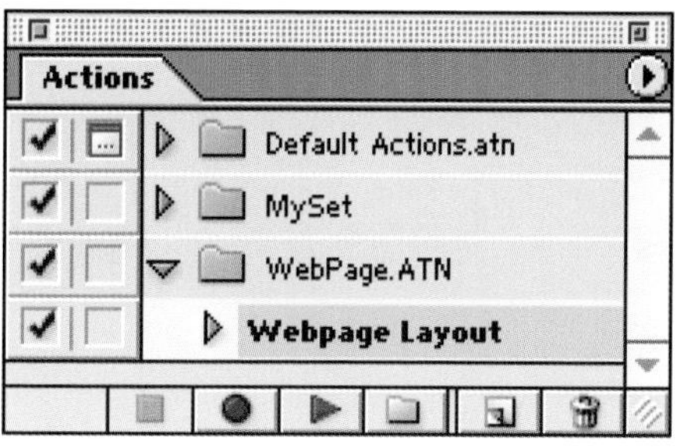

Choose the Webpage Layout Action in the Actions palette.

2 To edit an action, you need to make sure that you are viewing the Actions palette in Edit/List mode. Click the flyout menu in the Actions palette and make sure that Button Mode is not checked.

3 Pull down the Actions menu. Select Playback Options. In the dialog box, click the Pause For: option button and type **3** seconds as the pause time.

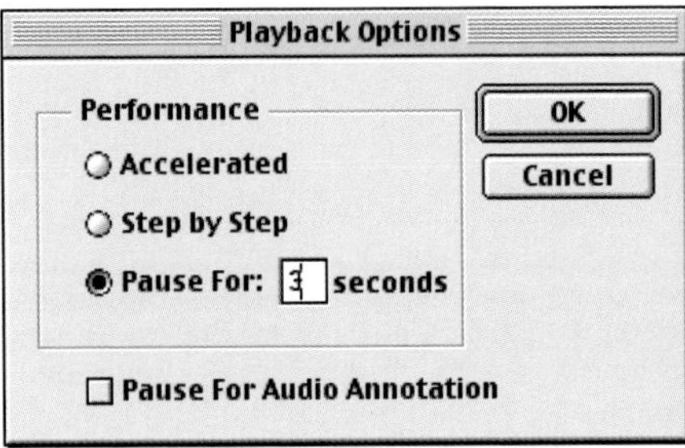

Change the Playback Options Performance mode to Pause For 3 seconds.

By default, the Action Playback Options Performance mode is set to Accelerated. This simply means that there is no delay between command operations during playback. In most cases, you can't tell what is happening with the image when you are working in Accelerated mode until the action has run its course. To successfully edit the action, you need to slow things down a bit to help isolate the commands that need to be changed. Setting the Playback Options with a three-second delay between commands might seem a bit short, but it really does give plenty of time to find the commands that you want to edit. Trust me—after you begin playing back a large action with a three-second delay between commands, the time it takes for the action to finish will seem like a *very* long time.

4 Play the action again with the time delay. Notice how the commands in the Actions palette scroll by. You can see the changes in the Layers palette and on the screen. Play the action completely one time.

Keep the completed image in the background as a reference. Comparing the replay to the completed image helps during the edit.

A First Edit

When you watched the actions scroll by, you probably saw only part of each command. You can see the entire command by enlarging the Actions palette (pull on its lower-right corner) and by clicking the arrow to the left of each Action step.

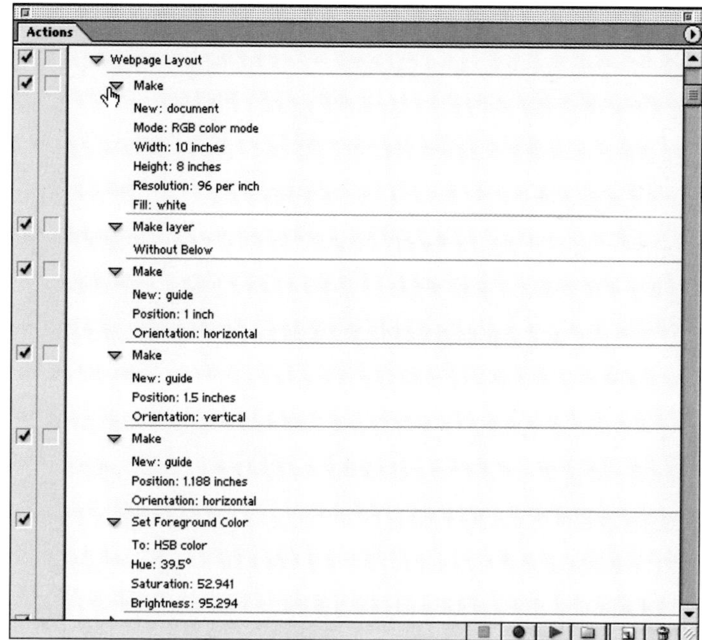

Click the arrow to the left of each step to see the entire recorded Action step.

To make changes to the action, you can work in one of two ways: You can read the Action steps to find what you want to change, or you can watch the action play to locate the steps you need to change. Because you have set the playback to Pause, you have the luxury of watching the Action work to locate the changes you want to make. I personally find that to be easier than scouring a list of commands.

Start the edit process with something easy. I used guides to help locate the areas where I needed to draw shapes on the screen. The position of those guides was recorded along with the action. However, now that the action is finished recording, it has also recorded the exact position of where to draw the shapes. The guides aren't needed anymore. In this section, you locate the steps that create guides and remove them from the action. Because you are modifying the action, you'll duplicate it first.

1 Click the arrow to the left to close the Webpage Layout action. Make sure that the Webpage Layout action is highlighted and then choose Duplicate from the Actions palette menu. Click the arrow to the left of the Webpage Layout copy to view all the steps.

  Duplicating the action before editing is a safety precaution and makes sure that you don't damage the original.

2 Play the action again and watch as the first commands scroll by. After you see the first guide appear on the image, click the Stop button. There are three Make commands that create the guides. If necessary, turn down the twisty arrows on Steps 3–5 to see these Make: New: guide steps.

The first two steps create a new document, set the attributes (size, resolution, fill color, and mode) of the Background layer, and create a new layer.

3 Drag each of the three Make: New: guide steps to the Trashcan icon at the bottom of the Actions palette.

This removes each Make: New: guide command from the action. When you play the action from the beginning again, you won't see the guides. (Don't play the action just yet.) The gradients will still appear where the action originally placed them.

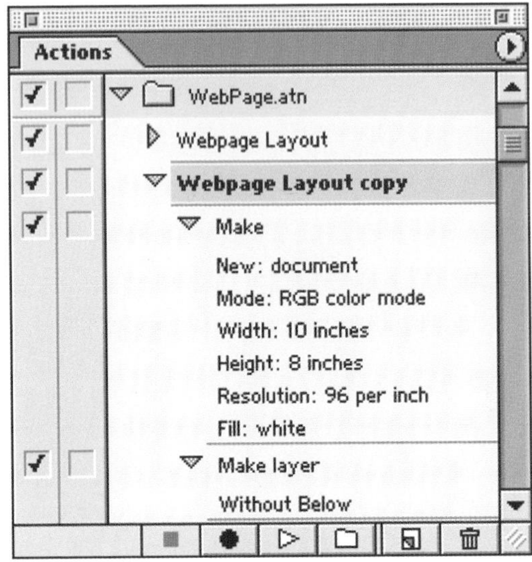

Play the action and watch the first two steps.

Note: You can select multiple steps by holding the Shift key as you click each step after your first selection.

Changing the Page Colors

Among the changes that you want to make to the page are changes to the colors of the web site. In this section, you modify the steps that set these colors for the page.

1 Drag the next two commands (Set Foreground Color and Set Background color) to the Actions palette Trashcan icon.

These steps set the foreground and background colors for the gradients in the web page. After you have deleted the steps, the next step, Subtract From Selection, is highlighted in the Actions palette.

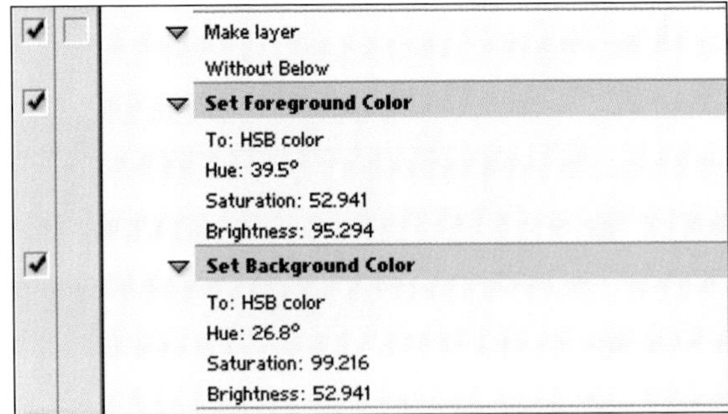

Highlight the steps that set the foreground and background colors and drag them to the Actions palette Trashcan icon.

2 Select the Make layer command above the Subtract From Selection step. Click the Begin recording button.

You can start recording new steps by positioning the command on the step above the place where you want the new steps to appear. You then press the Begin Recording button. This works in any previously recorded action. The steps already in the action don't play. You can simply add the new steps.

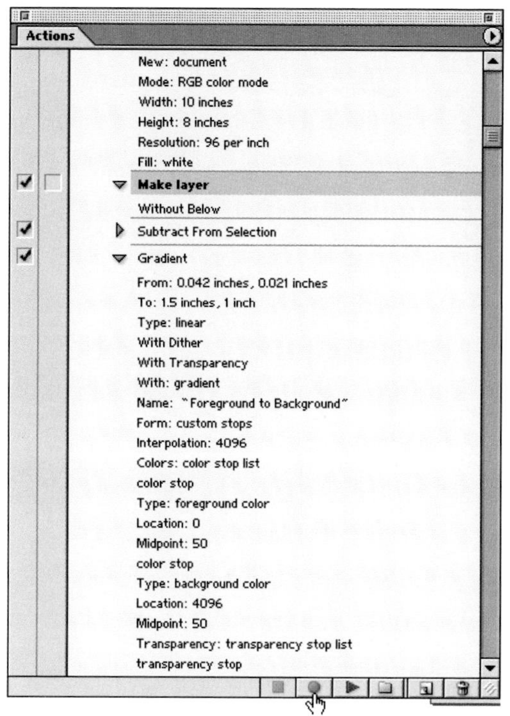

Click the Begin Recording button at the bottom of the Actions palette.

3 Click the Foreground color swatch in the Toolbox and select RGB 112, 157, and 171 from the Color Picker. Click the Background color swatch in the Toolbox and choose white (RGB 255, 255, and 255). Close the Color Picker. Click the Stop playing/recording button.

This step is critical. If you don't remember to do it, the Actions palette continues to follow you around, recording your every move. If you look at the Actions palette now, you'll see the two new steps that you just added.

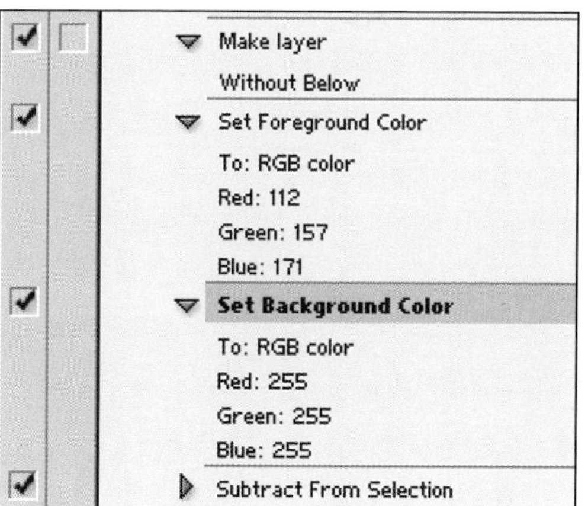

Click the Stop playing/recording button and view the two new commands.

4 Play the Webpage Layout copy action from the beginning again by clicking the Webpage Layout copy entry in the Actions palette. Do this until you see the Stroke command change your colors back to the original ones set in the action. Then, click the Stop playing/recoding button.

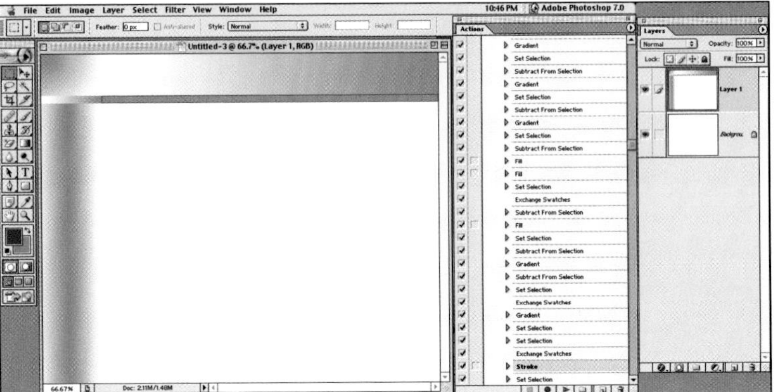

Play the action until the Stroke command executes.

Different Strokes

The Stroke command step poses a problem because it reverts the color back to the original brown, stroking an area that no longer requires it with a color that just doesn't work with the current design. To correct this, you need to remove several more commands.

1 Click the closest Set Selection command above the Stroke command. (It is directly above the Exchange Swatches command.) Press the Shift key and click the Stroke command step. Drag both commands to the Actions palette trashcan.

You can leave the Exchange Swatches step for now.

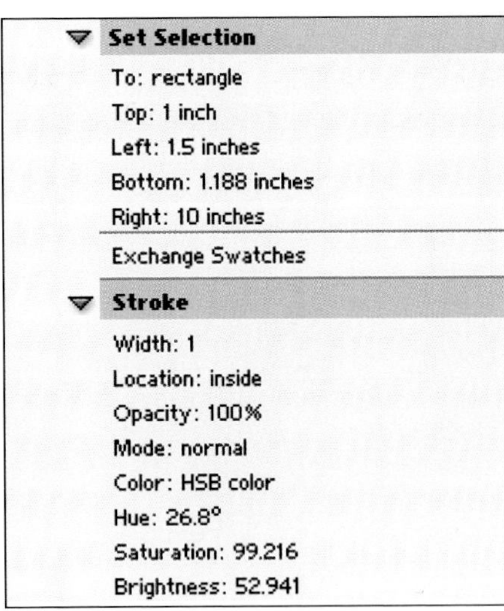

Delete the Set Selection and Stroke commands.

2. One step below the deleted Stroke command, you'll see a series of Set Selection and Stroke commands. Click the second Set Selection command that has this text: To Rectangle, Top: 0 Inches, Left: 0 Inches, Bottom: 1 inch, and Right: 1.5 Inches. Then press the Ctrl/Cmd key as you click the Set Selection command nine commands down in the list (just above the Make Fill Layer command). Drag the group to the Actions palette trashcan.

   The Ctrl/Cmd key enables you to select a contiguous group of steps at one time. The steps that you are deleting are no longer needed because you don't want to stroke the gradient in this design.

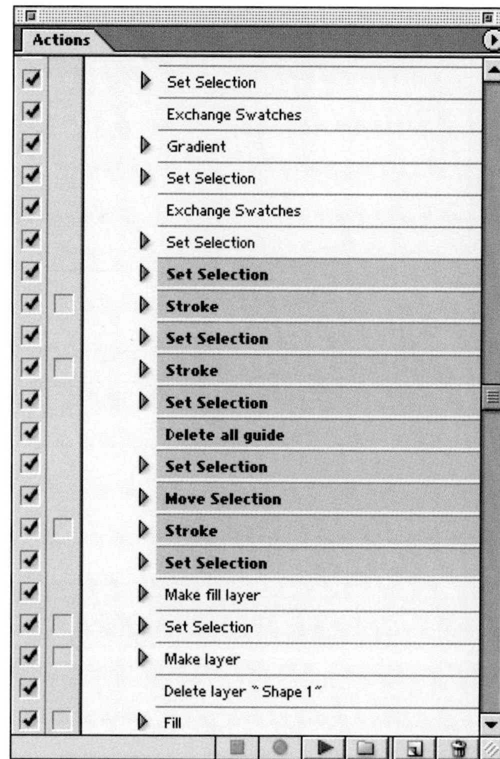

Select the group of Action steps shown here and delete them.

Body Work

Now that you have deleted some of the more obvious areas where the old action was not meeting your new requirements, you need to take a careful look at the new prototype web page to see how it compares to the original and what other changes are needed. The original version and the new version are shown here for comparison.

You can see that you no longer need the buttons on the left side of the page or the solid area in the center of the page. Your next task is to find these commands and remove them.

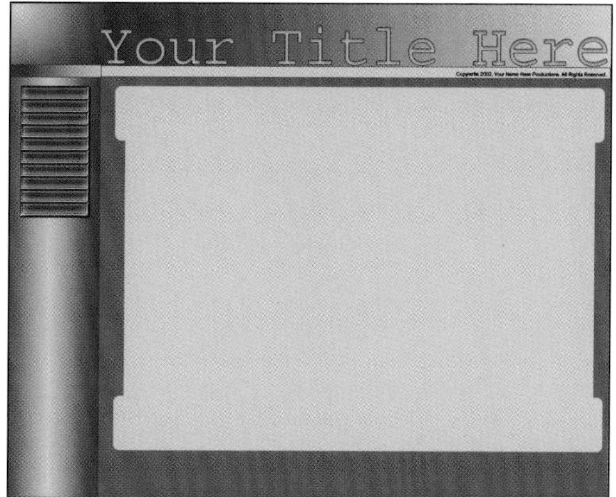

Here is the web page produced by the original action.

1. Close any previous copy of the edited action's output. Leave the original action's output open for comparison.

2. Click the Webpage Layout copy action and then click the Play button to start the action again. When the action creates its first new guide, click the Stop button.

   If the wait time seems too long to you, you might want to drop this down to a one- or two-second pause.

   You don't need the background shape in this design, although it is interesting to see how it was created. After you see the guides set again, you know that the background shape is complete and you can delete all the related steps.

3. Click the Set Selection step to highlight it and then scroll up the Actions list to the Make fill layer command. This was the first command that created the background shape. Hold the Command or Control key as you click that step. Drag the selected steps to the Actions palette trashcan.

4. Close the image that the edited action last produced. Click the Webpage Layout copy action again and click Play. Continue to allow the action to play until it finishes making the side menubar and begins to create the guides to place the text on the menubar. Stop the playback.

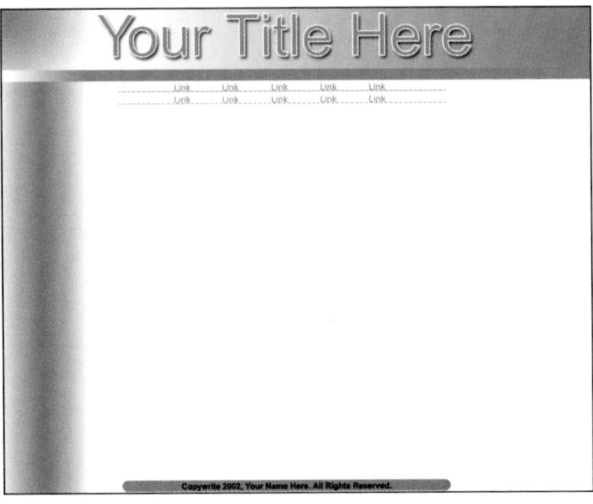

Here is the web page that you need to create.

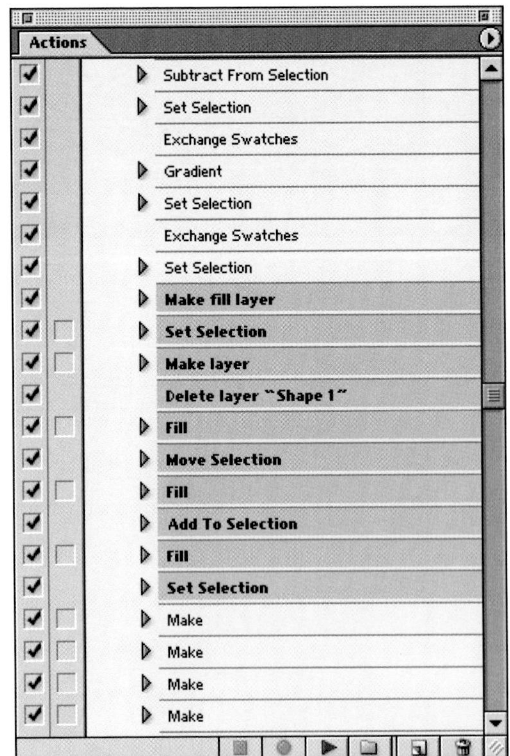

Drag the steps that make up the background shape on the original action to the Actions palette trashcan.

5 Click to select the step just above where the guide is created. That is the last Duplicate Current Layer entry. Then scroll up until you come to the start of that sequence, which is the Make command. Press the Command/Control key to select the range of commands and drag this group of statements to the Actions palette trashcan.

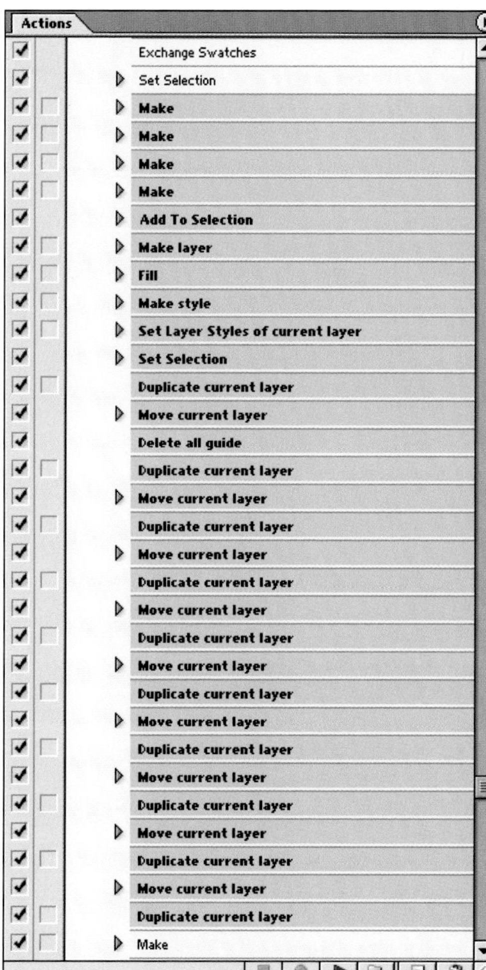

Delete the commands that create the buttons.

A New Title

You're coming down the home stretch now. You'll play the action again to see what is left to do (change the fonts and colors), and you'll delete and re-record these commands.

1 Close the previous copy of the edited action's output. Click the Action name and then click the Play button to start the action over. Let it play through until it stops.

The only new part of the action that is left to create is the title and the copyright notice. Neither element works in this design as is.

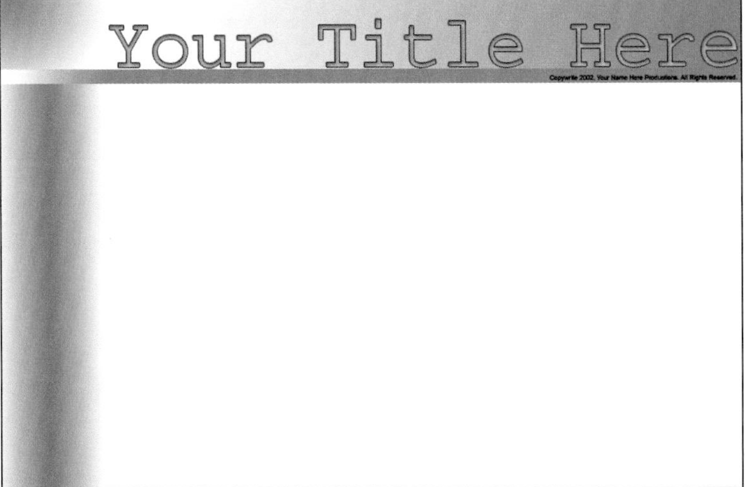

Play the action through to the end.

2 This time, don't close the image that is generated. Instead, delete the layers in the image with the exception of Layer 1 and the Background layer.

This puts you where you can re-record the text settings.

3 Double-click the first Make text layer entry in the Actions palette. Change the font to Arial MT, if you have it (or to whatever you prefer if you don't). Set the font size to 70. Click the Color swatch and set it to RGB 118, 151, and 168.

This is done in the image window rather than in the Actions palette. Double-clicking a step enables you to change the settings for that step.

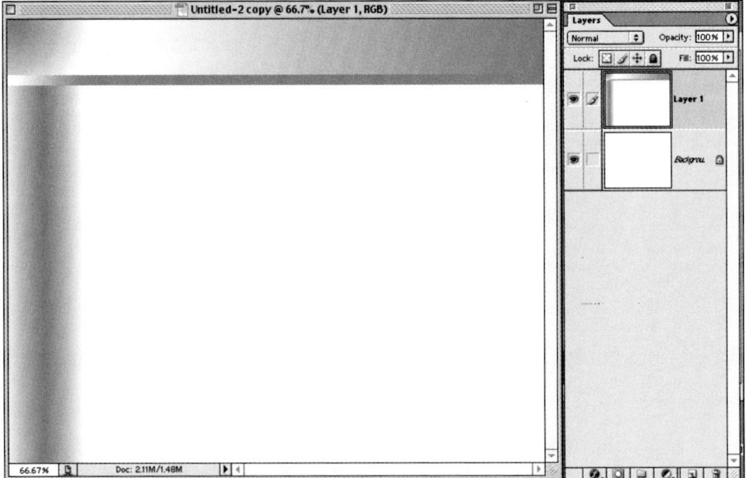

Delete all the layers in the image except for the Background layer and Layer 1.

4 Click the checkmark in the Options Bar to commit the changes to the text.

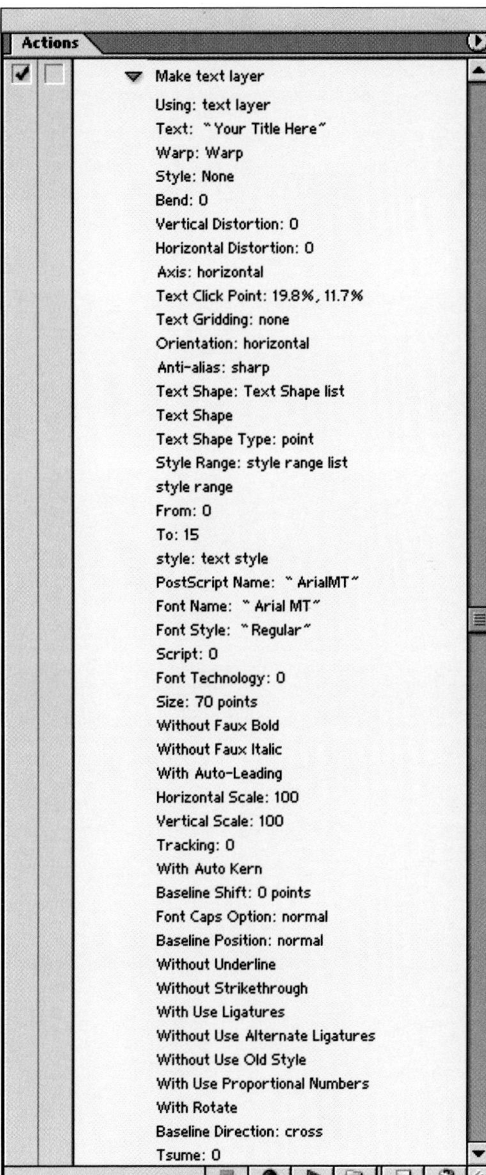

Shown here are the changes to the Make text layer step.

When you commit the text, the Actions palette registers the change and stops recording. The amount of detail that it records in the Actions palette for a text layer is little short of astounding.

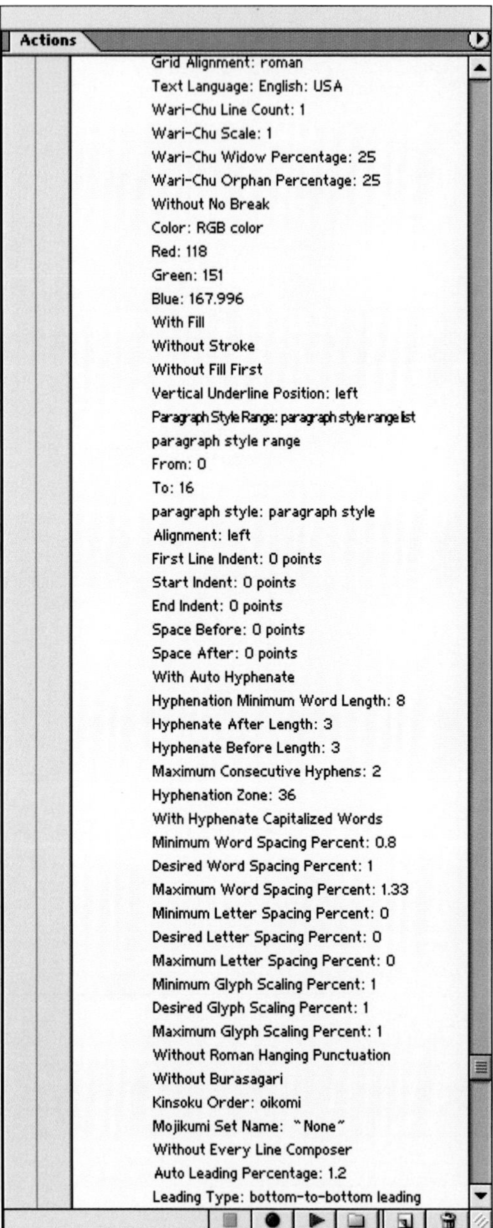

5 Leave the Make text layer step selected and click the Record button. Add a Drop Shadow style to the current text layer in the image. Use these settings:

Structure:

Blend Mode: Multiply

Color: RGB at 0, 0, 0

Opacity: 75%

Angle: 120 degrees

Use Global Light: Checked

Distance: 5 pixels

Spread: 0%

Size: 5 pixels

Quality:

Contour: Linear

Anti-aliased: Not checked

Noise: 0%

Layer Knocks Out Drop Shadow: Checked

Don't close the dialog box just yet.

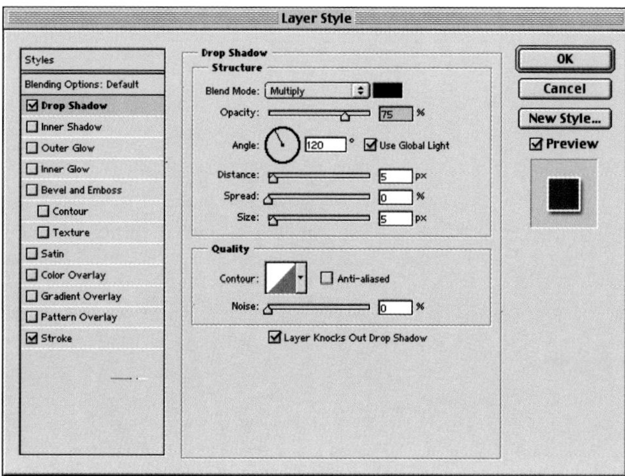

Record a Drop Shadow effect for the text title.

6 Click the Stroke effect in the Styles section of the dialog box on the left. Use these settings:

Size: 2 pixels

Position: Center

Blend Mode: Normal

Opacity: 100%

Fill Type: Color

Color: White (RGB at 255, 255, and 255)

You can now click OK to apply the effects.

7 Click the Stop button in the Actions palette.

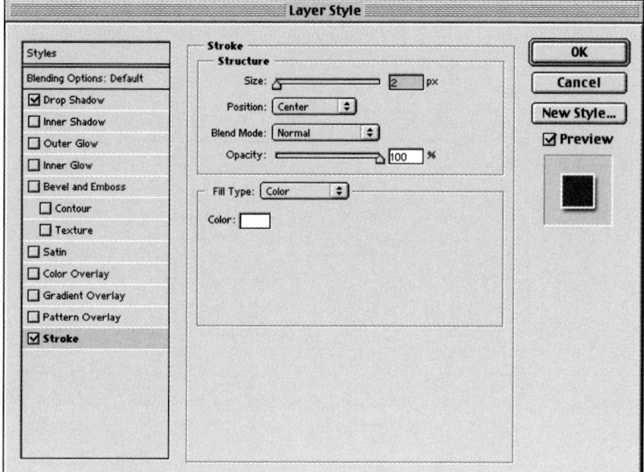

Record a Stroke effect for the text title.

The Finishing Touches

All that remains to be done is to change the location of the copyright notice and create new buttons. You'll do that now.

1. Select and delete all the steps that remain in the action after you added the new Layer styles to the text.

Note: It's easier to delete and then add the new steps than it is to change the settings of the steps in the action.

2. Turn on the Rulers (if you don't already have it on) and drag a guide from the vertical ruler on the side to the 190-pixel mark on the top ruler. Then drag out a horizontal guide to the 745-pixel mark on the side ruler.

   These guides mark the top-left corner of the copyright bar. Because you don't have the Record button on, you can drag these guides without needing to record their position in the action.

Note: You can double-click a ruler and change the units to pixels if you don't already have them set up that way.

3. Select the Rounded Rectangle tool. On the Options Bar, click the drop-down arrow to the right of the Shape tools. Change the Marquee Style to Fixed Size and enter the dimensions 537×20. Click to close the box. Set the radius of the rounded rectangle to 10 pixels.

   The size of the rounded rectangle is automatically recorded in the action when you place it. However, by setting up guides and making a fixed size before you record, the action that's recorded is cleaner than it would have been if you had just placed a shape and then moved it where you wanted it to go.

4. Click the Record button and place your cursor at the intersection of the two guides. Click to create the shape. Click the Stop button.

   The action records a fill layer with the size and placement you just created.

5 Drag another vertical guide to the 460-pixel tick mark on the top ruler.

This marks the center of the shape to show you where to place the text.

6 Click Record. Select the Text tool with Arial Bold (if you have it). Select 10 points, Strong, and Center Alignment, and select black as the text color. Click the guide and type **Copyright 2002. Your Name Here. All Rights Reserved.** Click the Stop button.

If you want to enter the copyright symbol instead, press Option+G on the Mac or hold the Alt key as you type **0169** in Windows.

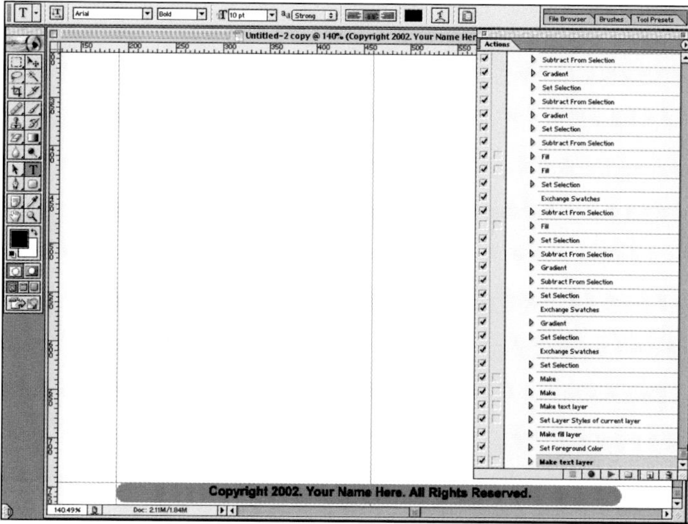

Record the text for the copyright notice.

7 Open the image NEWPAGE.psd from the accompanying CD-ROM. From that image, copy the placements and characteristics of the two lines under the links. Note the text characteristics of the link text and the placement. Record the lines and then the creation of the first link text layer. Drag the first link text to create the second link and use the Transform command to move it to the correct location. Use the combination of drag-copy-layer and Transform Again to place the remaining links and text. Stop recording.

8 Change the Playback option to Accelerated. Play the action from the top.

If you like what you see, you're done! If not, make any needed modifications.

9 Click the WebPage.atn folder and choose Save Actions from the Actions palette menu.

This ensures that your action is saved even if you need to reload the Preferences (which would cause you to lose all your loaded actions and presets).

Note: Create a backup set of all your presets—especially if you use the Photoshop Presets folder to store them. If you upgrade Photoshop, apply an interim release of the program, or reinstall the program, you likely will lose everything in the Presets folder. By creating a duplicate somewhere else every time you add a new preset, you preserve and safeguard all your work.

Modifications

Now that you have had some practice modifying an action, you might want to do more to it or write your own. Check out my web site at **www.actionfx.com** for a large variety of tips on creating your own actions and for links to the sites for which I write tutorials.

In the action you just modified, you might want to allow whoever uses it to dynamically choose the colors of the gradient and the text at the time the action is run. To do this, you need to make a few changes to the action (of course, you should work on a duplicate copy).

You need to insert a comment (Actions palette menu > Insert Stop) above the steps that set the foreground and background colors to tell the user to select a foreground color and a background color. Then click the checkmarks next to the two color selection steps to turn them off. Any step that is not checked is skipped when the action runs.

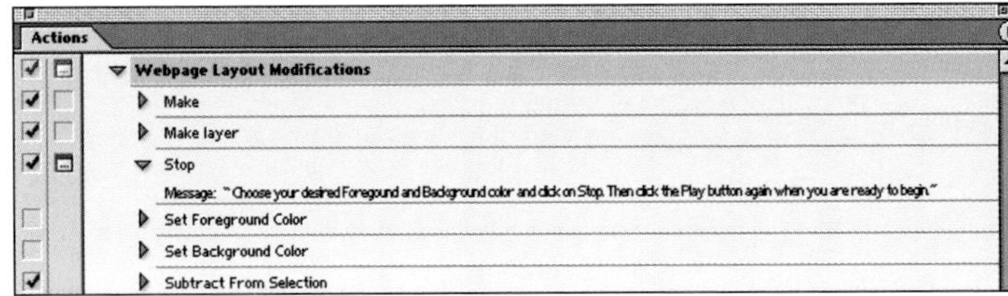

Add a comment and uncheck the two color selection steps.

The only other thing that needs to be changed is the text creation step that sets the title for the page. Click the empty well to the left of the Make text layer step to tell the action to wait for user input. When your action runs, it will pause here. You can change any of the text characteristics and the text color as the action runs. The action pauses for these changes until you click the checkmark on the Options Bar. If you find it hard to know that the action has paused, insert a comment prior to that step to remind the user to click to commit the text changes.

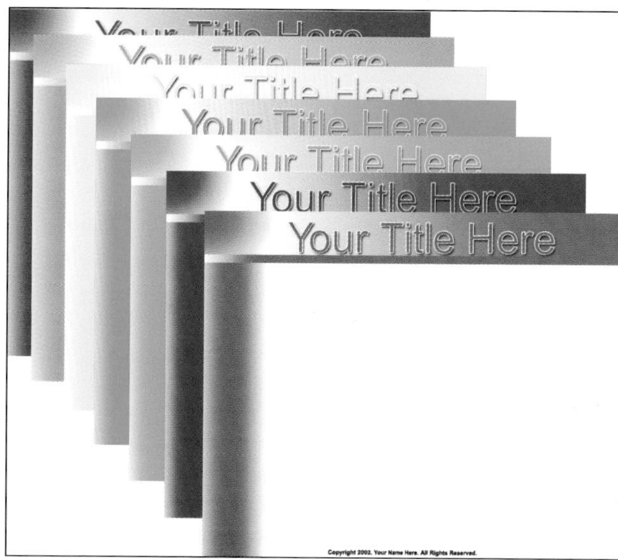

You can color code portions of your web site easily by making this simple modification.

COMPOSITING SEAMLESS PATTERNS

"When I'm working on a problem, I never think about beauty. I think only how to solve the problem. But when I have finished, if the solution is not beautiful, I know it is wrong."

—RICHARD BUCKMINSTER FULLER

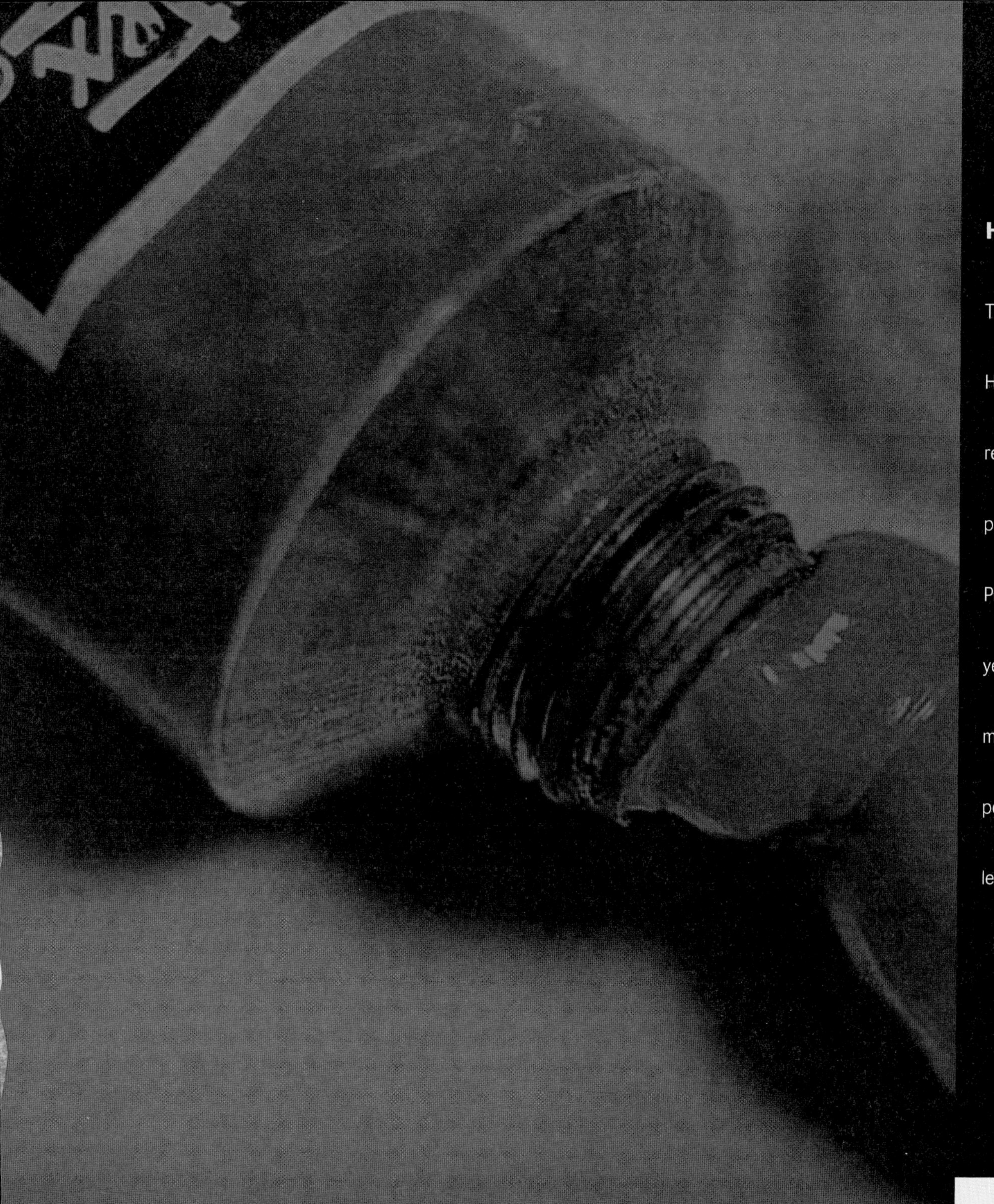

How I Spent My Christmas Vacation

The "endless pattern" has been almost like a Holy Grail. While designers have been creating repeat patterns since mankind was young, the photographic repeat is fairly new. It has to be. Photographs themselves are less than 200 years old. You have seen repeating patterns made from jellybeans or potatoes or nails or pennies or a thousand other things. Now you'll learn my methods of constructing one.

Project 11

Compositing Seamless Patterns

by Sherry London

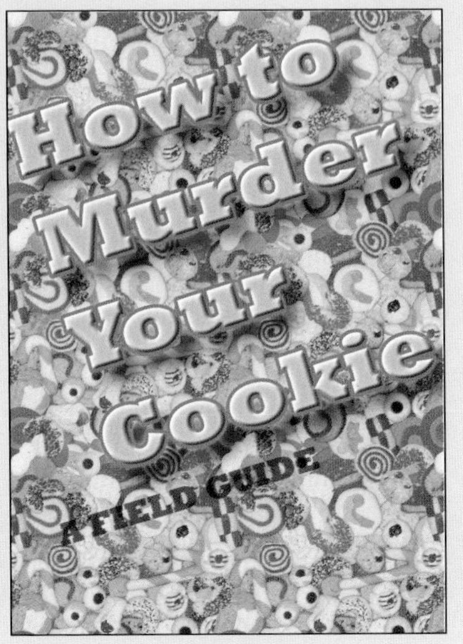

Getting Started

I became involved with computer graphics through my work as a fiber artist. I wanted to design knitware and needlework on the computer. Both fiber techniques—especially machine knitting—include the design of repeating patterns. It has become, over the years, a passion of mine.

I have explored many different ways to make patterns tile or repeat. I really like this method of creating an endless repeat from a photo. It's based on the fairly new command, Reveal All. This command makes it much easier to wrap pattern elements and create a seamless image.

In this project, you learn how to use the Reveal All command after you have placed elements along the borders of an image. You'll also learn how to prepare an image to be made seamless, some tips on doing your own photography, and how to make the added elements blend into the original photo.

PREPARING THE PLAYERS

The first requirement in creating an endless photo pattern is to find an appropriate photo that you want to make endless. I am not really being facetious as it sounds. An endless image has no clear top or bottom and no division lines when it is done.

Some images can be made seamless in that you don't see the hard line where one image ends and the other begins. However, they can never become endless because the image itself has a boundary or point of view.

You can't create an endless repeat of a person, an animal, or scenery. You can create an endless repeat only from objects that can logically be stacked or piled on top of one another. For example, candy, cookies, pennies, fruit, tools, and so on.

The contents of the individual bins of vegetables in a supermarket are excellent subjects for an endless pattern. A photo of the deli counter that includes the case is not. You need an image where you can suspend your doubt and believe that the item could go on forever.

You can get your source material in one of two ways: you can use a photo from a stock image collection, or you can take your own picture. If you take your own photos, you have total control over the results and can easily photograph spare parts for the composite.

For now, you'll start with a rectangular image of cookies. (These are my cookies—the recipes are available on request!) To get you started, I have already placed extra cookies in a layered file. If you were starting with a stock photo (or your own work), you would need to select, copy, and arrange individual whole elements in a file similar to this one. For example, if you were trying to create endless green beans, you would need to create a file that contained a variety of whole green beans, each in its own layer. The skills you need to do that are the ability to lasso or otherwise select individual elements in the image, copy them to a new layer in a different document, and soften the edges to remove any color contamination.

HOW PATTERNS WORK

Before I get into the mechanics of preparing a seamless tile, you need to understand what we are working toward. You need to be able to see the seam. The most common way to prepare a seamless tile is to use the Offset filter. Another way is to move the TileMaker filter from the ImageReady-only set of filters into the joint set of filters and try that. Neither solution works to give you a good seamless pattern.

Look at the images shown in this section. They illustrate the process and results of using the Offset filter or the TileMaker filter to create a repeat. There is nothing for you to do here but look at the images. I want you to be able to recognize pattern seams when you see them.

Note: To place the TileMaker filter so that you can use it in Photoshop, close Photoshop if it is open and locate the Photoshop application folder on your hard disk. On the Mac, drag Photoshop 7.0/Plug-Ins/Adobe ImageReady Only/Filters/Tile Maker and place it in Photoshop 7.0/Plug-Ins/Filters. In Windows, drag Photoshop 7.0/Plug-Ins/Adobe ImageReady Only/Filters/TileMaker and place it in Photoshop 7.0/Plug-Ins/Filters.

There is no reason not to place the Tile Maker plug-in in the common folder. The filter works equally well in either program.

Here is an image that I want to use to create an endless pattern.

You can see from the example shown here how the hard lines detract from the pattern. When I speak of making a pattern seamless, it means to create a pattern that does not have any visual clues as to where it tiles. Leave this image open—you will use it again.

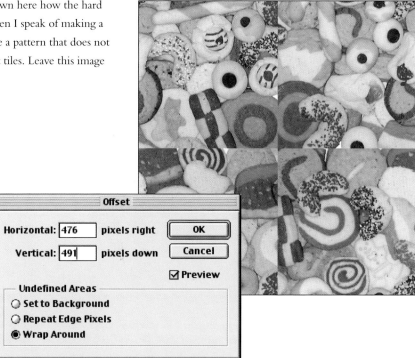

I used the Offset filter to offset the image in half using these settings.

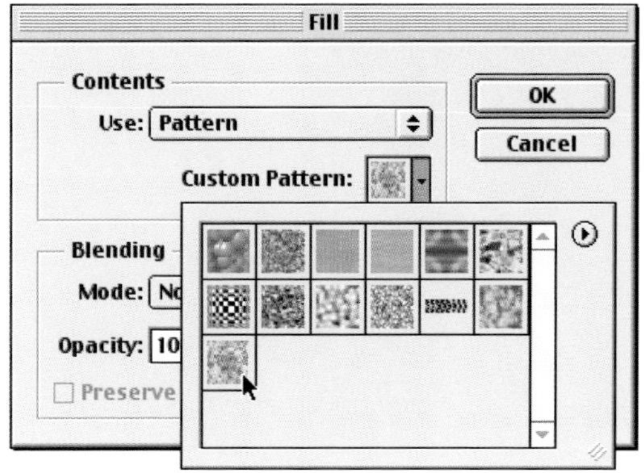

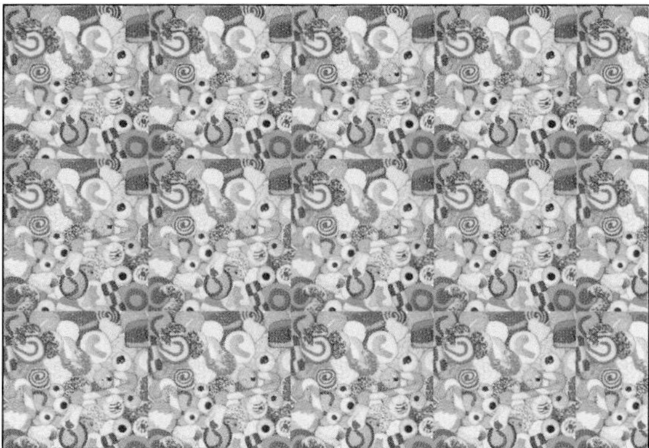

I filled an empty document with the pattern.

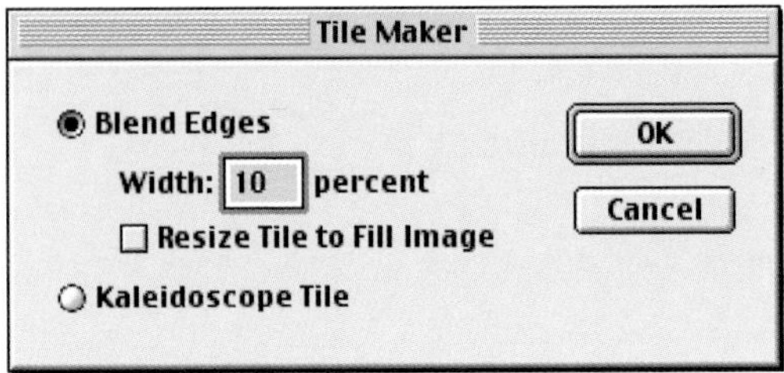

I applied the Tile Maker filter to the image using these settings.

You can see how the patterned image is shaded where the tiles repeat. That is not the look you want either.

I filled the large file with the new pattern.

Preparing the Images

My approach to making a seamless tile is different. If you actually use more cookies to patch over the seam, you will get a totally seamless tile that looks like it was supposed to be that way. You won't be able to locate the area where the tiles meet. To do that, you need to prepare extra pattern elements.

In this section, you examine the various cookies that you can use. You then check them for edge contamination. Of course, you will find at least one that needs some help! You'll then learn an easy way to quickly remove the edge problem.

1. Open the image morecookies.psd from the accompanying CD.

   This image has layers filled with additional cookies that you can use.

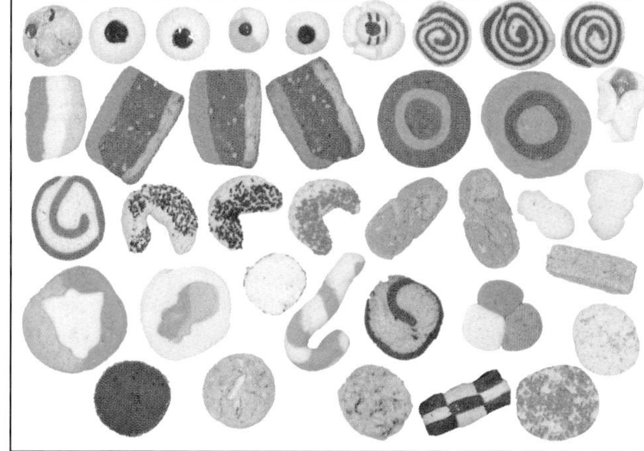

Use these extra cookies to help make the pattern seamless.

2. Make the Manufactured Cookie layer in the image active and add a new layer. Choose a strong blue (or any other bright color that isn't in the image) as your foreground color, and fill the new layer with it. Choose Layer > Arrange > Send to Back (Shift+Ctrl+left bracket/Shift+Cmd+left bracket) to place the layer at the bottom of the Layers list.

   This blue background is deliberately awful with the cookies. With it, however, you will be able to spot any problems with white edges on the cookies.

3. Click the Molasses Ginger layer. Then zoom in on the cookie to make it as large as possible on your monitor.

   The easiest way to figure out which cookie it is, is to look at the image in View > Fit on Screen view and turn the layer's Eye icon off and on. You'll see the correct cookie flicker. Notice the white around the edges of the cookie. You'll fix that next.

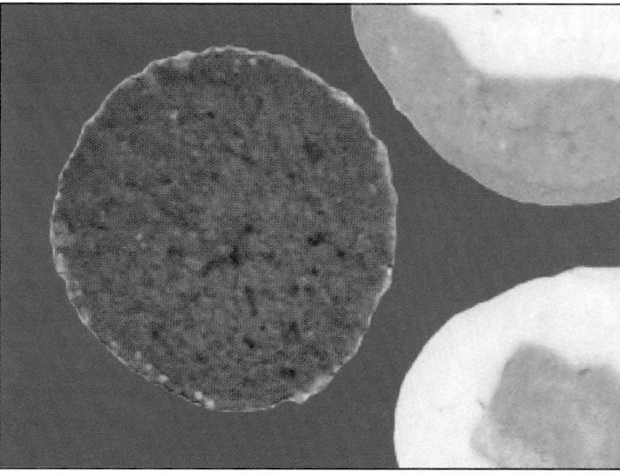

Zoom in on the molasses ginger cookie.

4 Select the Eraser tool in Paintbrush mode, and then select the Hard Round 9 pixels brush from the Brushes palette. Click the Brush Tip Shape settings, and change the Hardness to 50%.

Just like Goldilocks and the bears, hardness of 100% is too hard, 0% is too soft, but 50% is just right.

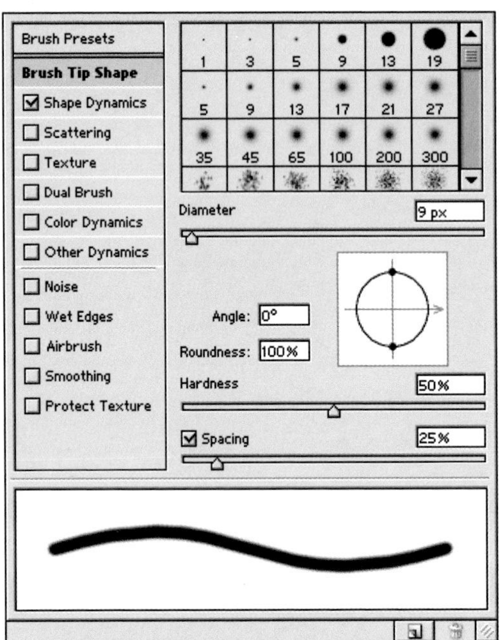

Change the hardness of the 9-pixel brush to 50%.

5 Carefully place the eraser outside the molasses ginger cookie, and let the edge of the brush eat away at the opaque light-colored pixels around the edge of the cookie.

This cookie has orange sugar crystals on its edge, so some lightness is expected. However, it also has white pixels that need to be removed. You can tell that you are getting some transparency on the edges when they turn a deeper blue. I prefer the Eraser tool for this to any other automated method of edge decontamination (you can use a Layer Mask if you prefer the safety). I will use automated techniques in other circumstances, but on these small cookies, this method gives me the most control.

Use the edge of the eraser to add some transparency to the edges of the cookie.

6 Carefully check the edges of the other cookies and fix them, if necessary.

I did a fairly decent job on the others. You can edit them or not. If this were your own work, you would take a careful look at all the edges now.

7 Remove the blue layer and save the file, but leave it open.

Adding the Extra Elements

Now comes the fun part! You get to be a food stylist. In this section, you add the cookies to the original image along the top edge and the left side. These extra cookies will hang off the edge of the canvas and in a later section, the areas outside the image will wrap to make the cookies seamless.

1 Open the original cookies1.psd image from the accompanying CD. Arrange the images on your monitor so that you can see both images at the same time.

2 Drag the snowman sugar cookie from the morecookies image to the top-left corner of the main cookies image so that it partially leaves the canvas. Place it carefully so that it does not go into the area to the left of the image and outside the image area itself.

On the image shown here, that area is labeled "Place Nothing Here." The gray transparency pattern shows the actual image area, and the white borders are the part of the image that is hidden from view because it is outside the printable boundary of the image. It is the area that Photoshop calls "Big Data." It's critical that you don't place any object in that corner area because it will not appear in the final repeat. Making sure that nothing intrudes on that tiny corner is a major challenge throughout this entire process. The snowman is perfect for that spot near the corner because he leans to the right. You will understand this better when you wrap the image in the next section.

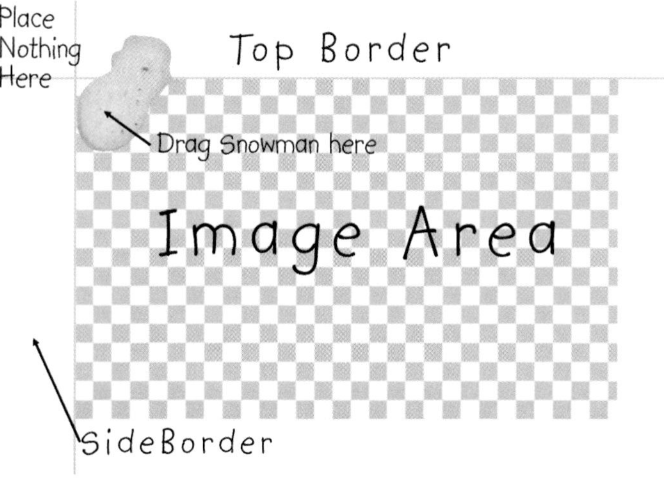

Drag the snowman sugar cookie to the right of the upper-left corner of the image so that only part of the cookie is visible.

3. Choose Image > Adjustments > Levels (Ctrl+L/ Cmd+L). Set the Gamma field (the center numeric field) to 1.54.

   As you place a cookie, you need to make sure that it doesn't pull your eye to it in the composite. The snowman was just a little bit too dark.

4. Locate the pink, chocolate, and green-striped cookie that is partially visible along the top border of the cookies1 image. Using the Lasso tool, make a selection around that cookie. In the morecookies image, make the Ribbon Cookie2 layer active, and load the transparency of the layer. Choose Edit > Copy. Make the cookies1 image active and choose Edit > Paste Into. Move the cookie until it is in approximately the same position as the original occupant of that spot. Using black as your foreground color and a very soft brush, paint in the Layer Mask to blend the two cookies.

   The Paste Into command creates a Layer Mask that you can edit. This technique works well to enable you to place a cookie so that it seems to go under another one. Your cookie patches will be very obvious on the finished pattern if all the cookies are full cookies on top of other cookies. This is an unnatural arrangement. Using a Layer Mask—created either by hand or by the Paste Into command—helps to avoid this problem.

Match the tone of this sugar cookie to another sugar cookie in the image.

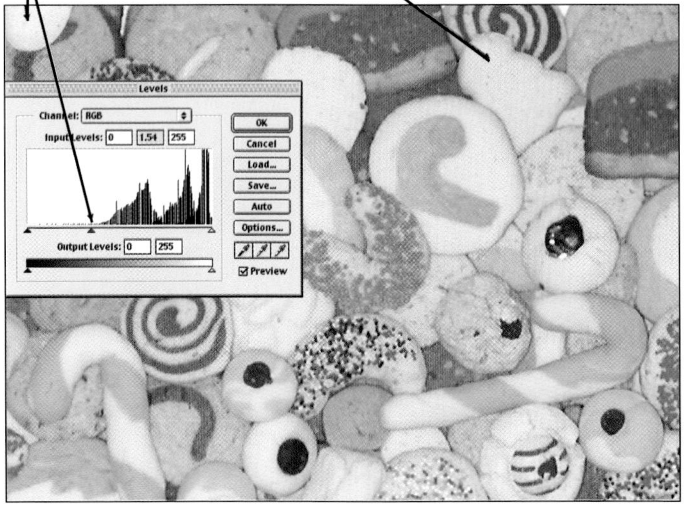

Match the tone of the placed sugar cookie to that of a nearby sugar cookie.

5 Drag the green peppermint kiss into the cookies1 image. Drag the layer below the ribbon cookie layer, and then move the peppermint kiss below the ribbon cookie in the image so that it looks as if it is sitting under it. Make sure that you have placed the cookie so that some of it extends beyond the visible area of the image and into the top border area.

This cookie covers the partial cookie that is at the top of the image. As you place cookies, you need to make sure that you substitute cookies that go into the top border for half-cookies on the original. The areas where the cookies go off the canvas will eventually wrap to the opposite side of the image to make the tile seamless.

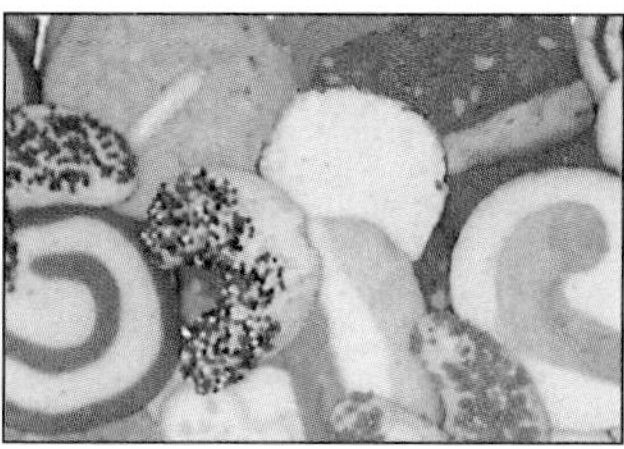

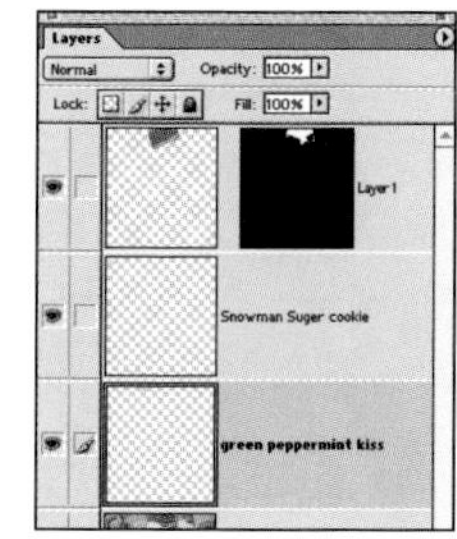

Place the green peppermint kiss underneath the previously placed ribbon cookie.

6 Continue to place cookies along only the top and left borders of the image as you have done so far.

You can choose the cookies because you like them or because they are continuations of the cookies already partially shown at the edges of the image. You might want to place some additional whole cookies into the image so that they cover the visible part of a "border" cookie. This keeps the border cookie from looking too perfect and whole. You can paste cookies into selections; you can even create a Layer Mask to blend a cookie after you have placed it.

Complete the top and left borders of the image.

Note: As you work, keep flipping the Eye icon on and off on the Background layer of the cookies1 image. This will show you where you have placed cookies and which areas still need cookies. I have found it faster to choose the Auto Select Layer option on the Move tool. I generally hate this option, but it works so much faster for clicking a cookie in the morecookies image and then dragging the cookie. Make sure that no cookie extends into the right or bottom border areas at all. If any part of a cookie does, you won't get a good seamless match.

THE FIRST SEAMLESS PASS

You are ready to make the first attempt at creating the seamless image. This is an iterative process, and it might take several tries to get it the way you want. You will use the Reveal All command to show you the cookies that were placed in the border areas. You'll then cut these cookies apart and move the border areas to the opposite side of the image.

1. Save the image as **cookies2.psd**. Then choose Image > Duplicate > OK. Don't select the Duplicate Merged Layers Only check box.

   Because you might need to change the position of the cookies, you don't want to touch the original composite.

2. Choose Select > All.

   You need to select the entire image so that after you use the Reveal All command in the next step, you can get back to the original image dimensions.

3. Choose Image > Reveal All. Click the Save Selection as Channel icon at the bottom of the Channels palette to create the Alpha 1 channel (or choose Select > Save Selection). The second option brings up a dialog box that the first does not.

   You need to select the image first and save the selection after you have used the Reveal All command because that is the only way to create a properly sized alpha channel to get back to your original image dimensions later. In the image shown here, the red areas at the top and left sides are the border areas uncovered by the Reveal All command.

Choose Image > Reveal All and then save the selection as a channel.

4 Turn off the Eye icon on the Background layer and look at the cookies that are left. Check to see if any of them need to be edited or remasked.

In the image shown here, you can see that the mask did not properly hide part of the cookie that had been under the border area. You would need to go back and add to that layer's mask to fix it. You will also need to fix any mask that you created by using the Paste Into command because the selection marquee makes the mask cut off the areas into the border. (The first ribbon cookie that you placed will have this problem.)

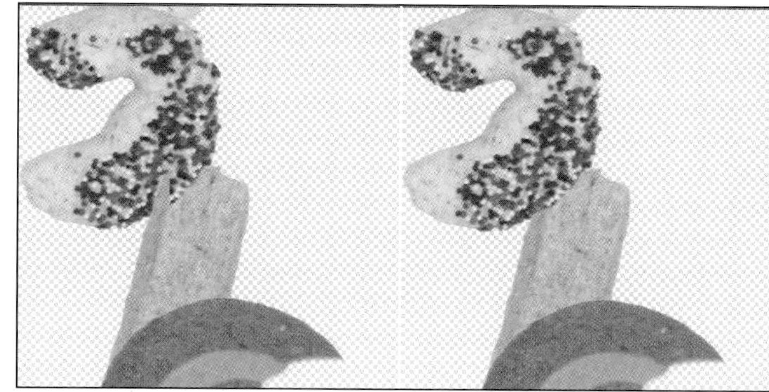

Fix any inconsistencies that you see in the cookies that you added to the image.

5 Choose Layer > Merge Visible.

This puts all the layers with the exception of the Background layer into the same layer. You need to make certain that you don't have the Background layer visible or active when you use this command.

6 Load Alpha 1 channel as a selection. Choose Select > Load Selection > Alpha 1 or Ctrl-click/Cmd-click the Alpha 1 channel in the Channels palette.

7 Choose Select > Inverse. Then choose Layer > New > Layer via Cut (Shift+Ctrl+J/Shift+Cmd+J). Rename the layer from which you cut the borders (the merged image layer) as **Stationery** and check the Lock Position icon on the Layers palette. Then make the new layer active again.

Cutting the area outside the original image puts the border wrap area on its own layer. You'll cut this layer in two in the next step.

8 Load the Alpha 1 channel as you did in Step 6. Select the Rectangular Marquee tool and after you start to move the selection marquee up, hold the Shift key to constrain the motion vertically. Drag the marquee until it reaches the top of the image. Choose Layer > New > Layer via Cut (Shift+Ctrl+J/Shift+Cmd+J).

You are using the rectangular selection in the Alpha 1 channel to choose the correct area of the cookies along the top edge of the image to cut its own layer. You now have one layer of cookies that belong to the horizontal border and another layer that belongs to the vertical border.

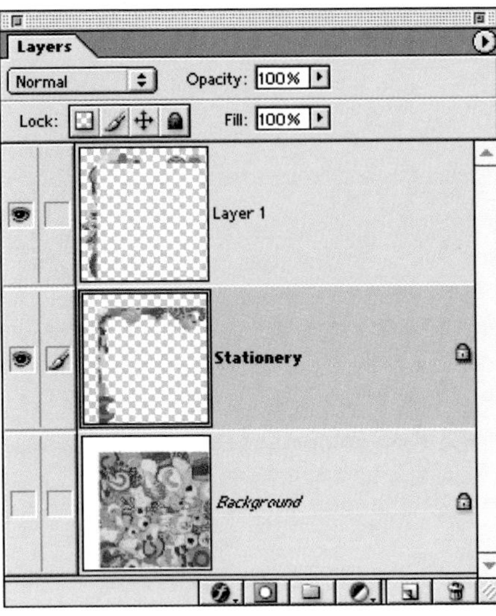

Cut the border area to its own layer.

9 Load the selection from the Alpha 1 channel again and look at the selection dimensions on the Info palette. Deselect (Ctrl+D/Cmd+D).

The selection is 952×982 pixels.

10 Make sure that Layer 2 is active. Choose Edit > Free Transform. On the Options Bar, click the icon between the X and Y position fields to turn on relative positioning. Then enter 982 in the Y: field and click the check mark on the Options Bar to commit the transformation.

Your border area moves to the bottom of the image to cover the cookies there. Turning on relative positioning enables you to avoid the math.

Use the Free Transform command to move the image on Layer 2 down 982 pixels.

11 Make Layer 1 active. Choose Edit > Free Transform. Relative positioning should still be set. Enter 952 in the X: field and click the check mark on the Options Bar to commit the transformation.

The Free Transform command seems to pick up most of the layer, but it doesn't matter. Just ignore the over-selection and enter the number to move the selection to the other side of the image.

12 Turn on the Eye icon on the Background layer. Load the Alpha 1 channel as a selection. Choose Image > Crop.

This makes the single pattern tile. The image should now be seamless when tiled.

13 Choose Edit > Define Pattern.

This pattern is very large. You might want to reduce your own work more than this. However, the more pattern repeats you have, the more obvious the tiling becomes. In addition, be aware of the resolution of the final project. If you make a pattern that is destined for 300 ppi printing too small, you lose all its impact. One way to judge on screen is to view your pattern at 25 percent. If it looks too small at that size, it will be too small when printed at 300 ppi.

14 Create a new image 6.5 inches wide and 6.5 inches high at 300 ppi and use RGB Color mode. (You can make the tile smaller and create a smaller image if this is too large a file for your RAM to handle.) Choose Layer > New Fill Layer > Pattern and select the cookie pattern that you just created.

Using a Pattern Fill layer enables you to make the pattern smaller if you want to see what it would look like with more repeats, and if this pattern is not optimal, you can easily switch it for a later version.

Load the alpha channel and crop your image back to its original dimensions.

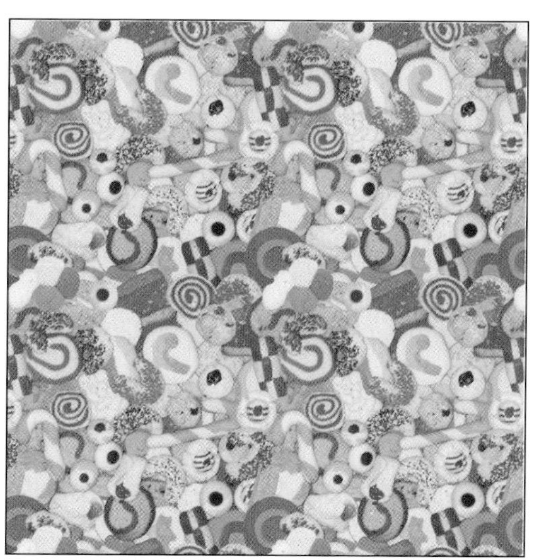

Fill an image with the new pattern using a Pattern Fill layer.

Perfecting the Tile

After you see the finished tile, you can evaluate the success of the completed pattern. My first effort, which was shown in the previous section, is successful in that you cannot see a pattern seam and there are no half-completed cookies that look disembodied.

However, there are some very subtle areas that could use improvement. Things to look for include the following:

- Seams
- Missing elements in the pattern wrap
- Missing shadows or edge definition
- Too many full cookies or cookies (pattern elements, if you are using your own image) on top, in a straight line

If you see seams, you need to go back to the saved cookies2 image and move elements around until you have an arrangement that gets rid of the seams. Seams are definitely a "no-no" here.

If you are missing parts of cookies in the wrap, you need to return to the cookies2 image and fix the masks. You could also bring in other cookies from the morecookies image.

If you see missing shadows that are really obvious, you can put them in using several methods. If you go back to the layered images, you can use the Drop Shadow. In this example, you would need a very small shadow toward the right. The Color Burn mode works well here. You could also create the same type of shadow and burnt edge by painting over the edge of the cookie very carefully in Color Burn mode with a tiny soft brush. If you do the entire cookie in one mouse press, you could then use the Edit > Fade command to reduce the opacity.

Finally, if you see an unnatural arrangement of cookies, you can add a cookie on top of it or add a mask to make one of the wrapped-around cookies on the bottom tuck under a cookie that was already there. The spot to look for this problem is at the bottom of the tile or along the right side. You can check for this before you create the pattern, but after you have moved the border areas so that they wrap.

In the beginning of this process, you added some cookies at the top or left side and maybe even used a mask. You might want to do both after the wrap as well. In the image shown here, I used a mask to tuck the ribbon cookie under the bear-in-the-center cookie that was already in the image. I also put a green almond crescent cookie over the too-bright clover cookie to make it less noticeable. Here, you can see the before-and-after images.

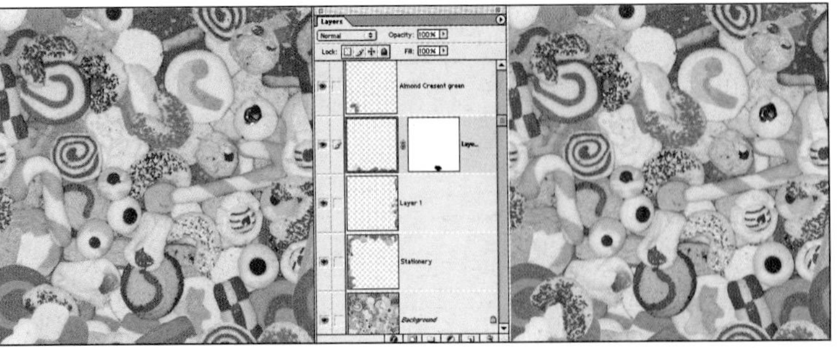

You can sink a cookie into a mask or add another cookie to reduce the effect of a regular line of cookies used to conceal the seam.

Modifications

I considered showing how endless potatoes or fruit would look and then thought, no, you can picture that easily enough. Instead, here is a camel from the ArtPartz clip art collection. The camel is painted with a texture brush (new to Photoshop 7), filled with the cookies pattern, and then textured with the Bevel and Emboss Texture style while using the cookies pattern. In addition to the texture on the brush, I also added Color Dynamics with a 45 percent Hue jitter. When I painted the image, I used this brush in Multiply mode to protect the black in the camel.

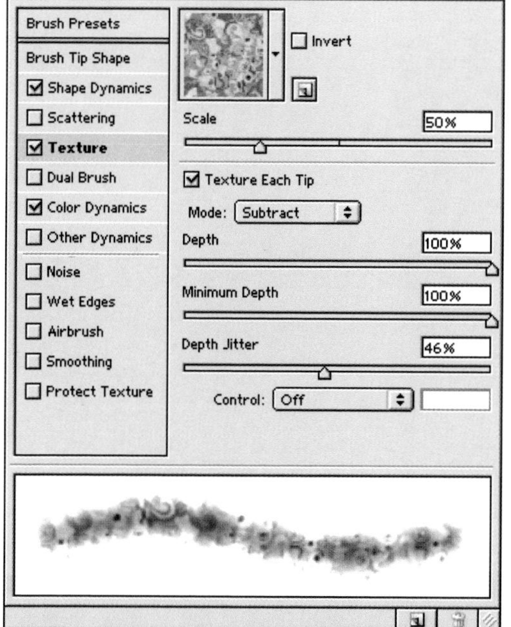

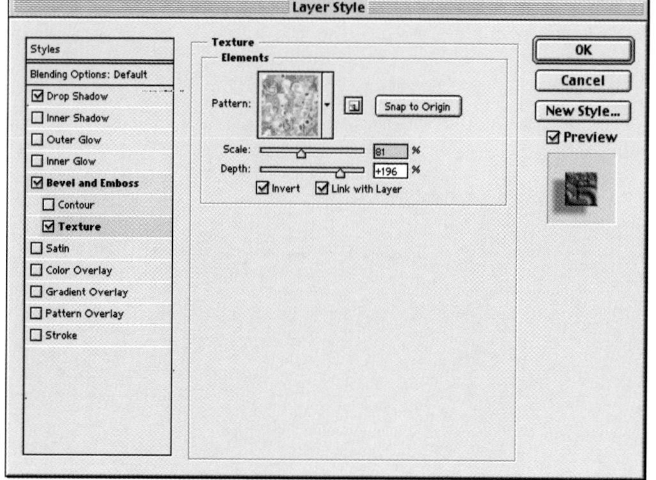

The camel was painted using the settings shown here.

DISTORTING WITH DISPLACEMENT MAPS

"Millions of men have lived to fight, build palaces and boundaries, shape destinies and societies; but the compelling force of all times has been the force of originality and creation profoundly affecting the roots of human spirit."

—ANSEL ADAMS

Applying Contour to Flat Images

It's deadline time and you've got a flat image that you need to overlay on another. You also need to make it follow the other image's contours. Don't pull your hair out; displacement maps will come to your rescue!

Project 12

Distorting with Displacement Maps

by Michel Bohbot

Getting Started

This project teaches you to be more assertive and push pixels around so that they don't push back! Seriously though, you'll map one image to another, using a grayscale image called a displacement map. Displacement maps are images designed to create custom distortion in other images. In this project, you use displacement maps for two different kinds of assignments. You'll make a flat emblem follow the flowing contours of a flag waving in the air, and you'll create reflections of a landscape in rippling water.

Creating a Displacement Map

First you turn the flag into a displacement map. Then you apply the flag shape to the emblem. To increase realism, you also use a blur and change the Blending mode between layers.

1 From the Projects folder on the accompanying CD-ROM, choose the Project 12 folder, and open the image Flag.psd. Turn on visibility of all three layers.

The image has three layers: a reddish sky, the original flag (actually a piece of fabric attached to a broom), and the emblem of our heroes.

Begin with the layered image of a flag.

2 Drag the original flag layer to the new layer symbol at the bottom of the Layers palette.

This makes a new layer called original flag copy.

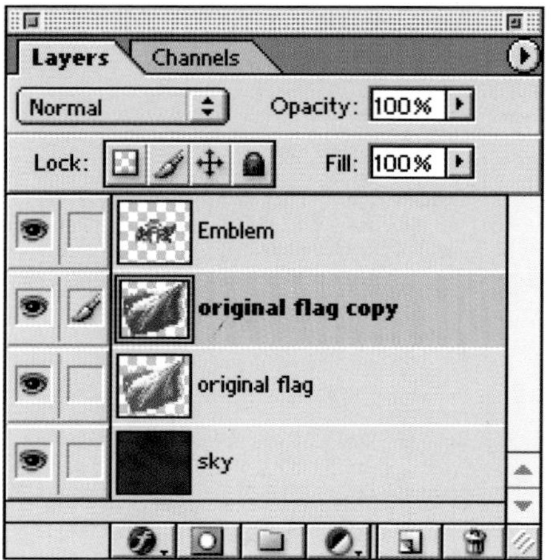

Duplicate the original flag layer.

3 With the new layer still selected, choose Image > Adjustments > Desaturate.

This eliminates color from the layer.

Desaturate the original flag copy layer.

4 Drag the desaturated original flag copy to the New Layer icon to create yet another layer. Set the Blending mode of this new layer to Multiply.

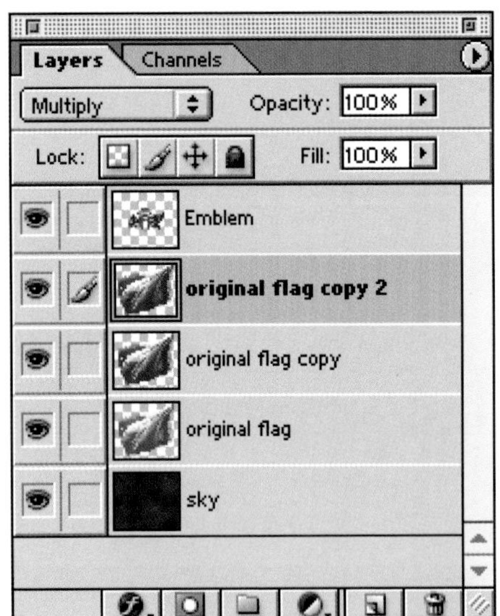

Make a second copy of the original flag.

This increases the contrast, which is useful because pixels that are 50% gray won't displace.

5 Turn off the view on all layers except the two flag copy layers. From the pop-up menu on the Layers palette, select Merge Visible.

6 Create a new layer. Fill it with white by making the foreground color white and then press Option+Delete/ Alt+Backspace.

7 Drag the white layer (called Layer 1) below the desaturated flag (the original flag copy 2 layer). Select Merge Visible.

Now there is a white background behind the flag.

Increase contrast with Multiply mode.

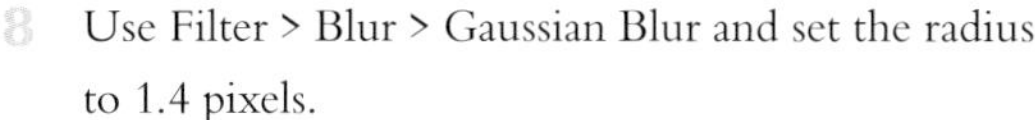

8 Use Filter > Blur > Gaussian Blur and set the radius to 1.4 pixels.

The blur serves to soften some of the wrinkles. This enables a smoother displacement effect later.

The following steps are for creating the custom displacement map.

9 Choose Select > All and choose Edit > Copy. Deselect.

The Copy command places the merged flag layer on the clipboard.

10 Choose File > New and name the file **flagdisplacementmap.psd** or whatever abbreviation works for you. Photoshop automatically provides the same dimensions as the image you copied. Click OK.

11 Choose Edit > Paste (Cmd+V/Ctrl+V). Flatten the image and save it in Photoshop format.

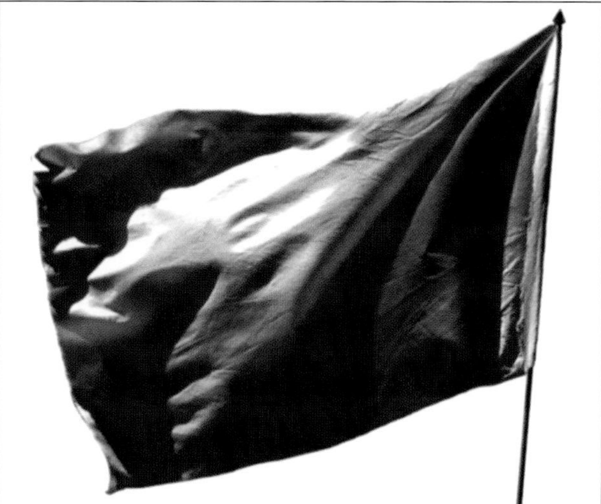

Apply Gaussian Blur.

Tip: It is important to save this image as a .psd file so that it can function as a displacement map. Only the luminosity (brightness) values are used in displacement, so you might want to convert this image to Grayscale mode before you save it.

Preparing the Emblem

Turn your attention to the layered image. You will skew the emblem to follow the angle of the flag. You then will apply the displacement effect.

1. Drag the Emblem layer to the New Layer icon to make a copy. Use Layer Properties to rename it **Skewed Emblem**.

Copy the Emblem layer and name it **Skewed Emblem**.

2. With the Skewed Emblem layer still active, click Edit > Transform > Skew. Place your cursor on the center handle of the right edge of the Transform bounding box and drag upwards until the top of the griffin's wing is roughly parallel to the top of the flag. Reposition the skewed emblem to the center of the flag. This can be done either before or after you commit the transform.

3. Drag the Skewed Emblem to the New Layer icon and rename the copy Displaced Emblem.

4. Hide the Skewed Emblem layer and all other layers between the Displaced Emblem and the original flag.

Skew the emblem.

5 Highlight the Displaced Emblem layer and choose Filter > Distort > Displace. In the Displace dialog box, type **5** in both the Horizontal Scale and Vertical Scale fields. Under Displacement Map, choose Stretch To Fit, and in Undefined Areas, choose Repeat Edge Pixels. Click OK.

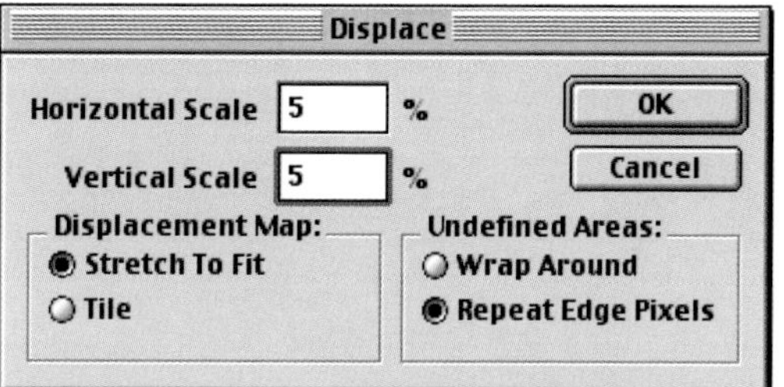

Enter settings for the Displacement filter.

6 When prompted to open a file to use for the displacement map, open the flagdisplacementmap.psd file you created earlier.

The pixels of the Displaced Emblem have been mapped to the luminosity of the flag. The higher the numbers you enter in the Scale fields, the greater the distortion. Thus, 5% produces only a slight displacement.

Apply Displacement to the emblem.

7. Change the Blending mode of the Displaced Emblem layer to Multiply.

   Realism is increased now that the displaced emblem has the same tonal variation as the flag. Note that Multiply mode darkened the emblem a little too much. It also created transparency in the white castle.

8. Make a copy of the Displaced Emblem layer and change its Blending mode to Color.

Change the Blending mode to Multiply.

Adding another emblem layer in Color mode fixed the problems caused by using Multiply. It also reestablished the original colors of the blue shield and the white castle. Now you're ready to storm the gates!

The finished image with layers intact, FlagEND.psd, is included for reference in the source folder for this project.

Adding Reflections to Water

In this exercise, you create a mirror image of some beautiful scenery from the Lake Tahoe area and add realistic ripples for the effect of a reflection in the water. The ripples will be the result of another custom displacement map.

1. From the Projects folder on the accompanying CD-ROM, choose the 12_Displacement Maps folder, and open the image tahoe.psd.

   That's my childhood buddy Howard on the rock, in case you're wondering.

2. Double-click Background in the Layers palette to convert it to a regular layer and name it **Land**.

3. Choose Image > Canvas Size, click the upper-middle square in the Anchor field, and change the Height field to 4 inches.

   You just added blank space to the bottom of the image to make room for the reflection.

Begin with the Tahoe photo.

4 Drag the Land layer to the New Layer icon to duplicate it. Name it **Reflection**.

5 Use Edit > Transform > Flip Vertical on the Reflection layer.

6 Change the stacking order of the layers in the Layers palette by dragging the Reflection layer down or the Land layer up.

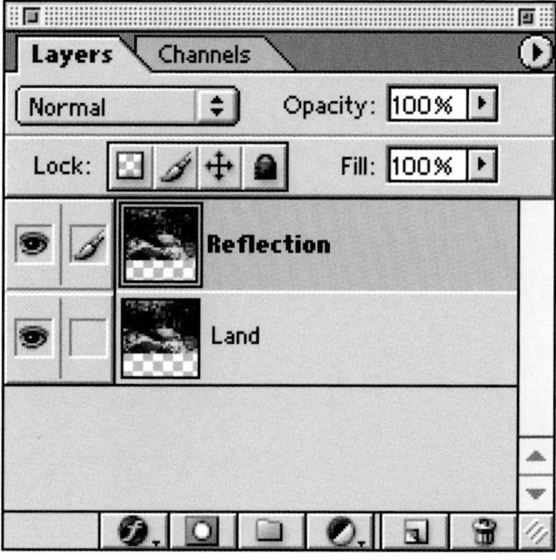

Duplicate the layer and rename it **Reflection**.

7 Use the Move tool to drag the Reflection layer down until it makes a mirror image of the Land layer.

Tip: To keep the layer from sliding around horizontally while you drag it vertically, constrain it with the Shift key.

8 Make a copy of the Reflection layer.

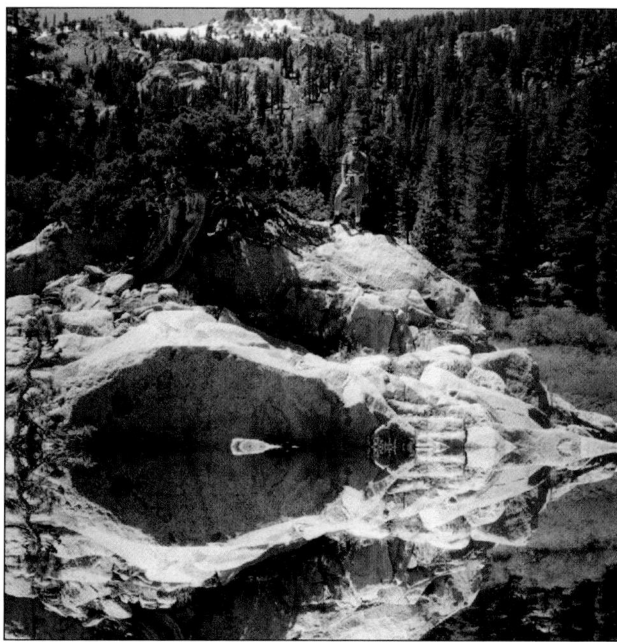

Flip and reposition the Reflection layer.

9 Create a Levels Adjustment layer. In the Levels dialog box, set Input Levels as follows (from left to right): Shadow 17, Midtones 0.77, and Highlights 255 (if necessary). Change Highlights in Output Levels by entering 239 in the right field.

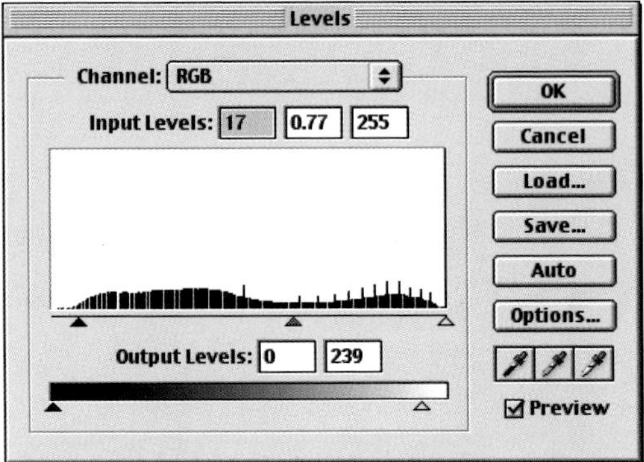

Reflections on water are usually darker than the items reflected. The Levels adjustment accomplished the darkness for you.

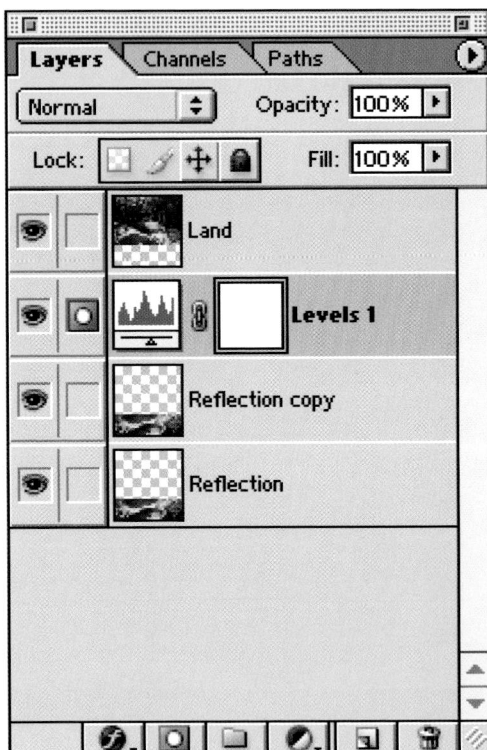

Add a Levels Adjustment layer.

Making Ripples

The illusion of ripples is essentially the result of a back-and-forth motion in the water. If you just used alternating bars of black and white as a displacement map, you would get that side-to-side distortion, but the perfect regularity would not look natural.

What will rescue you from this artificial reality? Noise! The Add Noise filter makes random speckles each time you choose it and that's what will save the day. When stretched out, these speckles make great ripples.

Avoid the unnatural look produced by too much regularity.

1. Create a new layer and name it Noise. Make a rectangular selection 48 pixels wide by 80 pixels tall. Fill the tiny selection with black.

Tip: An easy way to make an accurate selection is to use the Fixed Size style on the Options Bar for the Rectangular Marquee tool. Then enter the pixel dimensions you require. You can specify other units of measure if you prefer.

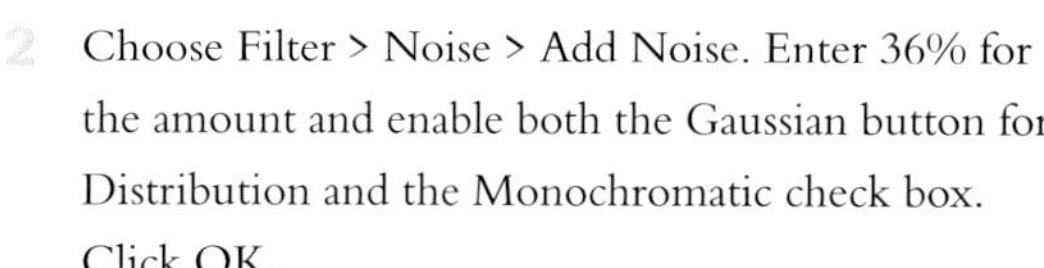

2. Choose Filter > Noise > Add Noise. Enter 36% for the amount and enable both the Gaussian button for Distribution and the Monochromatic check box. Click OK.

3. Hide the view on all layers except the Noise and Reflection copy layers.

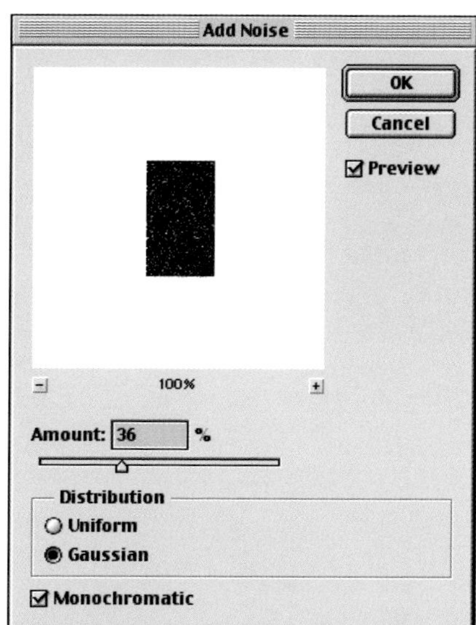

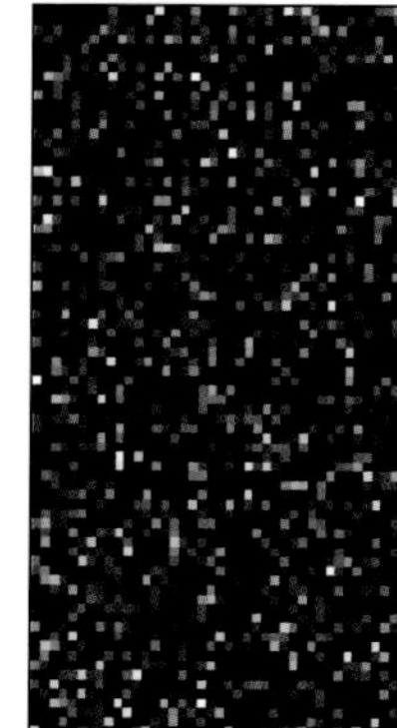

Add Noise to the black rectangle (shown at 500% magnification).

4 In General Preferences, be sure you have Bicubic (the default) chosen for Interpolation. Target the Noise layer and choose the Free Transform tool. Stretch the noise layer so that it is the same size as the reflection art.

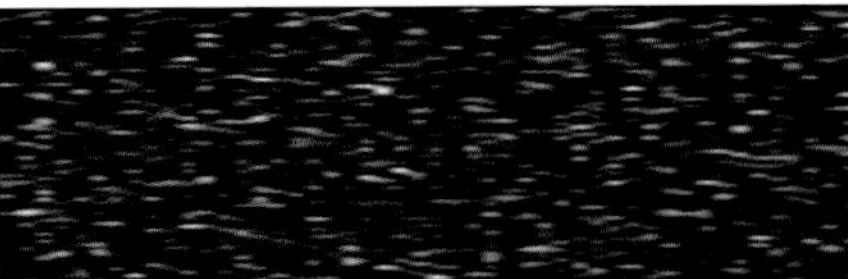

Enlarge the Noise rectangle to match the size of the Reflection copy.

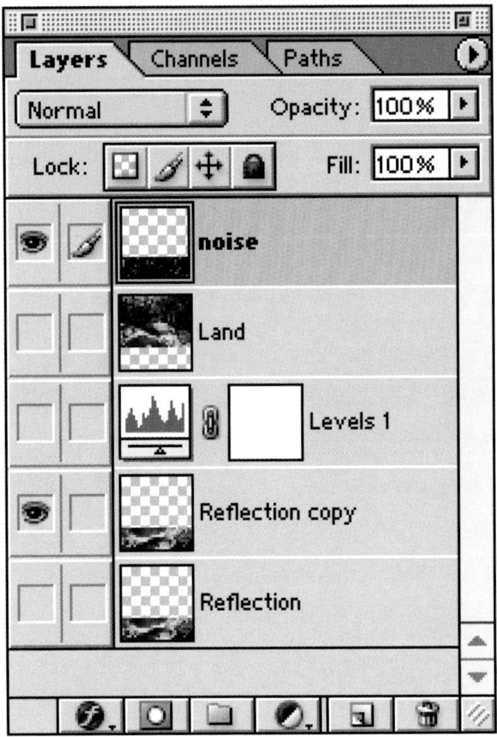

5 Add a little more contrast by using Image > Adjustments > Levels. Set these input numbers: Shadows 0, Midtones 0.94, and Highlights 94.

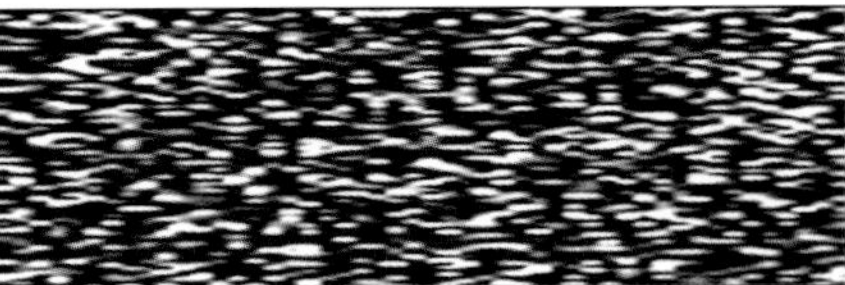

Add contrast to the Noise with Levels Adjustments.

6 Turn on visibility for the Land layer, choose a soft round brush, and set a 50% gray for your foreground color by using R 128, G 128, and B 128. Target the Noise layer and paint in Normal mode just below the small rock. Paint a gray shape that roughly corresponds to where the small rock's reflection falls on the water. This keeps that area from distorting so that the rock and its reflection line up.

Paint 50% gray where you want to minimize distortion.

7 Click the Noise layer in the Layers palette while pressing Ctrl/Cmd to select the portion of that layer containing an image. Copy and paste it into a new document. Save the image as **Ripple Map**, using the .psd file format.

8 Return to the Tahoe file. Ctrl-click/Cmd-click the Reflection copy layer to select only the portion of the layer containing image data. Transparent pixels remain unselected. Select Filter > Distort > Displace. Enter **15** in the Horizontal Scale field and **0** in the Vertical Scale field. As you did with the flag project, choose Stretch to Fit for Displacement Map and Repeat Edge Pixels for Undefined Areas. Assign Ripple Map.psd as the displacement map.

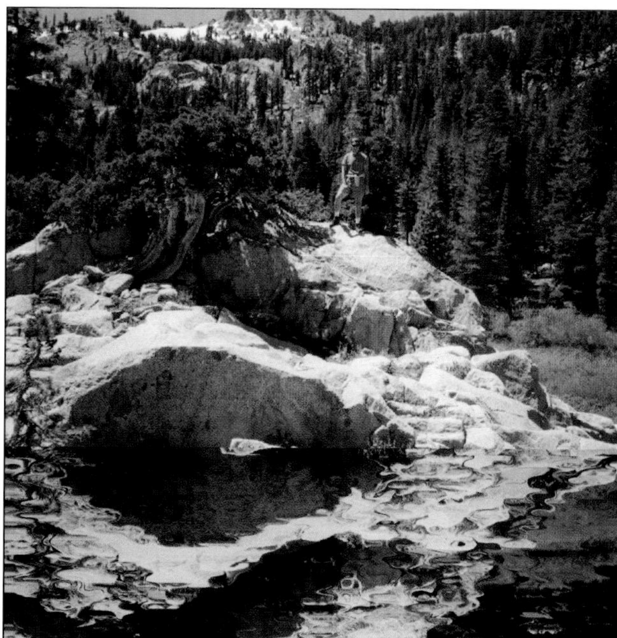

Apply the Displace filter, using the Ripple map.

If you had selected the entire layer, the ripple map would have stretched vertically as well as horizontally, spoiling the desired effect.

Now you have a more natural-looking ripple, but you're not quite there yet. You need to heighten the feeling of naturalism.

9 Flatten the image. Drag a horizontal selection across the entire image from just above to just below where the land meets the water. Feather the selection by 1 pixel.

10 Choose Filter > Blur > Gaussian Blur and set the Radius option to 1.

This softens the strong horizontal line just enough.

11 Deselect. Choose the Dodge tool with the soft, round, 5-pixel brush. Set Exposure to 43% and work in the Shadows Range. Click the left side of the art where the land meets the water and drag all the way to the right side while holding down the Shift key to constrain a straight line. Deselect.

This creates a little shimmer at the water's edge.

Blur the water's edge.

12 Change the brush preset for the Dodge tool to an irregular captured tip. Charcoal 14 pixels in the Natural Brushes group works fine. Drag a couple lines in the dark rock reflection to simulate a few insects or small fish slightly disturbing the water's surface.

Now you're ready to dive in after a long hike!

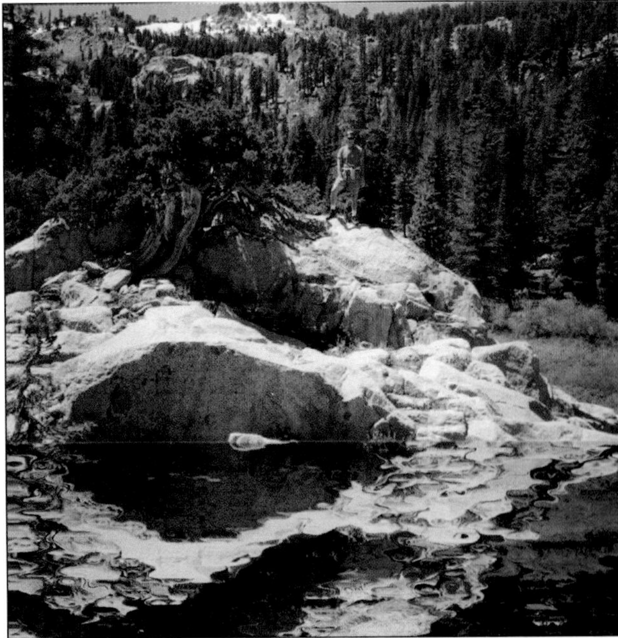

Add finishing touches with the Dodge tool.

Modifications

Distortions were used in this project to create realistic effects. The Displacement filter can also be used to make significant departures from reality. Here's a photo of a couple before and after some serious distortion using one of the off-the-rack displacement maps in the plug-ins folder of your Photoshop application.

The displacement map used to turn this ordinary portrait into a cubist painting is Random Strokes, with 25% for both Horizontal and Vertical Scale. The distortion was applied two more times by simply using Ctrl+F/Cmd+F, the keyboard shortcut for repeating the previous filter.

If you'd like more practice working with displacement maps, try Sherry's Project 5, "Marbled Backgrounds," on marbling.

Begin with a portrait photo.

Create a cubist painting with the Displacement filter.

IMAGE COMPOSITES USING EXTRACT IMAGE

"A doctor can bury his mistakes but an architect can only advise his client to plant vines."

—FRANK LLOYD WRIGHT

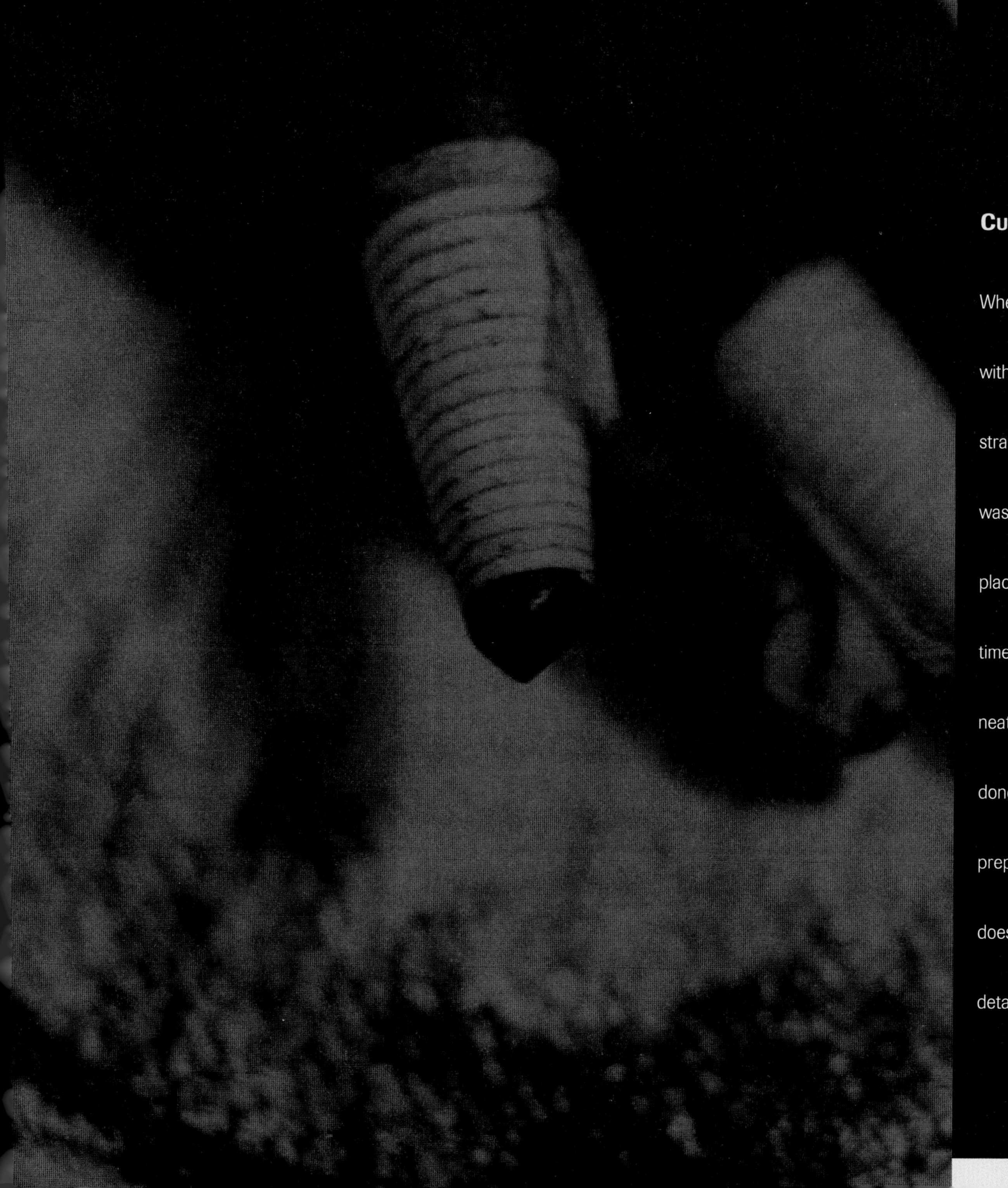

Cutting Out Judy

When I look in magazines and see a model with impeccably tailored hair and not a single strand out of place, I am fairly sure that she was photographed somewhere else and then placed into her current surroundings. There are times that you might need to "clean up" or neaten a hair-do, but all too often, it has been done for convenience because the artist who prepared the image doesn't know how or doesn't want to take the time to salvage the detail in the hair.

Project 13

Image Composites Using Extract Image

by Sherry London

Getting Started

Photoshop has many different ways to detach something from its background. The difficulty of accomplishing this task has given rise to both numerous methods and a vigorous third-party filter industry. The Extract Image command makes removing an object from its background a somewhat easier task. It's especially useful for images that are embedded in their backgrounds in areas of low contrast.

When you are handed a studio image that is shot against a solid background, it's easy to extract the image and preserve the detail of the hair, through a large number of different methods. However, when faced with the same task on a less-than-top-quality image (such as the image in this project, which is from a moderately priced digital camera), it becomes more challenging. For many of you, it will also be more realistic as well.

In this project, you remove Judy, an incredibly talented wearable artist, from this scene (which was shot in a fiber studio) and place her in more suitable surroundings where her handmade jacket and necklace show up better. You also learn some tricks for making Judy look as if she had been photographed in front of the fountain from the start. You'll also see how I structure a composite so that I keep my options open at all times.

Extract Image

The first step in this process is to extract Judy from the workshop. The original image is almost unbearably noisy. It's with great difficulty that I restrained myself from fixing it at this point. Try not to manipulate or fix the original until you place it into its final surroundings.

Because you need to match tone in its new background, you want to adjust the image as few times as possible. There are no adjustments that you can do now that you can't make later.

1. Open the image Judy.psd from the accompanying CD-ROM.
2. Duplicate the Background layer. Choose Filter > Extract.

   Keep your original image untouched.
3. Highlight around the sides and top of Judy's image using the Edge Highlighter tool in the Extract dialog box. Check the Smart Highlighting control. Start with a brush size of 25 at the bottom-left of the image and zoom in so that you can clearly see the edge you are trying to follow. Continue toward Judy's head until you reach her hair. Turn off Smart Highlighting and increase the brush size. Cover the entire transition area for the flyaway hair on the left. As you reach the area where you see a clear edge again, switch back to Smart Highlighting. Continue in this manner until you reach the bottom-right of the image.

Open the image Judy.psd from the accompanying CD.

Smart Highlighting draws a thin edge wherever possible. The width of the highlight line is the transition zone between the part of the image to keep and the part to toss. It should be as thin as possible. However, where you need to capture hair detail, you need to make the edge wider. Try to keep the highlight to the outside of the shape. You don't need to highlight along the bottom of the image.

Note: You can use all the shortcut keys here: B for Brush, E to choose the Eraser if you don't like the highlight, the spacebar to scroll, the Spacebar+Ctrl/Cmd to zoom in, the [or] key to make the brush larger or smaller, and Ctrl+Z/Cmd+Z to Undo.

4. When you have finished the highlighting, choose the Fill tool and fill the area to extract. If the blue leaks, you need to Undo and patch the outline. Set the Extraction Smooth control to 100.

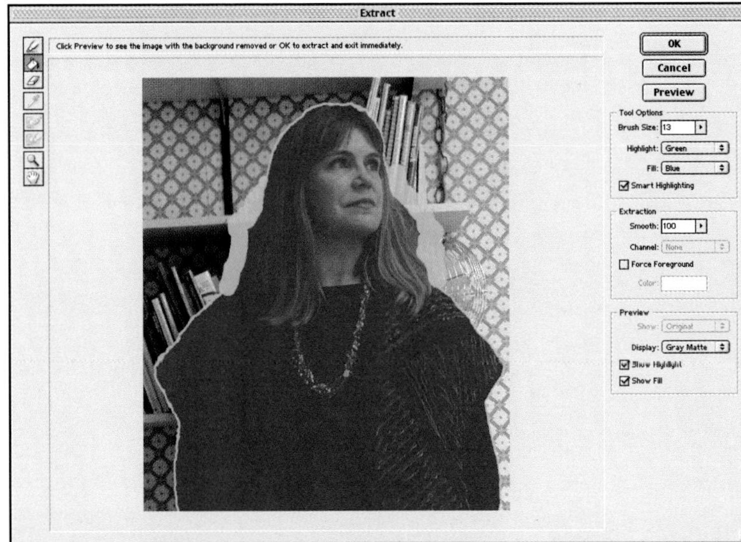

Fill the outline.

5 Click the Preview button to preview the extraction.

Don't panic. It is likely to look fairly awful, but you have other tools to use before you extract.

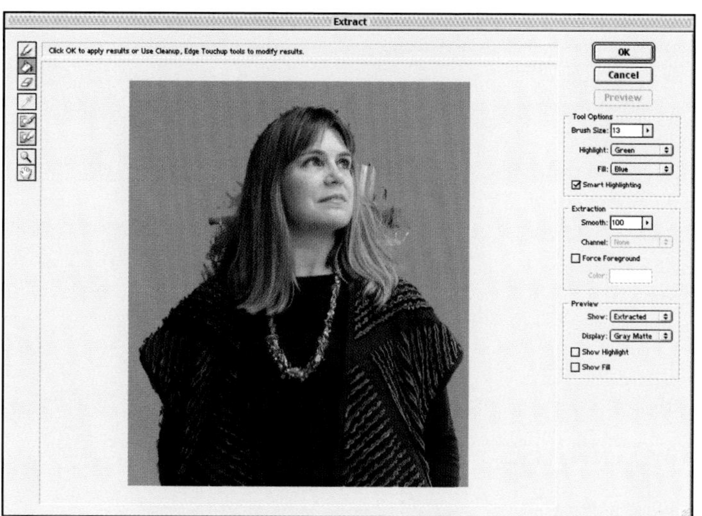

Preview the extraction.

6 Fix the edges of the area to extract.

You have two tools to use: the Cleanup tool (C) and the Edge Touchup tool (T). The Cleanup tool hides more of the image and is wonderful for making manual decisions of what to keep and what to toss. It works like the Quick Mask mode, except that you have no choice of color. Instead, to get back image areas that you lost, you can hold the Option or Alt key as you paint. The Edge Touchup tool helps to control the smoothness of the edge. For both tools, you can change the size of the brush and you can control the pressure of the tool by pressing a number from 0–9. You also might want to change the Display setting to White Matte. When in doubt, leave a little more of Judy's hair. After you have color-corrected the image, you can make the final adjustments.

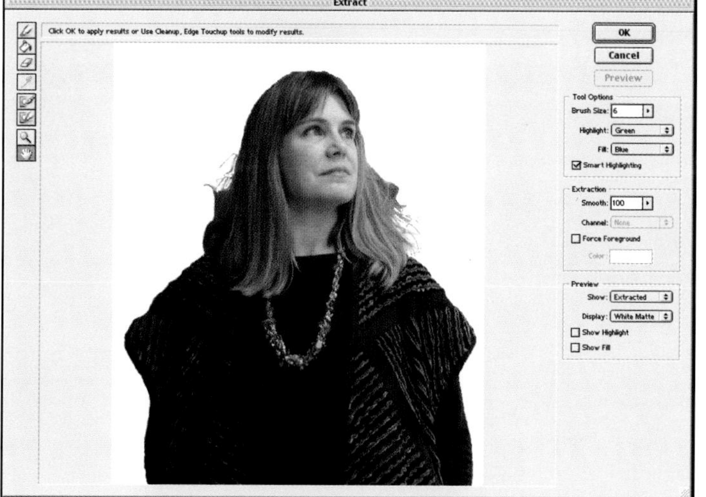

Fix the edges of the image using the Cleanup and Edge Touchup tools.

7 Commit by clicking OK.

Although it might seem that the Extract command has done nothing for you that you could not have done in Quick Mask mode or with the Magnetic Lasso tool, the Extract command has technology in it that also removes trace colors from the image edges. The areas where you use less than 100 percent pressure on the Cleanup and Edge Touchup tools leaves some transparency in the image. Turn off the Eye icon on the Background layer to see what your extracted image looks like.

Prepare Background Image

After you have Judy extracted from the background, your next step is to prepare the background image. You will be using adjustment layers to do the color correction.

When you look for an image that is a suitable background for a composite, you need to find one where the lighting is compatible and the shadows in the image won't conflict.

1 Open the image fountain.psd from the accompanying CD.

This image is actually in fairly good shape. Although it was taken with a digital camera, it has none of the multicolored noise that makes Judy's image such a problem.

2 Add a Levels Adjustment layer by selecting it from the Create New Fill or Adjustment Layer icon at the bottom of the Layers palette. Set the White Input slider to 246 and move the Gamma slider to 1.14. Click OK.

3 Double-click the name of the Adjustment layer in the Layers palette and change its name to **Fountain Adjustment**.

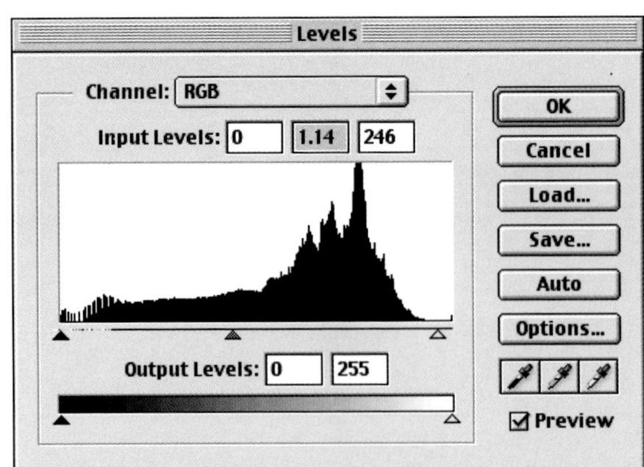

Add a Levels Adjustment layer to the background image.

Drag to a New Location

Now it's time to drag the extracted copy of Judy into her new home in front of the fountain.

1 Make Judy.psd active. Use the Move tool to drag her into the Fountain image above the Fountain Adjustment layer.

Place her head over the third fountain from the left. Make sure that she is grounded at the bottom of the image and not left floating disembodied in space.

Drag Judy into the Fountain image.

Add Depth of Field

Now that the two images are in place, you can see that in addition to the color mismatch problem, there is also a slight focus problem. The fountain image is sharper than Judy's image. If she had really been in front of the fountain, you would expect to see some slight blurring of the fountain on each side. This is the depth of field setting on a camera. We can add it here.

1 Duplicate the Background layer by dragging it to the New Layer icon in the Layers palette. Name the duplicate **Blurred Fountain**.

2 Choose Filter > Blur > Gaussian Blur, and use 3 pixels.

This setting might be too high, but you can reduce the opacity of the blur layer if necessary.

3 Add a Layer Mask to the Blurred Fountain layer. Select the Gradient tool and choose the Radial gradient with the Foreground to Background gradient. Press D to set the colors back to the default of black and white. (If black does not appear as your foreground color because you are in the Layer Mask, press X to swap colors. You need to have black as the foreground color.) Make sure that the mask is active and drag the gradient cursor from just below the neckline on Judy's dress to the top-left corner of the image.

This produces an instant depth-of-field effect.

4 Set Opacity of the Blurred Fountain layer to 85%.

This reduces the amount of blurring and adds a little more detail back to the water. The benefit of using layers this way is that you can manipulate the amount of blurring until you are satisfied and it's totally non-destructive.

Apply a Black to White Radial gradient in the Layer Mask.

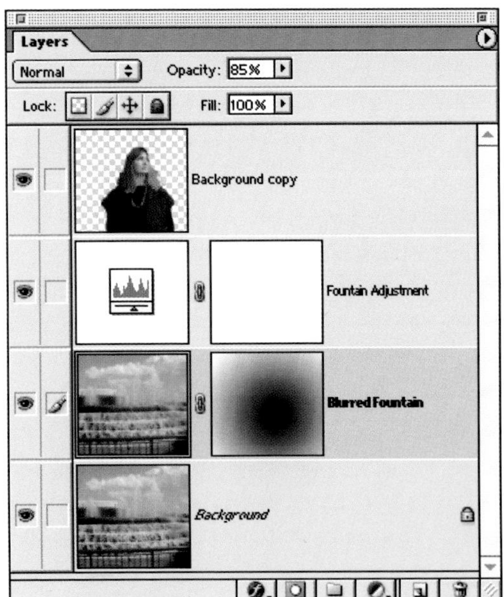

REMOVING CAMERA NOISE

At this point, you can fix the noise in Judy's image. This technique won't work magic, but it goes a long way in fixing much of the problem. You will make a "Judy Sandwich" and then merge the versions.

1 Rename Background copy as **Judy Base**. Choose New Snapshot from the History palette menu, name the snapshot **Judy Base**, and then click the Current Layer option. Move the History Brush icon to this new snapshot.

By creating this snapshot from Current Layer only, you can apply it to any layer you wish.

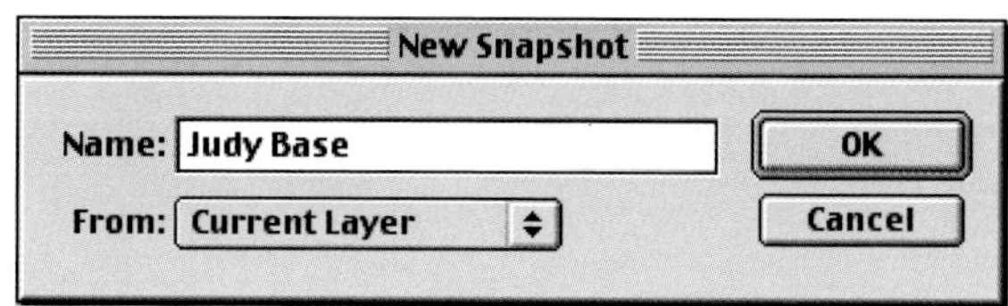

Create a snapshot from the Judy Base layer.

2 Drag the Judy Base layer to the New Layer icon at the bottom of the Layers palette. Name the new layer **Dust and Scratches Color 3**. Choose Filter > Noise > Dust & Scratches. Use a Radius of 3 and a Threshold of 0. Change the Blend mode to Color.

3 Duplicate the Dust and Scratches Color 3 layer. Change the name of the duplicate to **D&S Normal 50 percent**. Change the Blend mode to Normal at 50% Opacity.

4 Make the Judy Base layer active again. Duplicate it and drag the duplicate to the top of the Layers list. Name this layer **Despeckle 3x**. Choose Filter > Noise > Despeckle. Repeat this filter two more times on the layer. Change the layer's Opacity to 50%.

This basic "sandwich" gets rid of a lot of the color artifacts. It has made Judy's features just a bit too soft, though, so on the next step, you'll bring back some of the detail to her eyes, eyebrows, and lips.

5 Click the New Layer icon. Name the layer **Detail**. Choose the History Brush tool and an appropriately sized, soft-edged brush. Brush over Judy's eyebrows, eyes, and mouth.

If the effect is too strong, use the Blur tool at a very low pressure over the eyebrows and mouth. Leave the eyes as the image focus.

6 Turn off the Eye icons on the Background, Blurred Fountain, and Fountain Adjustment layers. Make the Detail layer active. Add a new layer above it. Hold the Shift+Option+Cmd keys on the Mac or the Shift+Alt+Ctrl keys on Windows and then, while still holding those three keys, press the E key.

The visible layers merge in the empty (active) layer and you have a single merged image with all your layers intact.

7 Make the Detail layer active and then click to link to the four layers below that. Choose Layer > New > Layer Set From Linked. Name the Layer Set **Noise Reduction Set** and then turn off its Eye icon. Turn the Eye icons back on for the bottom three layers and make the top layer active. Name the combined layer **Judy Less Noise**.

You have a layer set now that contains all the contributing layers and if you need to revert or try again, you have lost nothing.

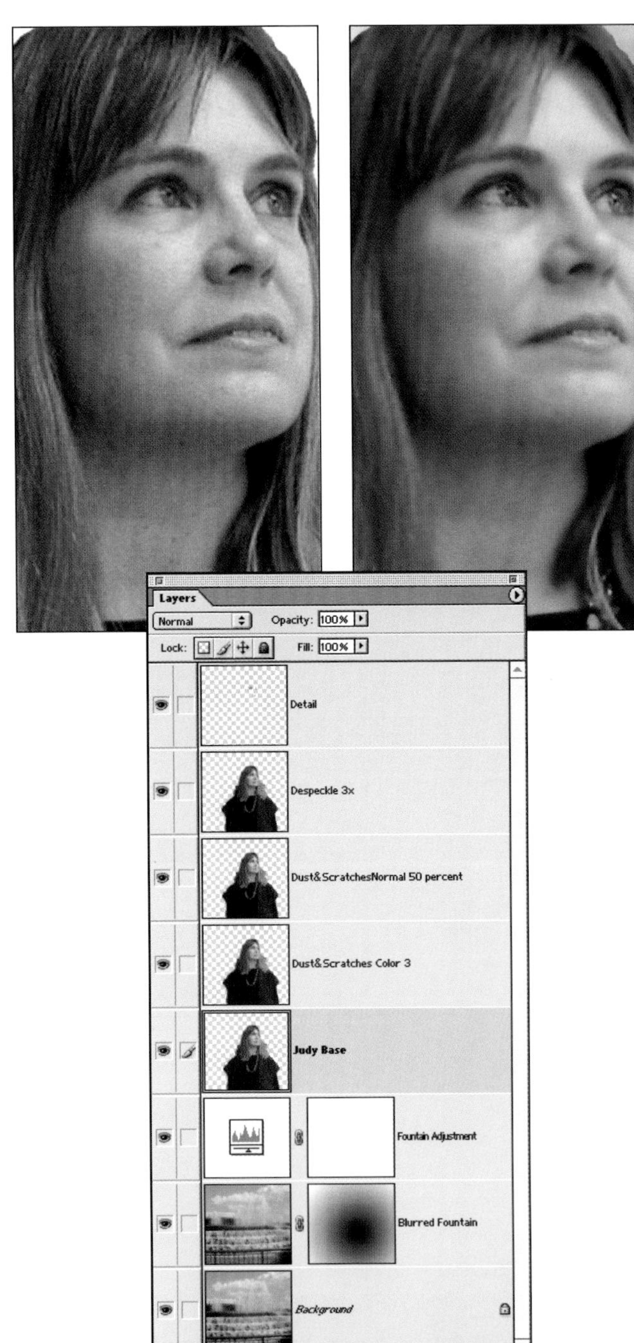

Judy before, Judy after, and the Layers palette.

Brighten the Jacket

Judy's wonderful coat does not show to its best advantage in the image. Even before you adjust the Levels in the image, you can brighten her jacket and jewelry. Again, you will use a nondestructive technique that you can adjust as needed.

1. Make the Judy Less Noise layer active. Add a new Solid Color Fill layer, filled with RGB at 128, 128, 128. Change the mode to Color Dodge and group (Ctrl+G/Cmd+G) the Color Fill layer to the Judy Less Noise layer below.

   The Group with Previous command keeps the Fill layer so that it affects only Judy, and the Color Dodge Blend mode when filled with neutral gray gives an excellent amount of brightness to the image.

2. Choose Image > Adjustments > Invert (Ctrl+I/Cmd+I).

   This makes the Fill Layer Mask black and removes the effect. Now you can point it just where it is needed.

3. With white and a medium-sized Paintbrush, brush over the colored areas of Judy's jacket. Change the brush Opacity to 20% and brush lightly over the arm on the right of the image to add just a hint of sunlight.

   You need not cover all the color areas of the jacket. If you leave some spots darker, it looks like shadow play. Be careful, though, not to brush over the black of her jacket. That needs to remain black.

Note: By Grouping to Judy rather than loading her as a selection and making that the Layer Mask, you can change Judy's edges to make them blend better into the background image. You will not disturb or need to recreate the Fill layer.

4. Change the brush Opacity back to 100%. Choose a smaller brush and brush over Judy's necklace in one brushstroke. Then choose Edit > Fade, and fade the brushstroke to 50–60%.

   Because the necklace will be much too bright, it's important that you reveal it in a single brushstroke that you can fade.

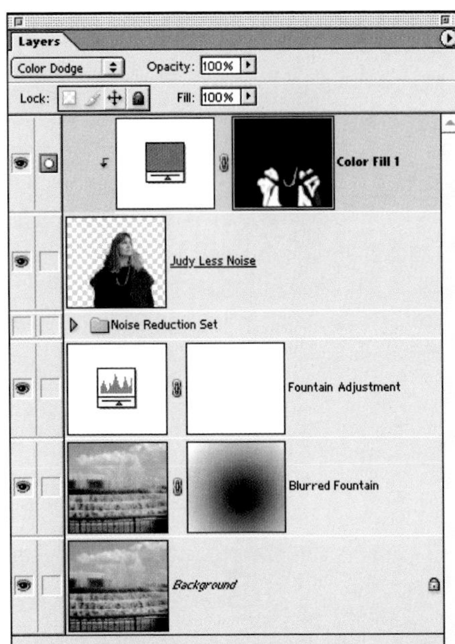

Brush over Judy's necklace in the Layer Mask using one stroke and then fade the stroke to about 50–60%.

Color Correct

Your next step is to add an Adjustment layer to color-correct Judy so that she looks correct in the new background image. This is a fairly easy task because the lighting is similar and the shadows work together.

1. Hold the Option key (Mac) or the Alt key (Windows) and select a Levels Adjustment layer from the New Fill or Adjustment layer icon at the bottom of the Layers palette. In the dialog box, choose Group with Previous. Click OK.

   The Option/Alt key shows you a dialog box so that you can add this layer to the clipping group to affect only Judy's image.

2 Press the Option or Alt key as you drag the white point Input slider to the left. The image turns black. When you start to see splotches of color or white, stop. It should be somewhere near level 243. Adjust the Gamma point to 1.35.

This trick, which is now built into Photoshop, shows you the areas that blow out to white. You need to be especially careful that you don't let any areas on Judy's forehead turn pure white. If you did, the printing would look wrong. If you need to lighten the image, you are somewhat safer moving the Gamma point a bit.

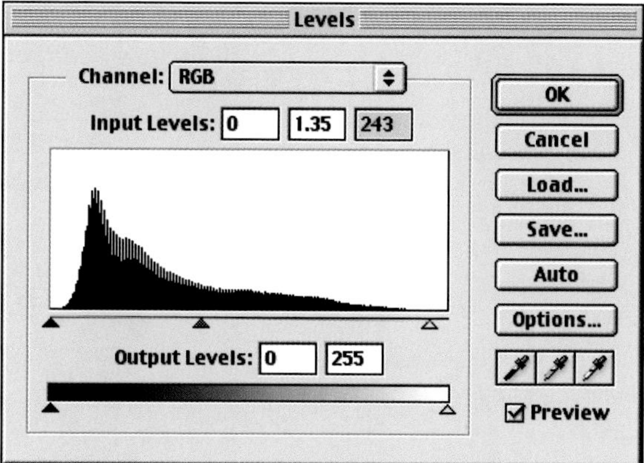

Set the White point and the Gamma point for the Levels Adjustment layer.

Fix Image Edges

"Finally," you say. Yes, it is time to make Judy's hair behave and to blend her into the image correctly.

1 Make the Judy Less Noise layer active. Load the transparency of the layer (Ctrl-click/Cmd-click the layer thumbnail in the Layers palette), and then choose Select > Modify > Contract > Contract by 1 pixel. Click the Add Layer Mask icon.

This chops the edge pixels off Judy's image and makes the blend smoother.

2 With the mask active, choose Filter > Blur Gaussian Blur. Use a Radius of 1.0.

This further helps to blend the edges.

3 Choose a small, soft-edged Paintbrush and black paint and touch up any edges that seem as if they were not well blended. Work along the clean areas of the hairline as well to blend these into the background.

There are few spots that need this, so use a light touch. Don't touch the fly-away hair just yet.

4 You need to create the wisps of hair by working with both small and large brushes and black paint. Change the opacity levels on the brush and change brush sizes to remove all but the small fly-away wisps of hair from the clumps that you left in the Extract command. With low opacity, brush over areas of wisps until they almost disappear. With 80–100 percent opacity and small brushes, clean up the areas that you want to totally remove. Finally, using a combination of small-to-medium brushes and low brush opacity, add some transparency to the area of hair that should see daylight through them. These areas are circled on the image, and you can see the gray shades on the mask.

Mask out all but the wisps of hair from the red-circled areas and add transparency to the hair in the yellow-circled areas.

Finishing Touches

In this section, you merge the layers to get a top layer that you can sharpen (while your other layers remain available). Then you'll sharpen the image itself.

1 Make any final changes to the hair. Add a new layer at the top of the image and, using the History brush with the Judy Base snapshot and 30% opacity, paint back some of the detail in Judy's hair. You might want to make more opaque streaks at full or near-full opacity.

You can paint back just what you need or want to see.

2 Make the Color Fill 1 layer active. Choose the Paintbrush tool. Using about 30 percent opacity and white, add a bit of lightness to Judy's hair to simulate the effect of the sun on it. Work in large areas on one brushstroke and fade the stroke until you like the result.

3 Make the top layer active. Add a new layer (not grouped). Hold the Shift+Option+Cmd keys on the Mac or the Shift+Alt+Ctrl keys on Windows and then, while still holding those three keys, press the E key.

As you did when you combined the Judy Sandwich, you now have a combined image that you can sharpen.

4 Choose Filter > Sharpen > Unsharp Mask with these settings:

Amount: 100%

Radius: 2.0 pixels

Threshold: 3 levels

This setting gives you enough sharpness for print without over sharpening.

5 Choose Edit > Fade Unsharp Mask and change the Blend mode to Luminosity. Leave the Opacity at 100%.

There is a loss of data when you transfer in and out of Lab mode, although most experts agree that sharpening the Luminosity channel of the image is the best way to sharpen an image. Fading to Luminosity does the same thing while staying in RGB mode.

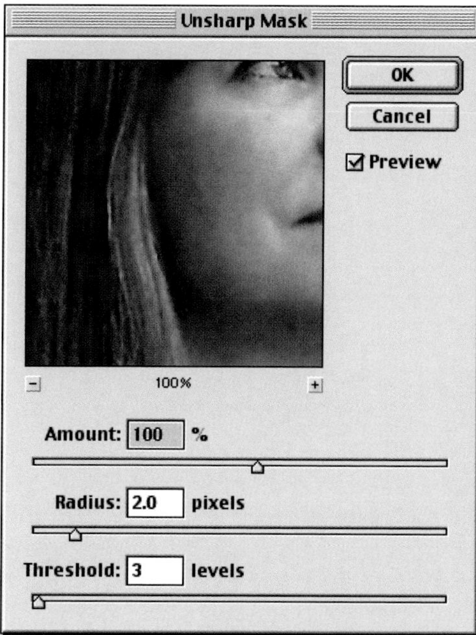

Sharpen the image with these settings.

Modifications

If you need to place the subject into an image with slightly different lighting conditions, you might need to do additional corrections or even add layer effects to help compensate.

In this image, taken in San Francisco, I added a Drop Shadow effect, but I used yellow for the shadow color and Screen mode. I positioned the shadow to look like sunlight behind Judy.

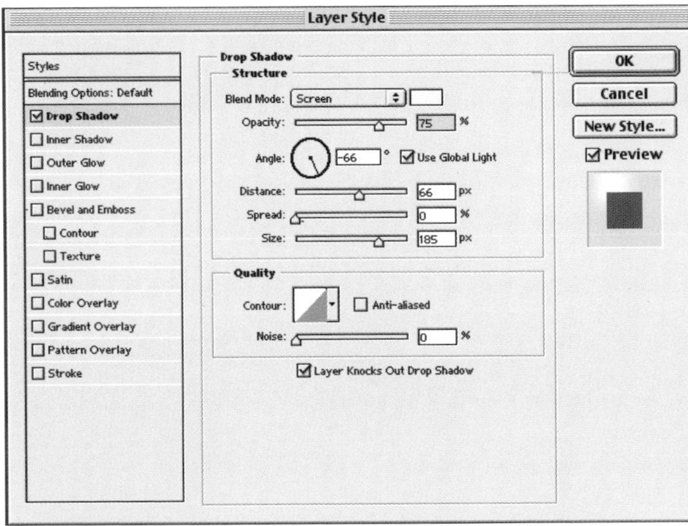

You can add light behind a subject with a modified Drop Shadow effect.

Judy is now visiting San Francisco.

In this image, I used an Inner Glow and Outer Glow effect. In addition, I added a Color Fill layer to make Judy blend into the pink of the image. The key ingredient in all these techniques is to always keep your options open. You need to create Adjustment layers, use Layer effects, Fill layers, and Layer Masks so that you can adjust the image at any point in time.

This image used two layer effects and a Fill layer to make Judy more pink.

FINDING AND APPLYING DETAIL

"The better work men do is always done under stress and at great personal cost."

—WILLIAM CARLOS WILLIAMS

Enhance Photoshop's Capability to Make Something from (Practically) Nothing

With the aid of some third-party plug-ins, you can tease detail out of minimal material and build a respectable image, layer by layer.

Project 14

Finding and Applying Detail

by Helen Golden

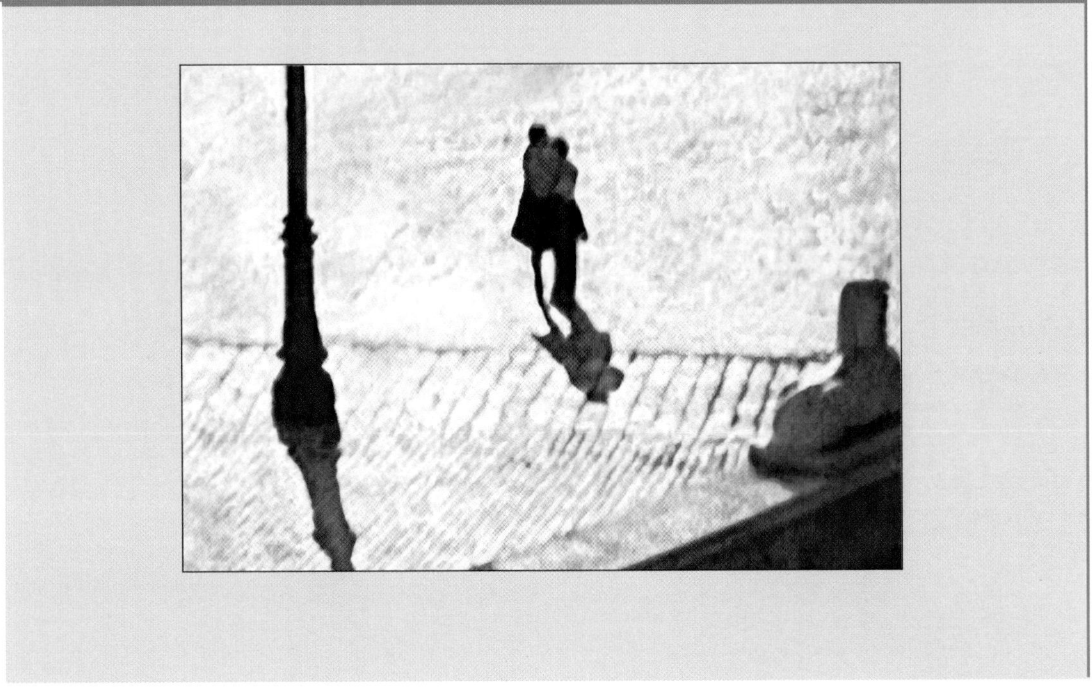

Getting Started

This technique involves developing an image from degraded material by finding hidden information in the image and gradually adding it to the original. You will enlarge and improve a small image several times.

The finished image, called "On The Plaza," was printed on 28×19-inch archival art paper at 150 ppi. The look of the finished piece is similar to that of a pastel painting. The most remarkable aspect of this project is the transformation of a tiny portion of a small photo to a work of art.

1 Copy the LucisArt plug-in from the *Photoshop 7 Magic* CD, as directed by the Read Me files accompanying the demo version of the software.

2. Copy the Genuine Fractals PrintPro plug-in to the Photoshop 7 folder on your hard drive. Follow the directions provided.

3. Quit Photoshop and launch it again. The LucisArt plug-in is now accessible from your Filter menu, and the GF PrintPro feature is available as an additional file format when you save an image.

Consider the Source

"On the Plaza" began as a small detail in a poor quality 35mm slide. The source photograph was taken with a camera that has a cheap plastic lens and that takes half-frame 35mm images. I used only a small part of that image because the forms and composition of that segment interested me.

1. Open the PlazaSource.psd image. With all three layers visible, you can see the entire original photo. The brighter rectangle near the lower right is the tiny section with which you will work.

2. Turn off the visibility of the bottom two layers.

3. The name of the remaining layer tells you the next step: "CopyThisAndMakeNewFile." Here's an efficient way to do that: Make it the active layer and Ctrl-click/Cmd-click the layer's name in the Layers palette. The layer must be made current before Ctrl-clicking it or Copy will not be available in Step 4. This selects the rectangle you want.

Tip: Any non-transparent pixels are selected in this way. Thus, if the portion of an image that you want to select is not easily managed as a rectangle, imagine what a handy shortcut this can be.

4. Choose Edit > Copy (Ctrl+C/Cmd+C) followed by File > New (Ctrl+N/Cmd+N). Click OK.

   Photoshop automatically provides dimensions to match the rectangle you copied.

5 Paste the copied rectangle into the new file (Ctrl+V/Cmd+V), and then flatten the image.

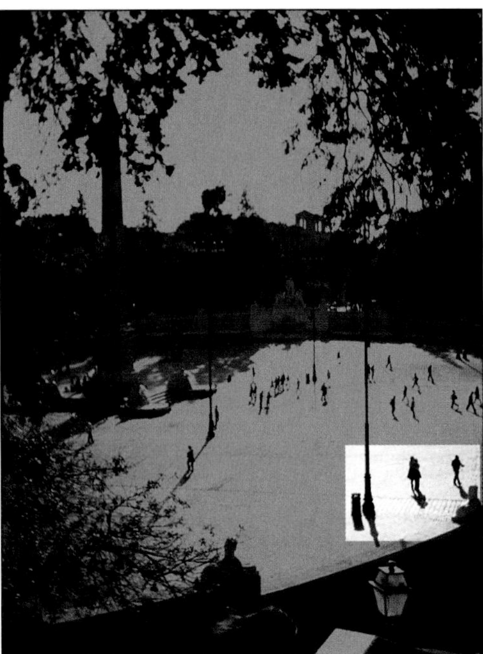

Copy the small detail to a new file.

6 Enlarge this tiny image fragment. Use Image > Image Size and make sure that Constrain Proportions and Resample Image are both enabled. The current image height is about one half inch. Enter 3 inches to increase the image dimensions by approximately 600%. Allow the resolution of 150 ppi to remain unchanged. Click OK but do not save the file.

Enlarge the cropped image by a factor of 6.

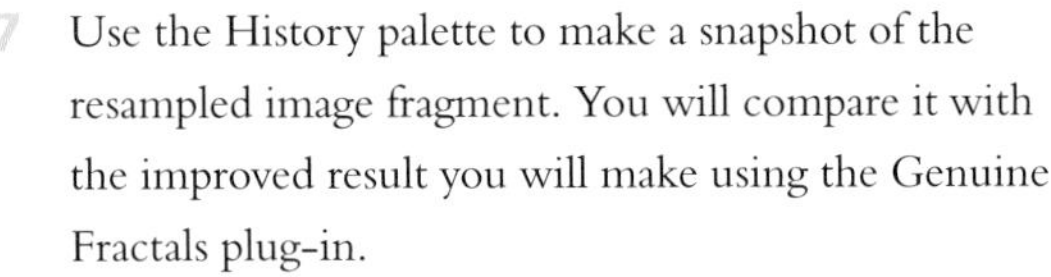

7 Use the History palette to make a snapshot of the resampled image fragment. You will compare it with the improved result you will make using the Genuine Fractals plug-in.

Note: I know what you're thinking. You're about to point out that resampling up is not an effective way to increase the quality of an image. You can't really add more information by simply increasing the resolution or dimensions of a small image. You are correct, of course, and the resulting image is fuzzy, as you would expect. In the next step, however, you will use the Genuine Fractals plug-in to sample up using a method that actually does improve the image quality!

8 Return to the previous state of the image—before enlargement.

9 Use Save As and choose the GF PrintPro (STN) file format in Lossless mode. This automatically saves a copy of the image and applies the .stn suffix. Name this image **FirstEnlargementA.stn**. Close the file.

10 Use File > Open (Ctrl+O/Cmd+O) to access the STN image you just saved. The Genuine Fractals PrintPro dialog box appears. Enter 600% in the Scale fields for Width and Height, which are at the lower left. Choose the Quality High radio button. Click OK. Save this version in PSD format. Name it **FirstEnlargementB.psd**.

Compare the quality of the two enlargements. The Genuine Fractals enlargement has eliminated most of the fuzziness.

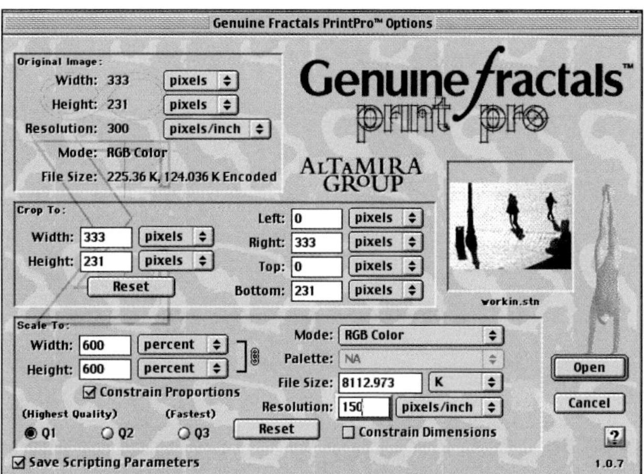

Enlarge the original cropped image with the Genuine Fractals plug-in.

Note: Genuine Fractals PrintPro was designed to increase the quality of images that are already at high resolution. As an artist, I like the idea of pushing the envelope; in this case, I'm using a tool for a purpose other than that for which it was intended.

I felt that the image would be stronger if it had fewer elements. The triangular arrangement of the lamp-post, the couple, and the statue intrigued me. Thus, I removed the other items with Photoshop's new Patch tool.

11 Make a rough Lasso selection around the trashcan and its shadow.

12 Choose the Patch tool. It shares a space on the toolbox with the new Healing Brush.

Compare the original image fragment with the Photoshop resampling and the Genuine Fractals enlargement.

13 Drag the selection to the right until it encloses a clean area of the background. Release your mouse button or stylus. In a moment, the trashcan will be covered by the background.

14 Use the Lasso and Patch tools again to eliminate the walking figure. Be sure to include his shadow in your selection.

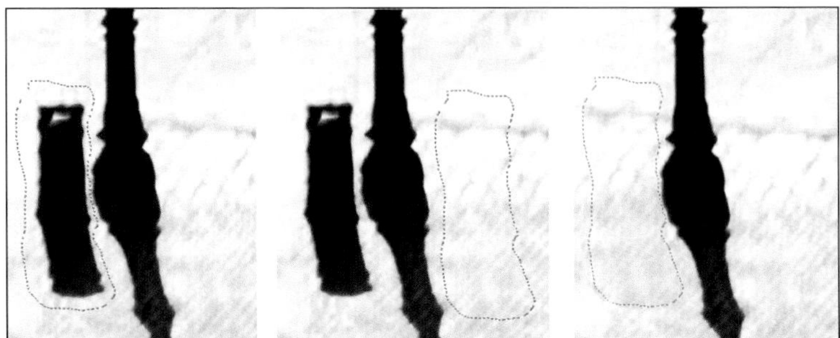

Remove the trashcan with the Patch tool.

15 Repair any imperfections or discolored spots with the Clone Stamp tool.

16 Use the Smudge tool around the edges of all the remaining subjects (lamppost, couple, and statue) to clean up and smooth them.

Remove the walking figure with the Lasso and Patch tools.

Preparing the Clean Image

Get rid of that greenish tinge. Shift toward some pinks and purples.

1 Select the subject areas and their shadows with the Magic Wand. Increase Tolerance to about 150, and turn the Contiguous option off. Click the darkest area of the lamppost. That should select the three subjects almost perfectly and leave all the background unselected.

2 Save the selection to a new channel named **Subjects plus Shadows**.

Save the selection and make it a new Alpha channel.

3 Apply Image > Adjustments > Levels to the selected areas. Make these changes for each color channel:

Red: 1, 1.49, and 230

Green: 0, 1.18, and 251

Blue: 0, 1.38, and 255

Improve the color of the subjects with Levels adjustments.

4 Select > Inverse and alter the color of the background with these settings in Image > Adjustments > Color Balance. Then deselect.

Shadows: +14, -56, and +73

Midtones: -86, -16, and -100

Highlights: -40, -100, and -83

5 Double-click Background in the Layers palette to make the image an independent layer. Rename it **Color Adjusted** and deselect (Ctrl+D/Cmd +D).

Apply Color Balance adjustments to the inverse selection.

Building Detail

In this set of steps, you add layers and use the LucisArt plug-in to tease out detail.

1. Press Ctrl+J/Cmd+J to make a New layer via copy. Name it **LucisArt Modified**, in anticipation of the next step.

2. Apply Filter > Lucis > LucisArt to the new layer. Choose the Exposure option at level three (third button from the left). Move the Mixing slider to 50%. Click the big purple check mark to apply the effect.

Mixing is the equivalent of opacity in Photoshop. Using 100% applies the process at full strength. At 50%, you mix equal parts of the effect and the original. The result is more contrast and enriching detail.

3 Apply the LucisArt Exposure effect to the new layer. Make a copy of the LucisArt Modified layer. Turn off its visibility. You will work with it later.

4 Target the first LucisArt Modified layer and set the Opacity to 25% in Normal mode.

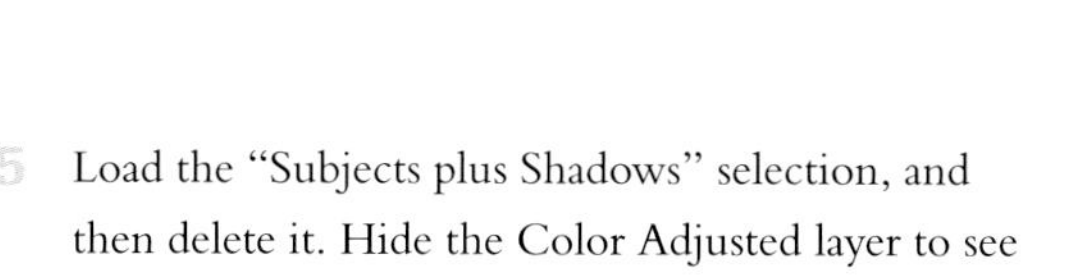

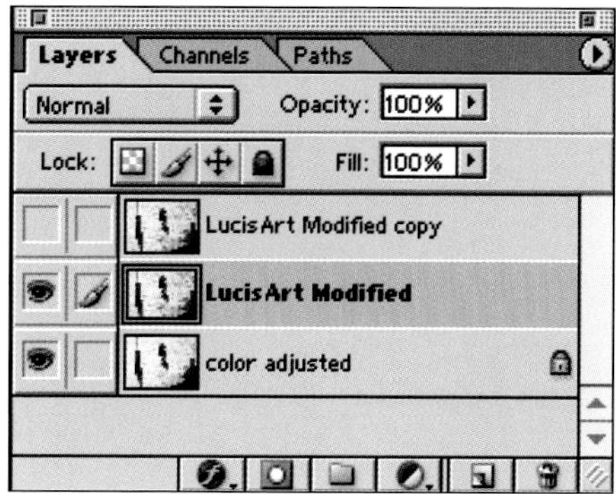

Make a copy of the LucisArt Modified layer.

5 Load the "Subjects plus Shadows" selection, and then delete it. Hide the Color Adjusted layer to see the results.

6 Choose the 25% opacity layer and merge down. Rename the layer **Color Adjust + LucisArt 25%**.

7 Load the "Subjects plus Shadows" selection again. Choose Select > Modify > Expand and enter 1 pixel for the amount. Feather the selection by 2 pixels.

This creates a smooth and soft transition into the surrounding areas when you apply the next effect.

Delete the subjects and shadows. The layer is shown at 100% opacity.

8 Apply a Levels adjustment, using the following values for the specified color channel:

Red: 0, 1.19, and 255

Green: 0, 1.34, and 252

Blue: 0, 1.31, and 255

The subject areas have been lightened a bit, and the colors have been shifted toward blue-green.

9 Now it's time to work with the copy of the LucisArt Modified layer you have been saving. Be sure it is placed over the layer you just altered. Choose Overlay mode and set the layer Opacity to 25%.

You will notice a subtle increase in contrast.

10 Make some artistic improvements using the Dodge tool to brighten highlights, and use the Sponge tool to increase saturation in spots.

11 Use the Clone Stamp tool in Color mode to apply color from one area to another, without changing the tonality of the target pixels.

12 Flatten the image and save it as a GF PrintPro file (in Lossless mode). Name it **SecondEnlargement.stn**. Close the file.

13 Open the file in Photoshop. The GF PrintPro dialog box appears, as expected. Enter 300% for the height and width. Open the file and save it in another format, such as .psd or .tif.

Adjust color levels of the subjects and shadows again.

Use the Clone Stamp, Dodge and Sponge tools as desired.

14 Zoom in to 100% and examine the image for any rough spots. Use the Smudge or Blur tools as needed for touchups.

15 Make any additional tweaks to color balance, and you are done.

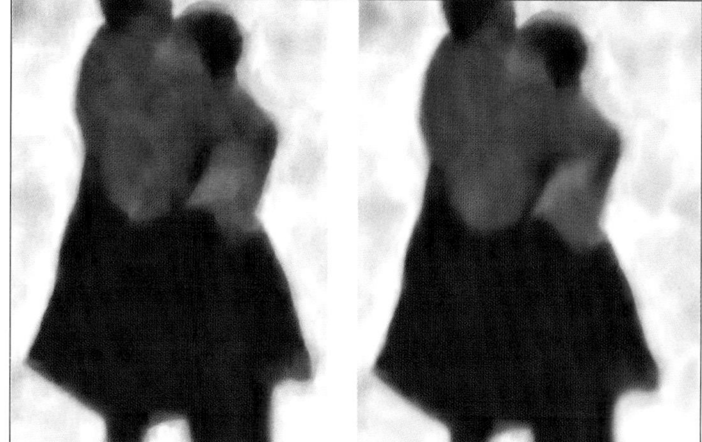

Use the Smudge and Blur tools as needed.

MODIFICATONS

This project should leave you wanting to search through old photos that might contain overlooked potential. Using these techniques, high resolution and detail are not required for source images. Practically any fragment of an image can be turned into a work of art.

Make a small rectangle with the Crop tool and drag it around an image. Look for a tiny section with a simple composition but with interesting contrasts in luminosity, shapes, and textures. The portion of the image that will be removed after you apply the Crop command is darkened, so you can more easily evaluate the selection.

Another project that involves selecting a small portion of an image is Project 6, "Liquid Painting."

SATIN BEVELED TYPE

"A bookstore is one of the only pieces of evidence we have that people are still thinking."

—JERRY SEINFELD

Turn Ordinary Type into an Exciting and Unique Title with Layer Effects

Photoshop offers robust live effects, such as Shadows, Bevel and Emboss, Glows, and Pattern Overlay. Each effect can be turned on and off independently, customized with a vast array of settings, and saved as New Style combinations. A Style can be applied to any layer and is especially effective when used on type or logos.

Project 15

Satin Beveled Type

by Cher Threinen-Pendarvis

Getting Started

The font used for this exercise is Arial Black, but you can use any bold sans serif font you'd like. It's not an exotic or unusual typeface.It is a bold sans serif face, and chances are, you already have it installed. Even if you have worked on Project 1, "Translucency in Typography," don't skip this one—it's completely different.

With Photoshop's Layer Styles options, you can create cool graphic effects for type and logos without the use of multiple channels and masks. Because the effects are live, you can quickly change the look of the effect as you develop it by making choices in the Layer Style dialog box.

Using cloud fills and Lighting Effects, you will create an environment for your title, right out of thin air!

Creating the Background

You will make a cloud-filled sky, enhanced by color and lighting effects. A special background is not really needed for this project, but working on a plain white surface is so boring!

1. Create a new RGB image 768 pixels high by 1074 pixels wide. There is no need to specify resolution.
2. Use the default foreground and background colors, and choose Filter > Render > Clouds. Photoshop generates a gray cloud fill on the background.
3. To color the clouds, add a new layer and fill it with sky blue (RGB 137, 197, 229). Composite this layer with the background using Color mode from the Blending Mode list in the Layers palette.

   Color mode is useful when you want to change hue while leaving brightness variation unchanged.

   Next you create a custom lighting effect.

Fill the background with clouds.

4 Choose Filter > Render > Lighting Effects and select 2 o'clock Spotlight from the pop-up Style menu. Drag the oval in the Preview box to change the direction of the light so that it points down and to the right. Use the other settings shown, and click OK.

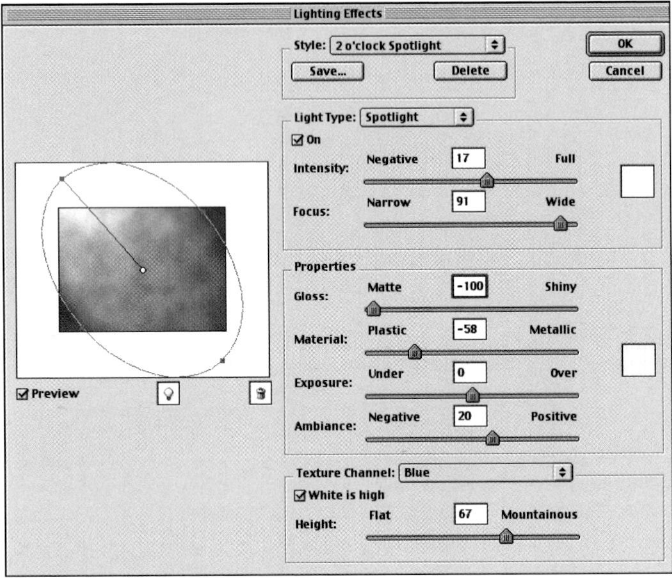

Apply custom lighting to the clouds.

Setting the Type

Now you will create the Type layer and work with Photoshop's text editing features. You can use any font you prefer, but a bold sans serif typeface is suggested.

1 Choose the Horizontal Type tool and click the Palettes button on the Options Bar to open the Character palette. Choose a bold font with wide even strokes from the font menu. Arial Black is used here.

2 Click the Color swatch in the Character palette and choose a foreground color that contrasts with your cloud background. I'll use Magenta with RGB 220, 65, 151. The text you create fills with this color.

The exact color you choose at this point is not critical. Later you apply a Color Overlay to the text in the Style palette.

3 Set the font size to 300 points with 235 for the leading. Type **good**, click Return, and type **style** on a second line. The type automatically occupies its own new layer.

A small value for leading, relative to the font size, makes the two lines fit together snugly.

Note: The Character palette offers sophisticated text editing controls. These include kerning (adjusting the space between two letters), tracking (spacing between all letters), leading (space between lines of type), baseline shift (adjusting the vertical position of selected letters), and independent controls for vertical and horizontal scaling.

You can make adjustments to all text variables on the Options Bar and Character palette, even after the type has been created. To tighten the spacing between two letters by small increments, highlight the letters with the Type tool, and then press the modifier key (Alt/Option) and the left-arrow key. Increase spacing between two letters with the right-arrow key.

4 Adjust kerning or other text attributes in the Character palette. Several letter pairs need kerning so that the letter spacing is optically correct.

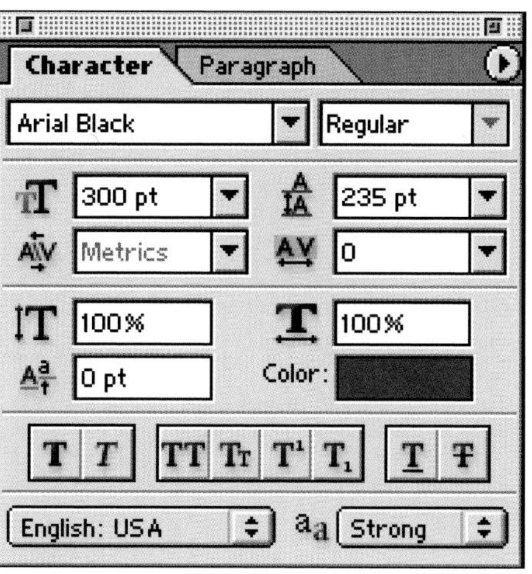

Set variables for the Type tool.

Type the "good style" title.

Adding Special Effects

This is the heart of the project! You'll apply several Layer Styles to your type and as you add each one, the "good style" title will develop more complexity and richness. Layer Styles can be applied in any order.

1 Choose Bevel and Emboss from the "f" pop-up menu at the bottom of the Layers palette. The "f" stands for "effects." Use the settings shown, but don't click OK just yet.

2 Some of the default settings for Bevel and Emboss can remain or can be adjusted slightly. Depth and Size are doubled to increase the bevel amount. The most dramatic departure from the default settings is made to the Shadow mode and color. Change from Multiply to Screen mode and click the Black color swatch to pick a pale (nearly white) blue. This gives the type a lustrous glow, even before any real Glow effect is applied.

Tip: Multiply mode always results in a darker color (unless it is combined with white). Screen mode lightens the color with which it is blended.

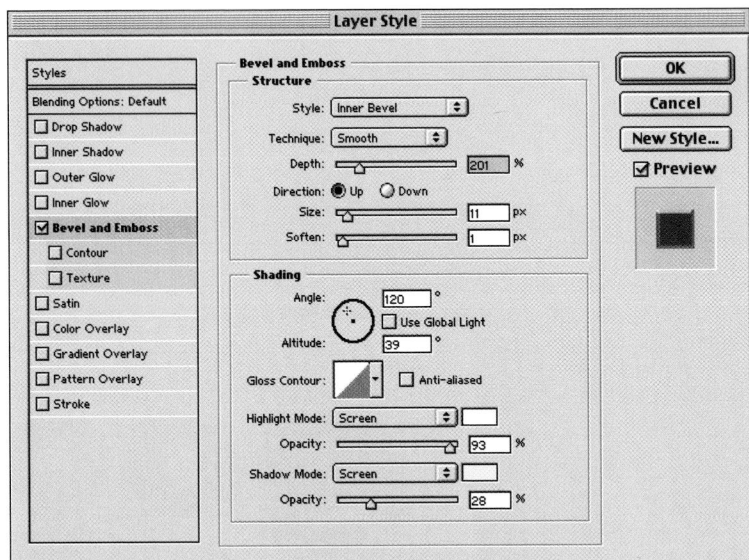

Customize the Bevel and Emboss settings.

Apply Bevel and Emboss to the text layer.

Continue adding Layer Style effects.

1. Apply Inner Glow.
2. There are three groups of settings. Major changes are required for the Structure section. Change Blend mode from Screen to Overlay, making the result darker. Choose the Gradient button instead of the solid-color button. Append the Metals gradient to the default gradients and choose the Gold preset.
3. In the Elements section, change Technique from Softer to Precise and increase the size from 5 to 6 pixels. The Quality settings should remain unchanged.
4. Apply Inner Shadow.
5. Change the shadow color from black to a deep burgundy with RGB 99, 41, 74.
6. Set Angle to 131 degrees, Distance to 7 pixels, Choke to 4%, and Size to 4 pixels.
7. Apply Satin.
8. Change the color from black to deep blue with RGB 74, 57, 165.

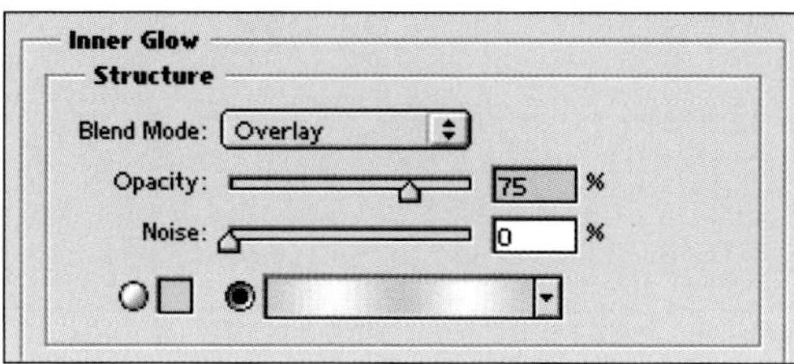

Customize Inner Glow settings.

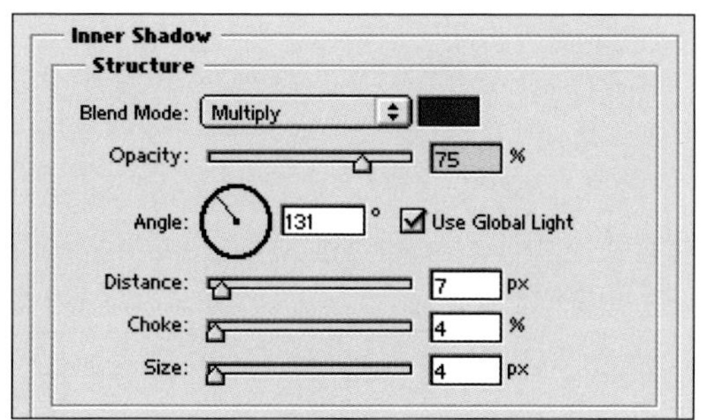

Adjust Inner Shadow values.

9 The most significant change here is in the Contour field. Open the pop-up Contour library and choose the Ring-Double style. This creates a dramatic difference from the default contour. To see exactly how the Satin effect contributes to this custom style, turn off the Layers palette visibility for the other effects.

10 Change the foreground color to a cool light gray with RGB 187, 187, 195.

11 Your choice of gradient strongly affects the result. Apply a Gradient Overlay.

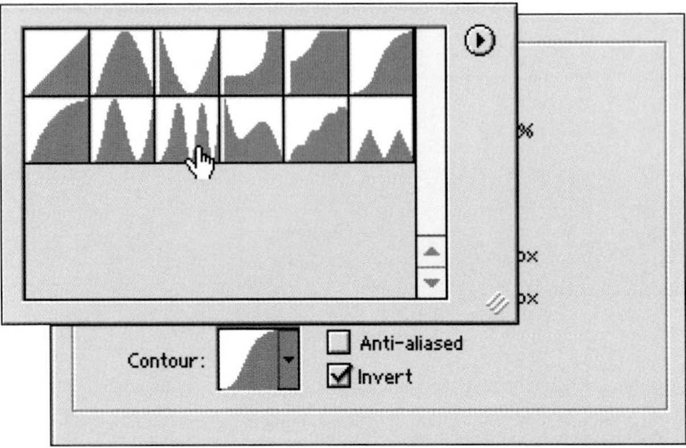

Choose the Ring-Double Contour for the Satin effect.

Enable visibility for the Satin effect only.

12 Now open the Gradient Overlay settings and choose Black, White from the Gradient pop-up menu. Enable Reverse.

13 Change Style from Linear to Radial. Use a 117-degree Angle and increase Scale to 129%.

14 Apply Color Overlay.

15 These settings are pretty basic. Just specify a color, a Blend mode and Opacity. Use purple (RGB 156, 41, 165) in Multiply mode at 100%. This creates more contrast for the Satin effect, and the rich luster of the type is completed.

16 Apply Drop Shadow.

17 Here's the finishing touch for your New Style. It adds to the illusion of depth and volume. Use the following settings:

Opacity: 50%

Angle: 131 degrees

Distance: 15 pixels

Spread: 15%

Size: 8 pixels

Other settings remain at their default values.

18 Save all Layer effects with the New Style button, naming them **Satin Bevel** or anything else you like. They will appear in your current Styles library and can be viewed as a thumbnail preview or by name.

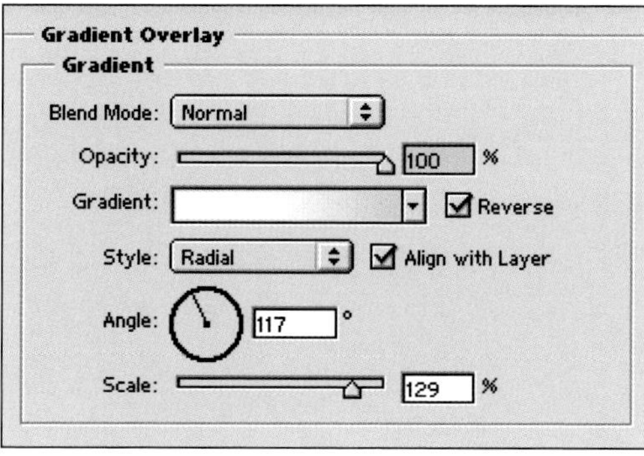

Customize the Gradient Overlay effect.

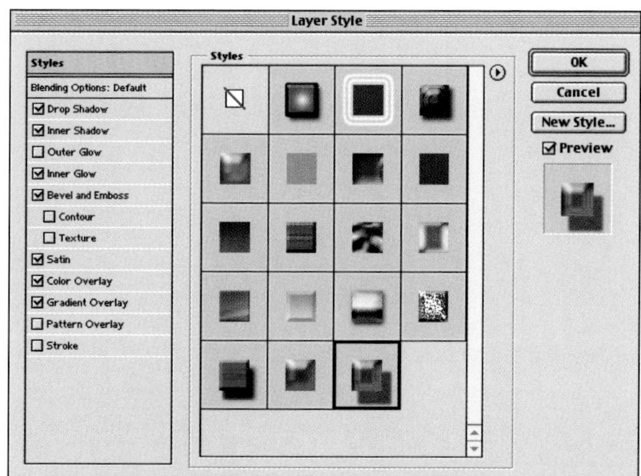

Add your custom effects to the Styles library.

MODIFICATIONS

Scaling live effects to fit: If you follow my settings and apply them to a different font and they don't look similar, consider scaling the effect to fit the width of your letterforms. Choose Layer > Layer Style > Scale Effects, and when the dialog box appears, type a larger or smaller percentage into the field to scale the effect. Continue to experiment with the scaling until you're pleased with the effect.

This style can be the source of several similar styles, each of which can be saved with a unique name. Gold Rush began with a font called Stanyan Bold. I typed it over a background made from the Gold gradient in the Metals Gradient library.

I wanted to see how the Satin Bevel style would work on a font with variables, shaky forms, and sketchy lines. The striations from the Satin effect, which look so smooth and even on Arial Black, are wavy and irregular when applied to this casual font. I felt the color needed to be much warmer, so I changed the Color Overlay from purple to golden yellow. The drop shadow needed adjustment, too. I moved the drop shadow closer to the letterforms, reduced its opacity, and chose Rounded Steps for the contour. I saved the changes as a New Style called Gold.

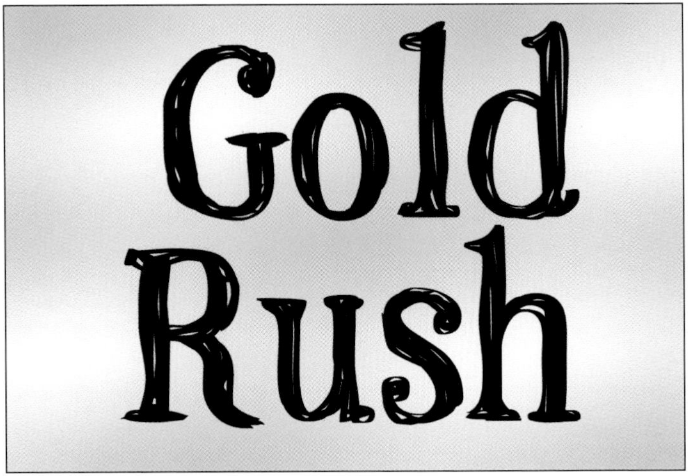

Begin with a sketchy or quirky font.

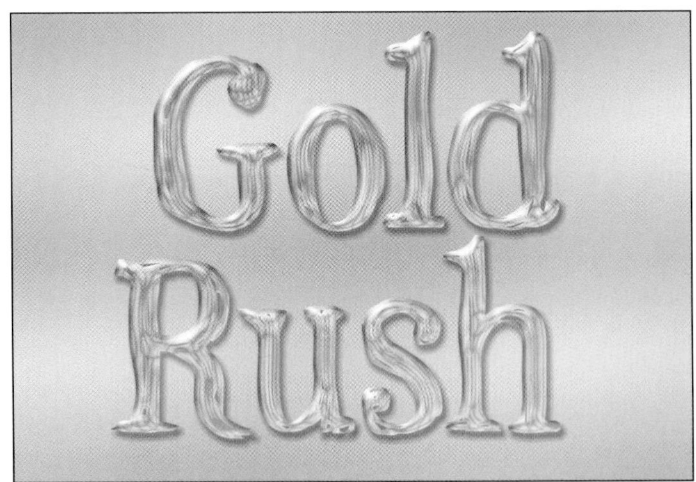

Change Color Overlay and Drop Shadow settings for a New Style.

Working with Sand, another quirky typeface that suggests the letters are melting or runny, I got the look of butter by simply turning off the Satin effect in the Gold style.

Remove the Satin component to get the Butter style.

Vivaldi is an elegant script font, and I wanted a cool, icy look this time. Using the Gold style, I simply changed the Color Overlay to a sky blue, and saved the New Style as Ice.

Change Color Overlay to blue for a cool, icy effect.

PUSHING AROUND COLOR

"There are no great things, only small things with great love. Happy are those."

—MOTHER THERESA

Creating Good Images from Bad Ones

I've made something of a career out of retrieving not-quite-good-enough and really-totally-awful images. For some reason, there are a lot more poor photos than good ones, but in the publishing world, you sometimes just have to use what you have and hope for the best. The key to all this, of course, is to push what Photoshop can do far beyond normal auto-correction.

Project 16

Pushing Around Color

by David Xenakis

Getting Started

Last spring, I needed a somewhat romantic-looking shot of someplace in Sioux Falls. I walked over to the river a couple of blocks from the office and took this photograph. Unfortunately, it was not a bright day, rather overcast and dull, and I was using 35mm slide film. After developing the film at a quick photo place, I scanned it on the drum scanner. There was starting to be a bit of grass, but I wanted a look that was cool and wet and just beginning to be green. My other problem with this image was that the water was muddy with the field run-off, and I needed to make it look not quite so disgusting. However, this is the image that I had, and I needed to make it into the image I envisioned.

In this project, I'll show you the best kind of magic—magic you can use in your everyday work to get more quality from your photographs than you might ever have thought possible. This is practical magic in what many think of as the "black art" of color correction.

START WITH A SCAN

Your scan is the most important resource that you have. You need to capture as much detail as possible in the scan because if it isn't in the scan, you don't have enough to work with. We have a Howtek 4500 drum scanner, and though it has fabulous software, I don't let my scanner operator do anything other than capture the raw data. In other words, I want all the data I can get, and the auto-correction routines built into the scanners just throw away too much data to enable me to push the images as far as I like. Later in this project, I will show you that because of the way I scanned this image, you still have a full range of unposterized data after you have done all your corrections.

There are three things that can help if you need to scan a poor quality original:

- Scan larger than you think necessary. That way, when you size down, you'll get much better detail. This is especially true if you have to work with photo prints (which are not my favorite—I much prefer to scan the film).
- Do not let the scanner auto-correct or sharpen or do anything. Just make it capture the data and give you everything it can see.
- If the image is really poor, and you have all the original data in it, you can put it into 48-bit mode and push the dickens out of it before you convert back and work normally. Bicubic interpolation is our friend!

Note: In the case of a poor original, it is much better to have the scanner dump it directly into 48-bit mode. However, if the scanner won't do that (although most of the newer ones do), changing it in Photoshop, working on it, and then changing it back makes a precision of adjustment that is almost not to be believed.

If you have never used 48-bit color, you might have no idea that Photoshop can deal with this at all. When you scan, generally you scan into 24-bit color space. This means that in an RGB image, each channel can hold 8-bit color, or 256 shades of gray. In 48-bit color, each channel can hold 16 bits worth of data. This is many more colors than is possible in Photoshop's normal working mode and gives you a huge latitude for correcting an image without losing data.

The downside of this is that Photoshop cannot use layers when you work in 16-bit mode. Therefore, you can't attach the Adjustment Layers that I prefer to use. However, you still can make the most of the adjustments that you need and then convert the image back into 8-bit mode. You make this conversion using the Image > Mode menu.

Note that when I am working in 48-bit color, I usually use a set of small adjustments instead of one large one. It just seems to work better, but I don't know why.

A Color Correction Action

I always use three Adjustment Layers for color correction: Levels, Color Balance, and Hue/Saturation. Because I use this trio all the time, I have made myself an action that automatically adds these layers. I think you will find it useful.

1. Create a new file that is 300-pixels square.

   The size doesn't matter at all on this. It is a throw-away file whose only purpose is to help you create the action.

2. Click the Create new action icon at the bottom of the Actions palette and name the action **Make Correction Layers**. Click the Record button.

3. Choose Levels from the Create new fill or adjustment layer menu at the bottom of the Layers palette. Don't make any changes to the Levels; simply click OK.

   All you are doing is adding blank Adjustment Layers that don't change your image. This is simply a shortcut so that you don't need to think about the order in which you need to place the Adjustment Layers.

4. Add a Color Balance layer from the Create new fill or adjustment layer menu at the bottom of the Layers palette. Again, make no changes to it. Finally, add a blank Hue/Saturation Adjustment Layer. Click the Stop playing/recording button to end the action.

5. Close the empty file. You won't need it again.

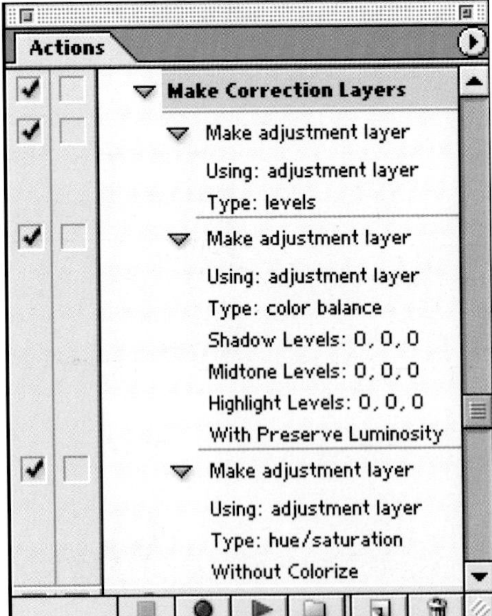

Create an action that adds blank Levels, Color Balance, and Hue/Saturation Adjustment Layers to your image.

6 Open the image spring.psd from the accompanying CD.

Open the image spring.psd.

7 Highlight the action that you just created and click the Play Selection button.

The action should automatically add the three Adjustment Layers.

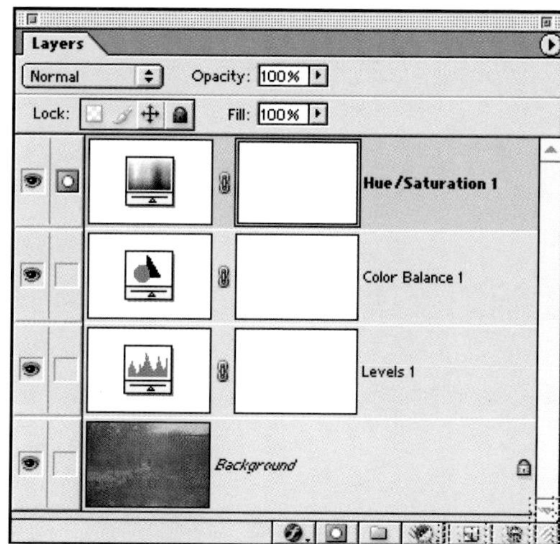

Play the Make Correction Layers action.

8 Choose Edit > Color Settings and change the Settings field to Color Management Off.

I don't like profiles and I don't think they work well. If you have a profile set in your system, you will see a strange version of the spring.psd image. If you absolutely don't want to change your color settings for this technique, choose View > Proof Setup > Monitor RGB.

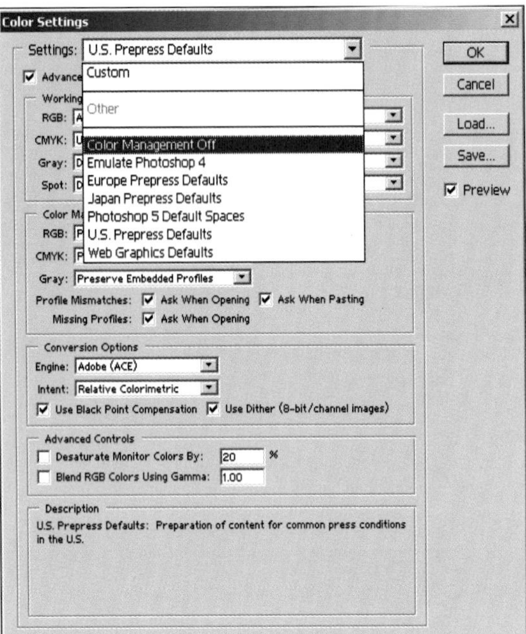

Turn off Photoshop's Color Management.

Applying Levels

In the Levels correction, you deliberately blow out the highlights. The sky is gray anyway and you need to create a strong contrast. The strong contrast also brings out a lot of the details that simply get lost otherwise. For example, it brings out the fine branches in the trees in the middle distance. In fact, without pushing the contrast, you have trouble seeing the ducks in the water.

You will adjust each channel individually.

1 Double-click the Levels 1 adjustment layer thumbnail to open the Levels dialog box.

You need to click the leftmost thumbnail icon on the layer—not on the Layer Mask.

2 Before you start to adjust anything, look at the Levels histogram. Hold the Option key on the Mac or the Alt key on Windows and drag the White point Input slider to the left until it is past the "hump" on the Histogram. Then drag it all the way back to the right so that you have made no changes.

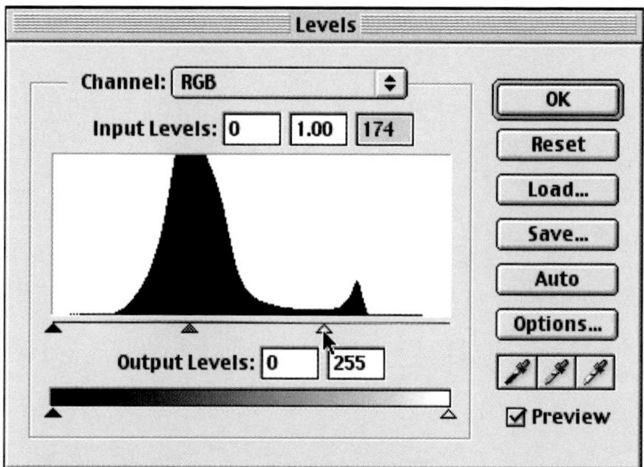

Holding the Option or Alt key, drag the White point Input slider to the left.

You'll notice that the area that turns white is the sky. That "hump" contains the values for the sky and for almost nothing else in the image. Taken as a whole, there is a huge lack of contrast in the histogram, with most of the values huddled to the left, just past center. There are no true whites or blacks. If you looked only at the Histogram and not at the image at all, you could have predicted a grayed-out, dull image simply by looking at the range of values. You need to explore the Histogram simply to get an idea of your correction strategy. You now know that you can cut off the hump in each channel and all you will do is blow out the sky (which you can repair later).

3 Make the Red channel active in the Levels dialog box by choosing it from the drop-down menu or by pressing Ctrl+1/Cmd+1. Set the White point Input slider to 186 and the Black point Input slider to 62. This looks weird right now, but it won't when you are done. Don't change the Gamma point of the channel.

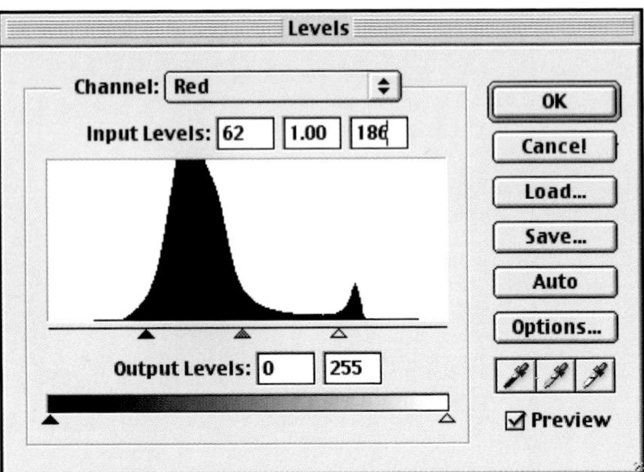

Set the Red channel values to 62, 1.0, 186.

4 Make the Green channel active in the Levels dialog box by choosing it from the drop-down menu or by pressing Ctrl+2/Cmd+2. Set the White point Input slider to 187 and the Black point Input slider to 52.

The Green channel has almost the same histogram shape as the Red channel, and you are moving the sliders to the same approximate locations along the shape of the histogram.

5 Make the Blue channel active in the Levels dialog box by choosing it from the drop-down menu or by pressing Ctrl+3/Cmd+3. Set the White point Input slider to 179 and the Black point Input slider to 40.

If you switch back to the composite channel, you'll notice that the Histogram has changed to show you the new levels. You have a full range of color with a very mild posterization (which we will fix later). You have spread out your values without creating a huge spike at the white end of the scale.

6 Click OK to exit the Levels dialog box.

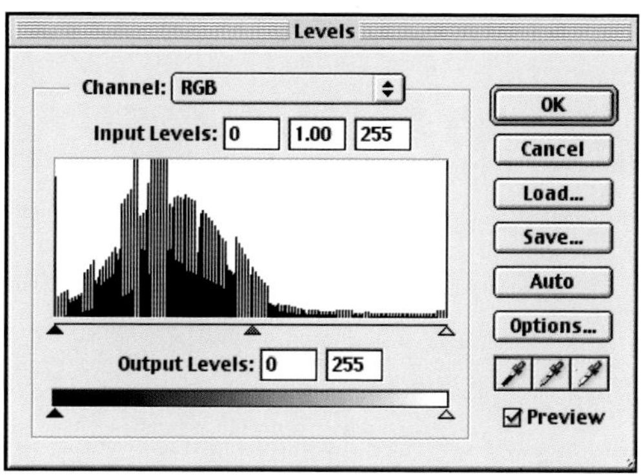

Check the composite channel to see the result of the three channel adjustments.

Color Balance

Although there is some green in this image, there is too much red. In the Color Balance layer, you will push green and yellow (and cyan) into the highlights and midtones. You then will pump a little red back into the shadows to keep them from becoming too blue-casted.

1 Double-click the thumbnail icon on the Color Balance 1 layer to open the Color Balance dialog box.

Color Balance enables you to make adjustments to compensate for color casts more successfully than you could do in the Levels dialog box, in my opinion. You can adjust the shadows, midtones, and highlights independently.

2 Click the Highlights option button and check the Preserve Luminosity check box. Change the color sliders to +2 on the Magenta to Green slider and to –11 on the Yellow to Blue slider. Don't change the Cyan to Red slider.

You are adding some additional green and yellow to the highlights of the image.

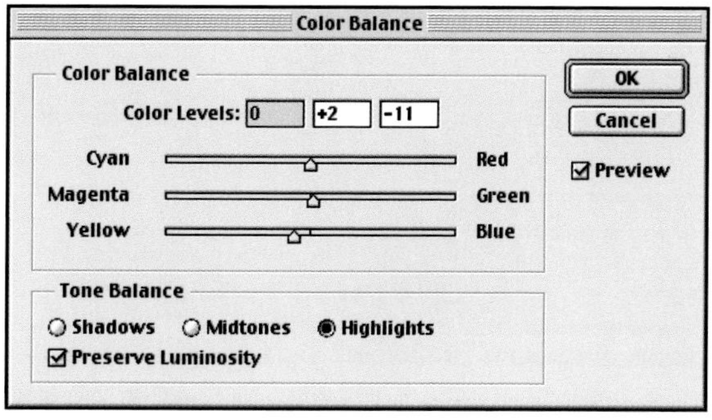

Change the Highlights Color Balance option to 0, +2, –11.

Note: I always start by adjusting the Highlights. The upper Midtones and lower Highlights are all in that very visible range where any correction is easily visible. It always seems to me that if I do things the other way, I have to go back and do it again. If I start with highlights, it's all done in three steps.

3 Click the Midtones option button. Change the color sliders to –6 on the Cyan to Red slider, +7 on the Magenta to Green slider, and to –11 on the Yellow to Blue slider.

This removes some red from the image while bumping up the green and yellow, giving the images a much healthier spring cast. Don't close the dialog box yet.

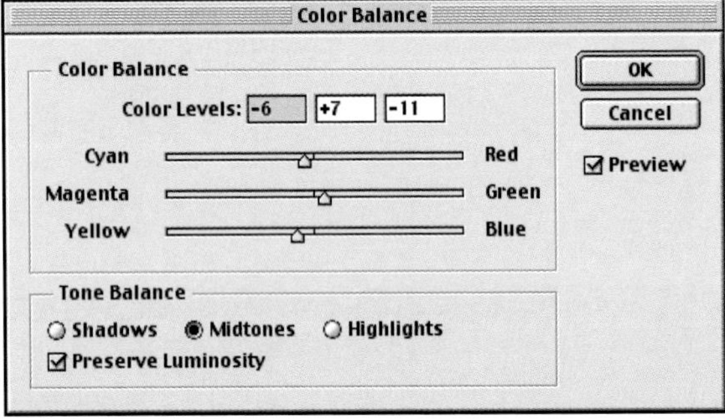

Change the Midtones Color Balance to –6, +7, and –11.

4 Click the Shadows option button. Change the Cyan to Red slider to +8, the Magenta to Green slider to +5, and the Yellow to Blue slider to –3. Click OK to save your changes and exit the dialog box.

You are adding some additional red, green, and yellow to the shadow areas of the image. Notice how this pumps the greens and yellows, but they are now a bit too bright for the lighting conditions in the image. This is not a problem. I almost always pump the color on this step because I know that I can modify it with the Hue/Saturation layer.

Hue/Saturation

In the Hue/Saturation layer, you will give the colors a fine tweak. You will desaturate and darken the green a tiny amount and saturate and darken the blue a bit. This yields the appropriate shades for the water and the grass. It also adds a hint of green to the trees (which was not in evidence before).

1. Double-click the icon for the Hue/Saturation layer to open the dialog box. Select Greens from the Edit drop-down menu. Set the Saturation slider to –16 and the Lightness slider to –13. Don't close the dialog box yet.

   This change will be most noticeable under the trees on the upper hillside, which is on the left side of the image.

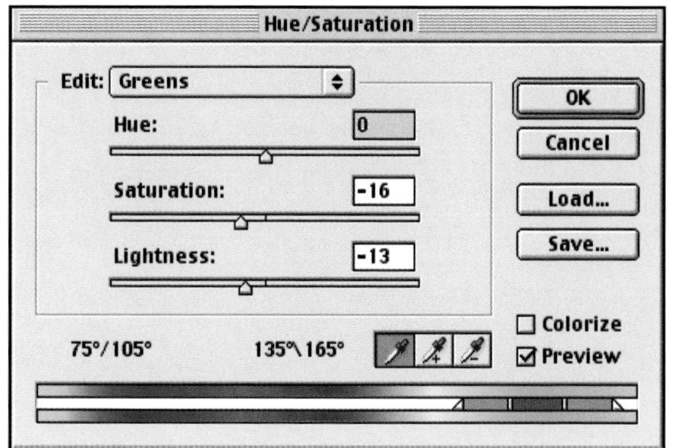

Set the Saturation slider to –16 and the Lightness slider to –13 for the Greens in the Hue/Saturation layer.

2. Select Blues from the Edit drop-down menu. Set the Saturation slider to +12 and the Lightness slider to –13.

3. The Blues settings actually control most of the color in the trees. You can tell this by dragging the Saturation slider all the way to the right before you give it the final settings.

4. In the Master Hue/Saturation controls, bump the Saturation slider to +2. Click OK to close the dialog box.

Creating a New Sky

Next, I need to give a hint of blue to the sky for this cool light to work. There doesn't have to be much color, just enough so that the sky isn't white. You'll use the Select > Color Range command to select the sky and then use a Quick Mask to touch up the selection. Finally, you'll add a Color Fill layer for this selection.

1 Make the Background layer active. Choose Select > Color Range. Drag the Fuzziness slider back to 0, and then click in the center of the sky area. You should see the preview of the sky appear in the dialog box, clearing out any existing selection. Now drag the Fuzziness slider to 60. Click OK to exit the Color Range command.

You pick up the sky and not much else when you set the Fuzziness slider to 60.

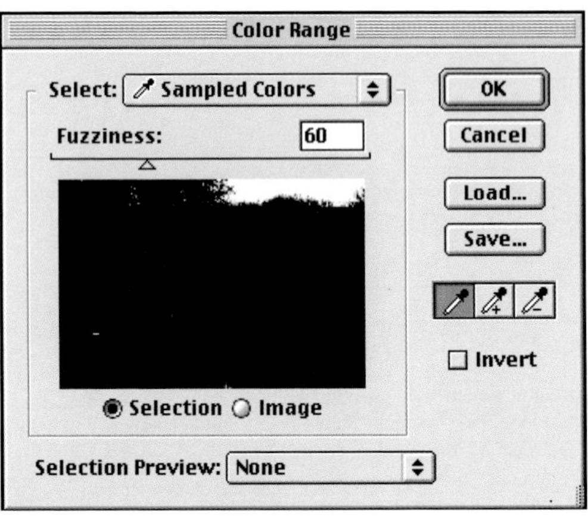

Using the Select > Color Range command, click the sky and set the Fuzziness slider to 60.

2 Press Q to enter Quick Mask mode. Use a hard-edged brush with black as your foreground color (or use the Lasso or Rectangular Marquee tool) and remove from the selection any areas that are not part of the sky. (The arrow in the image shows where many of the stray pixels are located.) Don't go back to Normal selection mode just yet.

Note: You will see the Quick Mask for this step more easily if you double-click its entry in the Channels palette and change Opacity to 80%. That will make it mostly red so that you can tell exactly what is red-coated and what is not.

Remove from the selection all areas that are not part of the sky.

3. Choose Filter>Blur>Gaussian Blur. Give it a Radius of 1. Click OK. Then press Q to return to Normal selection mode.

   I use a tiny Gaussian Blur almost every time to make the edges of the selection merge more easily with what it adjoins. One reason that I prefer to use Quick Mask is that I can also apply whatever blurring is needed to make a smooth selection.

4. Make the top layer active. Your selection is still active as well. Add a new Solid Color Fill layer from the Create new fill or adjustment layer menu at the bottom of the Layers palette. Set the color to RGB 0, 219, 170. Leave the Blend mode at Normal but change the Opacity to 5%.

   Even though it's hard to see, this sky color gives credibility to all the blue and green tones I pumped into the darker areas of the photo. In addition, because I blurred the selection, you can see that the blue cancels the little bit of red fringing on the silhouetted branches against the sky.

Give the Quick Mask a Gaussian Blur with a radius of 1 pixel.

Note: I use this technique all the time in other ways to pump the color in an image—use the fill that is complimentary to the tone you want to pump and then put it at 15% Opacity and either Color or Saturation mode. It's great!

SHARPENING THE IMAGE

Before you convert your image to CMYK for printing, you need to sharpen it. This image was shot with 35mm film, and when you make a scan this large and push the contrast as far as we did, all the film grain shows up (which is not a benefit).

Here's how I handle film grain. I run the Despeckle filter, and then use the Unsharp mask. Here is the general formula: Amount = Image Resolution × .66. In this case, 300 ppi × .66 = 200. Radius = Amount × .005, or 200 × .005 = 1. Threshold is something I always leave at 0.

If you try to apply that much sharpening to the original, you'll find that it intensifies the film grain and looks awful. However, on top of the Despeckle, it looks good. Because Knitter's is now printed CTP (computer-to-plate) with stochastic screens, we've found that we have to be much more careful in using the Unsharp Mask filter.

With the amount of apparent resolution you get with stochastic screens, if you sharpen too much, the halo and the anti-halo actually show up on the press, which makes the image look like a bad X-acto composite job.

1. Drag the Background layer to the Create a new layer icon at the bottom of the Layers palette to duplicate the layer.

   I like to keep my original image as the Background layer.

2. Choose Filter > Noise > Despeckle.

   This is a one-step filter and has no settings. However, the Despeckle filter fills in almost all the gaps in any image left by the Levels adjustments.

3. Choose Filter > Sharpen > Unsharp Mask, and then make these selections:

   Amount: 200%

   Radius: 1 pixel

   Threshold: 0 levels

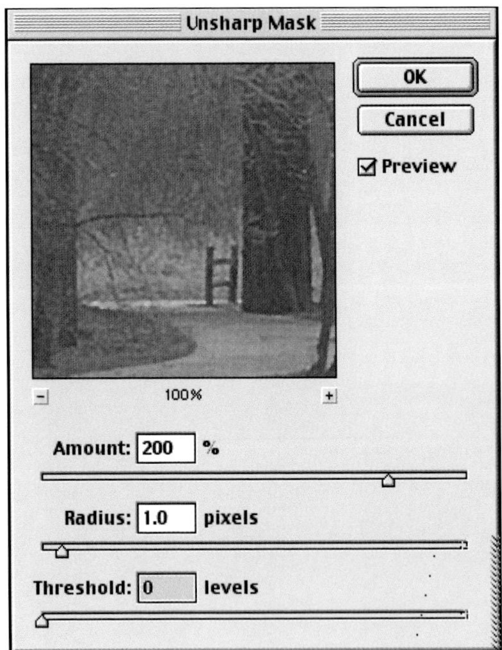

Choose Filter > Sharpen > Unsharp Mask and use an Amount of 200, a Radius of 1, and a Threshold of 0.

I used the formula explained previously to arrive at these settings. If you need to resize your image after you have done the color correction layers, don't use the Unsharp Mask filter until you have made the image the correct size. Otherwise, you lose some of your sharpening to Bicubic Interpolation.

Convert to CMYK

When you convert your image to CMYK, you should consult with your printer for the settings that are best for the press that will be used. However, if you are unable to get any direction from your printer or are looking for general purpose settings, you can use the settings that I give you in this section.

The setting in the following steps is a general purpose setting for coated stock. It prints dynamite press proofs on the digital proofer, and you can nail those in the pressroom. Set the separations to GCR, Light Black Generation, 26% Dot Gain, 300% Total Ink, and 10% UCA.

Here's how to set this up:

1. Choose Edit > Color Settings. Choose Custom CMYK from the Working Spaces CMYK drop-down menu. Use these settings:

   Ink Colors: SWOP (Coated)

   Dot Gain: Standard 26%

   Separation Type: GCR

   Black Generation: Light

   Black Ink Limit: 100%

   Total Ink Limit: 300%

   UCA Amount: 10%

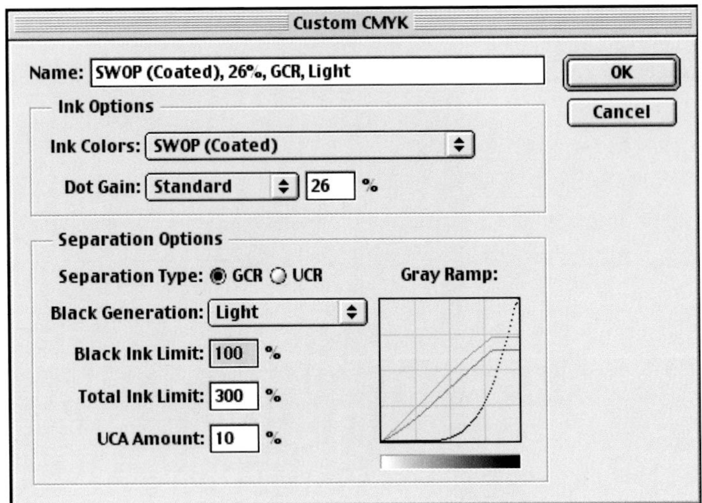

Create a new CMYK separation with these settings.

Note: You have pushed this color around and now have more quality than was in the original. However, if you were to add a new Levels Adjustment layer as the top layer in the image, you would see that you still have a full range of tones with no gaps or posterization.

Modifications

Now that you have an idea of how to color correct images, you can try your hand with this small, terrible photo of a dining room. In reality, the table is mahogany and the rug is beige-off-white. The cake is pink, and the fruit consists of oranges, green grapes, and strawberries. The before (diningroom.psd) and after (diningroomdone.psd) files are on the accompanying CD-ROM. For good measure, also open the Falls.psd image and look at the corrections. My notes about the image are embedded in the Notes icon for the file.

Can you change this...

to this?

"You shall know the truth, and the truth shall make you mad."

—ALDOUS HUXLEY

APPENDIX A

What's on the CD-ROM

The accompanying CD-ROM is packed with all sorts of exercise files and products to help you work with this book and with Photoshop 7. The following sections contain detailed descriptions of the CD's contents.

For more information about the use of this CD, please review the ReadMe.txt file in the root directory. This file includes important disclaimer information, as well as information about installation, system requirements, troubleshooting, and technical support.

Technical Support Issues

If you have any difficulties with this CD, you can access our web site at **www.newriders.com**.

System Requirements

This CD-ROM was configured for use on systems running Windows NT Workstation, Windows 95, Windows 98, Windows 2000, and Macintosh. Your machine will need to meet the following system requirements for this CD to operate properly:

Processor: 486DX or higher

OS: Microsoft Windows 95/98/NT or higher/MAC OS8.x or higher

Memory: 24MB

Monitor: VGA, 800×600 or higher with 256 color or higher

Free Space: 10MB minimum (will vary depending on installation)

Software: Latest Media Player by Microsoft (for Mac and PC)

Other: Mouse/Pointing device, soundcard, and speakers

Browser: IE 5.5 or higher or Netscape 6 or higher

Optional: Internet connection

Loading the CD Files

To load the files from the CD, insert the disc into your CD-ROM drive. If Autoplay is enabled on your machine, the CD-ROM setup program starts automatically the first time you insert the disc. You may copy the files to your hard drive or use them right off the disc.

Note: This CD-ROM uses long and mixed-case filenames, requiring the use of a protected mode CD-ROM driver.

Exercise Files

This CD contains all the files you'll need to complete the exercises in *Photoshop 7 Magic*. These files can be found in the root directory's Projects folder. There are no files for Project 15.

Third-Party Programs

This CD also contains several third-party programs and demos from leading industry companies. These programs have been carefully selected to help you strengthen your professional skills in Photoshop 7.

Please note that some of the programs included on this CD-ROM are shareware "try-before-you-buy" software. Please support these independent vendors by purchasing or registering any shareware software that you use for more than 30 days. Check with the documentation provided with the software on where and how to register the product.

- **Super Flip!.** By Kutuzov, Inc. Full version. Flip! is a flexible WIN 95/98/NT program for interlacing graphic images to fit a lenticular screen. Flip! can be used to make winkie-blinkie flip images, motion, or 3D lenticulars. **www.flipsigns.com.** Directory: Software.
- Genuine Fractals Print Pro 2.5. By Lizard Tech, Inc. Trial version. Genuine Fractals Print Pro enables you to increase the resolution and size of your images while preserving original sharpness and detail. **www.lizardtech.com**. Directory: Software.

- **Lucis Art 2.0.X.** By Image Content Technology. Demonstration version. Lucis is so easy to use that training time and expense are virtually eliminated. It has unparalleled flexibility. Lucis reveals detail other methods can't. Detail is enhanced in shadows and highlights simultaneously, so Lucis can repair both underexposed and overexposed images. **www.imagecontent.com**. Directory: Software.
- **SuperBladePro.** By Flaming Pear. Trial version. Quickly create tarnish, iridescence, and glassiness for appealingly 'touchable' 3D looks. SuperBladePro's features include waterstains, moss, abrasion, spotlighting, dust, grit, embossing, fractal blotches, and smooth Gaussian bevels. **www.flamingpear.com**. Directory: Software.

Read This Before Opening the Software

By opening the CD package, you agree to be bound by the following agreement:

You may not copy or redistribute the entire CD-ROM as a whole. Copying and redistribution of individual software programs on the CD-ROM is governed by terms set by individual copyright holders.

The installer, code, images, actions, and brushes from the authors are copyrighted by the publisher and the authors.

This software is sold as-is, without warranty of any kind, either expressed or implied, including but not limited to the implied warranties of merchantability and fitness for a particular purpose. Neither the publisher nor its dealers or distributors assume any liability for any alleged or actual damages arising from the use of this program. (Some states do not allow for the exclusion of implied warranties, so the exclusion may not apply to you.)

INDEX

F

G-H

M

N-O

P

Q-R

S

T

U-V

W-Z

PHOTOSHOP® 7

Photoshop 7
Down & Dirty Tricks
Scott Kelby, Felix Nelson
0735712379
$39.99

Photoshop 7 Magic
Sherry London,
Rhoda Grossman
0735712646
$45.00

Photoshop 7 Artistry
Barry Haynes,
Wendy Crumpler
0735712409
$55.00

Photoshop 7 Killer Tips
Scott Kelby, Felix Nelson
0735713006
$39.99

Inside Photoshop 7
Gary Bouton, Robert Stanley,
J. Scott Hamlin,
Daniel Will-Harris,
Mara Nathanson
0735712417
$49.99

Photoshop Studio with Bert Monroy
Bert Monroy
0735712468
$45.00

Photoshop
Restoration and Retouching
Katrin Eismann
0789723182
$49.99

Photoshop Type Effects Visual Encyclopedia
Roger Pring
0735711909
$45.00

Creative Thinking in Photoshop
Sharon Steuer
0735711224
$45.00

VOICES THAT MATTER™

HOW TO CONTACT US

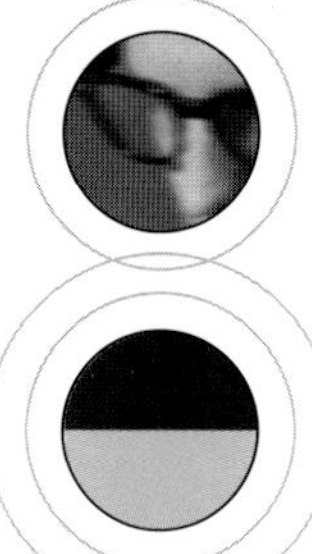

VOICES THAT MATTER

VISIT OUR WEB SITE

WWW.NEWRIDERS.COM

On our web site, you'll find information about our other books, authors, tables of contents, and book errata. You will also find information about book registration and how to purchase our books, both domestically and internationally.

EMAIL US

Contact us at: **nrfeedback@newriders.com**

- If you have comments or questions about this book
- To report errors that you have found in this book
- If you have a book proposal to submit or are interested in writing for New Riders
- If you are an expert in a computer topic or technology and are interested in being a technical editor who reviews manuscripts for technical accuracy

Contact us at: **nreducation@newriders.com**

- If you are an instructor from an educational institution who wants to preview New Riders books for classroom use. Email should include your name, title, school, department, address, phone number, office days/hours, text in use, and enrollment, along with your request for desk/examination copies and/or additional information.

Contact us at: **nrmedia@newriders.com**

- If you are a member of the media who is interested in reviewing copies of New Riders books. Send your name, mailing address, and email address, along with the name of the publication or web site you work for.

BULK PURCHASES/CORPORATE SALES

If you are interested in buying 10 or more copies of a title or want to set up an account for your company to purchase directly from the publisher at a substantial discount, contact us at 800-382-3419 or email your contact information to `corpsales@pearsontechgroup.com`. A sales representative will contact you with more information.

WRITE TO US

New Riders Publishing
201 W. 103rd St.
Indianapolis, IN 46290-1097

CALL/FAX US

Toll-free (800) 571-5840
If outside U.S. (317) 581-3500
Ask for New Riders
FAX: (317) 581-4663

WWW.NEWRIDERS.COM

THE PHOTOSHOP 7 MAGIC CD

The CD that accompanies this book contains valuable resources for anyone using Photoshop, not the least of which are:

- **Project files:** All the example files provided by the authors enable you to work through the step-by-step projects.
- **Software-related third-party software:** Demo versions of cutting-edge software and plug-ins that can be used with Photoshop.

Accessing the Project Files from the CD

The majority of projects in this book use pre-built Photoshop files that contain preset parameters, artwork, audio, or other important information you need to work through and build the final project.

All the project files are conveniently located in the CD's Projects directory. To access the project files for the "Abstract Figures and Portraits" project (Project 3), for example, locate the following directory on the accompanying CD: Projects\Project 03.

We recommend that you copy the project files to your hard drive, but this is not absolutely necessary if you don't intend to save the project files.

For a complete list of the CD-ROM contents, please see Appendix A, "What's on the CD-ROM."

Colophon

Photoshop 7 Magic was laid out and produced with the help of Microsoft Word, Adobe Acrobat, Adobe Photoshop, Collage Complete, and QuarkXpress on a variety of systems, including a Macintosh G4. With the exception of pages that were printed out for proofreading, all files—text, images, and project files—were transferred via email or ftp and edited on-screen.

All body text was set in the Bergamo family. All headings, figure captions, and cover text were set in the Imago family. The Symbol and Sean's Symbol typefaces were used throughout for special symbols and bullets.

Photoshop 7 Magic was printed on 60# Mead Web Dull at GAC (Graphic Art Center) in Indianapolis, IN. Prepress consisted of PostScript computer-to-plate technology (filmless process). The cover was printed on 12pt. coated on one side at Moore Langen Printing Company in Terre Haute, IN.